ENDORSEMENTS FOR *WO...*

"As a World War II Navy veteran, a Navigator, and a personal friend of Bob Evans, I'm pleased to see Bob's story being told to inspire a new generation of disciple makers. Bob and other heroic men and women of his era have made a lasting mark on modern Christianity. Their heart to reach people for Christ, fueled by passion for God and a willingness to make great sacrifices, has grown into worldwide movements of the gospel that still transform lives. I pray this book will ignite a similar passion and determination in young people today to carry on the great legacy of Bob Evans and begin new movements of the gospel in Europe and around the world."

JIM DOWNING
Veteran of World War II and Pearl Harbor, friend of Bob Evans, and author of *The Other Side of Infamy*

"Compelling. Timely. Convicting. At the heart of the Passion movement is the desire to see young people leverage their lives for what matters most—the name and fame of Jesus. I am so grateful for people like John Gilberts and Jazz Jones Becker who remind us that Jesus' words are just as true today as they were when he first told his followers that the harvest is plentiful but the workers are few. I believe *Worth the Risk* will encourage a rising generation to join in the harvest work in Europe and beyond."

LOUIE GIGLIO
Pastor of Passion City Church, founder of Passion Conferences, and author of *The Comeback*

Worth the Risk is the engaging story of two missionaries with one compelling message: no matter the cost, knowing Jesus— and making Jesus known—is infinitely worth it all.

DR. DAVID FLEMING
Senior pastor, Champion Forest Baptist Church

WORTH THE RISK

WHAT WOULD YOU PUT ON THE LINE TO SHARE GOD'S LOVE IN EUROPE?

JOHN GILBERTS & JAZZ JONES BECKER

Greater Europe Mission

18950 BASE CAMP RD, MONUMENT, CO 80132

INTRODUCTION

GREATER EUROPE MISSION'S PRESIDENT, Jon Burns, often likes to remind people, "When God calls, he always equips." He usually says this in conjunction with a biblical example to emphasize the point.

The idea seems straightforward and reassuring, yet the butterflies in our stomachs warn us otherwise. How do mere mortals like you and me find the courage to take a leap of faith in serving God?

I suspect the hesitation comes because of stories we've heard. Yes, Jesus ultimately built his Church through Peter, but not before a late-night swimming lesson and the cry of a rooster. Yes, God crystallized New Testament theology through the apostle Paul, but not before knocking him off his high horse and leaving him blind on the side of the road. The gut check comes from the chapters between the call and the victory, and we wonder if our comfortable suburban Christianity has prepared us to work closely with the wildness of our Creator.

Reading stories of God's faithfulness can help us. Faithfulness in the beginning and the end, certainly, but more importantly, faithfulness in the middle. That's what this book is about. First and foremost, it's about God's faithfulness to the people of Europe, with whom he desires a relationship. Second, it's about his faithfulness to his followers—to use our lives for his great purposes and to make us holy in the process.

GEM's founder, Bob Evans, was an ordinary yet heroic man whose European journey began when he asked his World War II commanding officer why chaplains didn't accompany the invasion force.

Bob's story is juxtaposed with Jazz Jones Becker's story. Jazz, a modern-day missionary, left the peaceful beaches of Hawaii to serve God in the idyllic City of Light and quickly discovered that missionary life wasn't as safe as she expected.

Yes, God called and equipped Bob and Jazz, but as you read their stories, you'll find out how he changed their lives along the way . . . and that may be the biggest miracle of all.

Many of us spend our lives loitering near the doorway to a grand Kingdom adventure. We think we hear the whisper of God's call coming from beyond the threshold, but we're not sure we have what it takes to respond when the obstacles come. And so we wait.

But every once in a while, someone hears that whisper, pushes forward, and dives headlong into the adventure.

Bob and Jazz beckon us to join them in making our lives count for the Kingdom—in Europe or wherever God calls. Who knows? The next great story might be yours.

John Gilberts

Paris, France
November 13, 2015

JAZZ JONES

CHAPTER I

EUROPE'S FAVORITE SPORT

ANTICIPATION PULSED THROUGH THE STADIUM like electricity as Sven and I arrived at our seating section. France was matching up against Germany tonight, and one thing I'd learned from my earlier years of living in Europe was that Europeans take their football very seriously. And this wasn't just any game—the rivalry between France and Germany is legendary.

The muscles in our thighs burned from climbing flight after flight of stairs toward the highest level, where our seats and a group of friends from language school waited. We pushed through throngs of people milling about the stadium's corridors buying beer, bratwurst, and team souvenirs and made it out into the bright lights and concentric circles of seats surrounding us.

When we located our row, we carefully inched sideways past spectators who had arrived before us, hoping to avoid stepping on toes or spilling drinks. We greeted the others in our group who were already there, and we finally sank into our seats, stowed our backpacks under our chairs, and absorbed the sight before us.

The carefully manicured field seemed like it was a mile below us in the enormous Stade de France. All around us people sported blue, white, and red clothing, football scarves, and French flags. We saw children decked out in team colors with flags painted on their small cheeks. The aroma of food and the taunting invitations of snack vendors filled the air. Music and announcements blared from the speakers above us. On the scoreboard at each end of the massive field, the clock counted down the minutes and seconds to game time.

The enthusiasm and patriotism of the thousands of French soccer fans around me was contagious, causing a love for Paris and France to swell in my chest. This was a moment to savor.

My fiancé, Sven, turned toward me. Seeing the excitement in my eyes, he asked, "Would you like to have a French flag?"

"Yes, I'd love one! Thank you." It was just like Sven to know what I wanted before I'd even said anything out loud.

Sven again edged past the row of other spectators, who were slightly irritated at being further inconvenienced, and merged back into the stream of fans. He returned ten minutes later with a French flag for me, and we settled in to wait for the game to begin.

There was a thunderous roar from the crowd when the two teams emerged from the locker rooms and took their place on the field. Germany won the toss and chose to kick off, and moments later, the whistle blew, signaling the start of ninety minutes of intense athleticism.

Throughout the game, one section of the stadium would start "the wave"; however, for some reason, Section 275 refused to play along. When the wave died there time after time, a playful, disappointed moan would resonate from the rest of the spectators, who, undeterred, would make another attempt at a complete circuit. The mission was eventually accomplished, and the wave went around and around in a sea of national colors. Each time it came to our section, I jumped to my feet, waving my French flag and cheering along with the rest of the fans. With Sven at my side and our friends Beki and Jeremy next to us, the night couldn't have been more perfect.

After a long week of French classes at the Sorbonne, the four of us were eager to celebrate the weekend by going to the big France vs. Germany game. We'd been planning this outing with a dozen of our fellow French-language students for weeks, and the day was finally here.

When classes had dismissed for the day, Sven took the train to my flat, and our best friends from language school, Beki and Jeremy, picked up dinner from "my" crêpe guys so we could eat before we headed to the game.

It was Beki and Jeremy's first visit to my flat, and as a new missionary, I still lacked some basic household furniture. But I did have a dining table, so the four of us gathered around, sitting on two dining chairs and two makeshift stools. We asked God to bless the food and prayed for a great evening at the game. Then I waited for the looks of sublime joy to appear on Beki and Jeremy's faces when they took their first bite of the crêpes. I was not disappointed.

The crêpes from the stand on my street are unlike anything you'd find in other parts of the world. My favorite is a crêpe stuffed with seasoned chicken, tomatoes, onions, and a generous helping of shredded cheese. The cheese spills over the edge of the crêpe, forming a crisp, brown edge. The stand also sells the spectacular sweet crêpes that France is known for the world over. It's an effort of sheer willpower to pass by on my way home and limit myself to eating there only occasionally.

Surrounded by friends after a long but satisfying week, and feeling confident that I was right where God wanted me to be, I was overwhelmed by a deep sense of gratitude. When I signed up to be a missionary with Greater Europe Mission (GEM) three years ago, I never would have imagined that serving God could also include moments of pure enjoyment like this.

+ + +

Suddenly a familiar but unwelcome odor assaulted our nostrils, bringing me out of my reverie.

"Do you smell that?" I shot my friend Beki a sardonic smile. "It smells like cigarette smoke. But it couldn't be, could it?"

Earlier, in the security inspection line, we were surprised

when a female security guard pulled a small rectangular package from Beki's bag. She asked Beki, "*Qu'est-ce que c'est?*" ("What is this?")

"*Un paquet de cartes*" ("A deck of playing cards"), Beki answered truthfully, confused about why she was being asked a seemingly obvious question.

We were even more surprised when Beki's reply didn't convince the guard. The uniformed woman opened the box and thoroughly inspected the contents. "*Les cigarettes sont interdites dans le stade*" ("Cigarettes are strictly forbidden in the stadium"), she said sternly.

Finally satisfied that Beki wasn't smuggling contraband into the stadium, the guard returned the cards to Beki and asked to see our other bags.

Having experienced the lengths stadium authorities went to in order to deter cigarettes in the facility, we were taken aback by the aroma of smoke. Yet Beki agreed that what we were smelling was cigarettes. Scanning the area for the offender, we spotted a man sitting farther down the row smoking. The four of us looked at each other in astonishment. How had this man made it into the stadium with forbidden goods? Here we had been detained over playing cards, and he was brazenly smoking in sight of the whole stadium.

We shrugged in amusement at the inconsistency of the situation and turned our attention back to the game.

I've played soccer since elementary school, and even though I don't devotedly follow a particular team, I always love watching a great football match in person. This particular match interested me because Sven is German and I've claimed France as my second home ever since I became a missionary in Paris. Secretly, I like both teams, but I wasn't going to tell Sven that and spoil our friendly rivalry.

Sven and I had met several months earlier, at the Les Cèdres French language school. In between sessions, I signed up to welcome two new students to the school and show them around. One of them was Sven. We bonded immediately over a shared knowledge of the German language, and soon we were doing homework together, playing volleyball and soccer with other friends from school, going on walks, and geocaching.

It wasn't long before we realized we had more than just a friendship, but neither of us wanted to start a dating relationship unless we knew God was leading us to marry each other. So we did a lot of praying and fasting, and we sought godly advice from family and friends.

In early October, I went to Germany with Sven to meet his family and friends. That trip felt like it confirmed so many things in our relationship, and about a week later, God revealed to us that he was directing us to serve him in marriage together. Sven proposed to me shortly after that, and I eagerly said yes—in French, German, and English! Now here we were, watching one of our favorite sports as an engaged couple.

A few times, when I wasn't paying close attention to the game, I inadvertently cheered for some of Germany's good plays. These slips didn't escape Sven's notice.

"I like that you're cheering so much for the German team," he said, a grin lifting the corner of his mouth.

I feigned innocence. "Of course!" I gave him a playful nudge. "Germany's my home team too, after all."

There was some truth to this statement. I was two years old when the US military relocated my family from Virginia to Germany. Over the course of my life, I've lived in Germany three different times for a total of seven years. Europe has always had a special place in my heart, so it's no surprise that throughout my life God was preparing me to be a missionary here. Even so, I never would have dreamed I'd be in the final months of language school, training to be an evangelist and disciple maker in Paris.

The teams continued to battle it out on the field. The French team advanced toward the German goal. The tension in the crowd intensified with every pass, every kick. The theme song from *Pirates of the Caribbean* blared from the stadium speakers, fueling the fans' excitement.

Suddenly a boom shook the stadium. I felt more than heard the muffled thump. At first the sound seemed to come from the stadium's speakers, as if there were some technical glitch. Sven was too engrossed in what was happening on the field to notice the disturbance, but Beki's eyes met mine. We had both heard the sound, and we knew something was wrong.

"What was that?"

"I'm not sure," Beki replied. "Maybe it was something outside the stadium."

We refocused our attention on the game. A minute later, a second boom followed.

"There it is again!" I exclaimed.

She nodded. "I don't like it. I hope it doesn't happen again." Her forehead creased with worry.

Despite the celebratory atmosphere, I felt fear begin to take root in my heart.

Sven saw our expressions and tried to ease the tension. Not thinking anything really was wrong, he calmly suggested, "Maybe it's just fireworks or something outside."

Perhaps, I thought. But it seemed like the sounds came from inside the stadium through the sound system. I forced myself to put the concerns out of my mind and to refocus on the game. *Maybe it's just some technical problem.*

As the game continued into the second half and nothing seemed to be out of the ordinary, I allowed myself to relax. With thirty minutes left in the game, a few of our friends near the aisle got our attention. They told us they were going to head back to Massy, the town they lived in, south of Paris. We and the others in our group bid them *au revoir* and continued watching the rest of the game. We wondered why they'd left early, since it was such a thrilling match, but we didn't think too much of it. It was getting late, after all.

Just a few minutes later, the Frenchman with the cigarettes signaled for our attention and attempted to show us something on his phone. His heavily accented French was difficult for us to understand, especially in the din of the stadium. We realized he was showing us a news feed, but his hands were gesturing so wildly as he talked that we couldn't decipher what he was trying to show us.

Then something near the field caught my attention. Previously, the stadium security guards in their highlighter-yellow vests had been sitting on short stools around the perimeter of the field, facing the crowd with bored expressions. However, now there were twice as many guards as before, and they all stood rigidly at attention, intensely scanning the crowd. Some had binoculars, and others talked urgently into walkie-talkies.

Well, that's interesting, I thought. *Not to mention unsettling.*

Scanning the stadium myself, my eyes landed on two security guards who were talking to each other and gesturing toward the crowd. They seemed to be discussing something important. Now my senses were on full alert.

What was going on?

CHAPTER 2

FLIGHT

IT QUICKLY BECAME CLEAR that this was not a case of friendly fireworks outside the stadium.

Our phones started chiming and buzzing like a tiny orchestra. Incoming text messages read, "Are you okay? Is everyone safe?"

We read conflicting news reports: some reported shootings; some claimed there was a hostage situation; others said there had been bombings near the stadium. We couldn't make sense of what was going on or where the drama was unfolding.

As I eyed the lower levels of the stadium, I saw security guards huddled in groups. Then some of them made their way into the stands, as if they were intently searching for something . . . or someone. Additional security personnel started to arrive. And then it hit me: *Is all this connected to the booms from earlier?*

Despite the tense situation that was unfolding off the

field, the soccer game played to its conclusion. As soon as the game ended, with France as the victor, the announcer instructed everyone to leave from specific exits due to "an incident" outside the stadium. I still didn't know what had happened, but I began to pray we could just get home. Then we could check the news from there. Our whole group stayed close together as we walked down the first flight of stairs toward the exit.

Looking down, we could see the crowd just outside the security area on the ground level, with some people heading to the left, in the direction of the train station. Then, in a split second, people started screaming and fleeing for their lives. We could almost smell the terror and panic permeating the crowd. Some people ran in the opposite direction; others tried desperately to return to the stadium.

Everyone on the stairs froze, knowing something was terribly wrong. But we had no idea what had just happened. Had someone or something dangerous just been spotted? No shots had been heard, and no more explosions had gone off, but we could see the terror on the faces of the people below us. Whatever had happened, people wanted to get as far away as possible, as quickly as possible.

I felt pangs of terror begin to rise in my stomach.

The next several minutes played out like a scene from a movie. My heart pounded furiously, and I could hardly hear anything above the pulsing in my ears. My grip on Sven's hand was so tight my knuckles were white with the effort.

Oh, Lord! I cried silently. *Is this the end? Will we make it out of here alive?* Suddenly the huge stadium felt like a trap, and I wondered if this was what it was like for those trying to escape the Twin Towers on September 11, 2001.

When we were about halfway down, people at the bottom of the stairs started yelling and madly motioning for everyone to go back up and into the stadium. Sven and I turned around with the rest of the pressing crowd and started climbing up again. We made it only a few steps before the people behind us started throwing themselves facedown on the stairs. In a domino-like effect, everyone on the stairs followed suit, including Jeremy and Beki and the others in our group. Sven pulled me down with him, his arm across my back.

My heart raced as I crouched down on the stairs. I felt paralyzed. I feared that at any moment I would hear another boom go off or that someone would spray the crowd with a shower of bullets.

A million thoughts flashed through my mind: *Am I going to die? Will I ever see my family again? How will they react when they find out something happened to me? What if something happens to Sven? I don't think I could stand to lose him! I haven't even started full-time ministry yet! What about all my supporters and partners?*

Suddenly someone yelled for us to get up and run into the stadium. Almost as one, we stood up and rushed to the top of the stairs, some people pushing and shoving, others stumbling in the chaos. People pressed on me from behind, and more than once I would have been trampled if not for my hand on the railing and Sven pulling me onward.

Sven and I reached the top together, just behind our friends Jeremy and Beki. In one part of the stadium, we spotted an open section of wall, and our whole group hurried to it for some semblance of shelter. Beki and I pressed our backs against the wall while Jeremy and Sven stood in front of us. Some of the others from our group hunkered down between the rows of seats. I clutched Sven's arm and prayed silently. I glanced at Beki and could see my own fear and helplessness mirrored in her eyes.

Sven pulled away slightly to look at me. "Is it okay if I try to find out what's going on?" He gestured with his head to the low wall next to the staircase, which would provide him with a view of the area below.

Are you out of your mind? Of course not! I screamed silently.

But all I managed to get out was a single word: "No." I pulled him closer to me. Sven was just curious, but all I could think of was some deranged person with a gun shooting into the crowd and Sven getting hit as he looked over the railing.

Just then we heard people yelling, telling everyone to go back farther into the stadium. We hesitated, not knowing if that would actually be safer or more exposed. Plus, we wanted to make sure everyone in our group was accounted for. Doing a head count, Sven quickly realized that no one knew where our friend Jacob was. We scanned the mass of people around us and those still on the stairs, but no luck. Jacob had been right behind us on the stairs, and we all thought he'd come with us when the crowds pushed upward.

As we looked at the crowds below us, we realized that whatever had scared people seemed to no longer be a threat, and everyone was beginning to exit the stadium again. For the first time since we'd left our seats, my heart began to slow itself. I stood beside Sven, scanning the crowd for Jacob.

"Let's pray that we find him," Sven suggested. Our small group gathered in a circle and grasped each other's hands as Sven asked God to intervene and help us find Jacob in the mass of people. About five seconds later, while Sven was still praying, I felt God prompt me to open my eyes. When I did, I immediately saw Jacob standing on the ground level, just beyond the entrance to the stairs. Praise the Lord! Jacob was calmly standing there, searching the stadium for us.

"Sven! There he is!" I exclaimed.

The two of us rushed down the stairs, shouting Jacob's name. Jacob must have heard us, because he began looking in every direction for the source. He'd looked fairly calm standing there, but the relief in his eyes was apparent when he spotted us descending the stairs toward him.

"I'm so glad we found you!" I gave him a hug. "We thought you were still with us after we went up the stairs."

"Yeah, I don't know what happened." Jacob's Australian accent seemed even stronger than usual in the intensity of the moment. "I'm really glad you found me, because I was beginning to think I'd have to make my way back home alone."

The three of us climbed up the first flight of stairs and rejoined our friends to discuss how we were going to get home. Figuring the train would be packed, we considered taking taxis to get away from the stadium as quickly as possible. In the end, ten of us decided to take the train back into Paris and then south to Massy. One family with two young boys decided to stay and take shelter in the stadium, where they thought it would be safer.

The decision made, our group joined the throng of people making their way toward the train station. The pavement was littered with shoes, most without a match. High heels, kids' shoes, even loosely tied sneakers had fallen off as people fled the area. Souvenir flags that people had been waving proudly a short time ago now lay abandoned around the stadium.

The tension in the air was palpable as people hurried toward the entrance to the station. Despite the masses of people on the street, the city was quiet. People's voices were subdued, muted by the heaviness of the situation. All around us, police officers guarded blocked-off alleys and side streets, funneling the crowd down the main street toward the train station. Ambulances and countless police vehicles lined the streets. In the distance, we could hear a shrill symphony of sirens echoing off the buildings.

When we arrived at the station, we saw a train waiting on the track, and we were informed that it would be the last train leaving the station that night for Paris. However, no one could board until the police officers permitted passengers to enter. I looked ahead at the long line of people pressed together in front of us, straining to reach the train, and wondered if we would make it. I began to pray that we would make it onto the train and safely home.

I just want to be home. I just want to be home, I silently repeated to God and myself.

At last we reached the steps of the train and were waved aboard. The cars were jammed to capacity—standing room only—but when the doors closed and the train pulled away from the station, all ten of us in our party were present.

Our prayers were answered. We were going home.

CHAPTER 3

THE LONG WAY HOME

THE TRAIN LURCHED as it slowed for the first stop at Gare du Nord, jolting me to the reality of our situation. The evening had ended so differently from the carefree way it had begun. Mere hours earlier, I had lifted my hands toward the sky and shouted, "Finally Friday!" as I exited the school. In that moment, I never could have imagined the current scene in front of me.

As soon as the train stopped, a voice came over the intercom, instructing everyone to leave the train and exit the station—and to do so quickly and calmly. Everyone on the train asked the same question, either aloud or with their eyes: "What's going on now?"

We had no idea, and we received no answers—just police officers and train station workers directing the crowd toward the exit. As we joined yet another mass exodus, we sensed a change in the emotional temperature around us. Nerves were beginning to fray, and the original panic that had set in at the stadium became anger and frustration. Stoic security guards guided people to specific exits, but they didn't allow people to stop and ask questions for fear of log jamming the large crowd. That left hundreds of passengers stranded, faced with the daunting task of making their way home at nearly midnight.

Okay. So now what? I asked myself.

Standing outside the station, our small group considered our options. The trains and metros had been shut down. The streets were mostly empty of automobile traffic, so finding a taxi would be difficult. While my friends discussed the options, I took the opportunity to contact some of the people who had been trying repeatedly to reach me.

"Hi, Mama. It's me."

"So good to hear from you, J." My mother's voice was mixed with concern and relief. Hearing that familiar sound from four thousand miles away made me instantly tear up. I hadn't realized how hard I'd been working to contain my emotions. It took me a few seconds to swallow my tears before I could explain our current predicament.

"I'm glad you're with friends. Just be careful on your way home. And let me know when you're home safe, okay?"

"Of course I will, Mama. I love you so much." As I hung up, the tears again threatened to crumble my composure.

With all forms of public transportation closed, we really had only one option left: to walk.

Thankfully our cell phones had GPS, and we were able to find the best route using Google Maps. To conserve our precious batteries, we put our phones on airplane mode. Then when we needed to consult the map again, we used just one of the phones. As is usually the case in emergency situations, once the initial panic is over, someone in the group rises to the occasion and thinks through contingencies such as saving batteries. In our group, that was Chris. With the plan formed, we were soon walking south through the empty streets of central Paris.

Even though our group was made up mostly of men, I still felt uneasy as we walked through the dark, deserted streets. Not knowing exactly what was going on in the city around us sowed seeds of "What if?" in my imagination. *What if we stumble into the middle of something dangerous? What if some of the people around us are terrorists? What if that group of guys standing on the corner is part of this?*

Without meaning to, we could easily end up at the wrong place at the wrong time. In a word, I felt exposed. If something happened, there would be no place for us to hide. Yet for the most part, all we saw as we navigated through the city was the occasional late-night dog walker or a few stragglers making their way home after being out late at a bar or café.

My thoughts raged; emotions flooded my heart. They warred for my attention, but I couldn't focus or begin to organize my internal world in that moment. I wanted solitude, and I *didn't* want to talk. To anyone.

A few times Sven tried to start a conversation with me in an effort to keep my mind off of our current situation: "What would you like to do this weekend?" Or "When do you think we should go to Germany next to visit my family?"

"Sven, I know what you are trying to do, and I appreciate it," I finally told him. "But I really just need to think right now."

Other people in the group were talking and making jokes, keeping the atmosphere light. But I couldn't handle being part of a conversation while processing what was going on inside me. I'm sure I seemed aloof to my friends, but in that moment, I just couldn't get out from under the storm cloud that seemed to be brewing over Paris.

CHAPTER 4

HOME

WE ARRIVED at my street just past 1:30 a.m., after ninety minutes and nearly six kilometers of empty, lonely city streets.
Sven and Beki walked me to the door of my building while
the others continued making their way to the place where
another member of our language class had arranged to meet
them and drive them home to Massy.

I fumbled with my keys and couldn't quite make myself
unlock the door and walk inside alone. The queasiness swirling in my stomach must have registered on my face as well.

"Are you okay, Jazz?" Sven asked with concern.

"Would you rather come stay with us this weekend?" Beki
chimed in. "I don't think I would want to be home alone
tonight either."

"I don't want to be alone," I answered. "But I think I want
to be in my own home. We have no idea what else is going
to happen."

Beki nodded.

"I could stay with you, if you want, and sleep in the living room," Sven offered.

I felt some of the tension lift from my shoulders with the offer, and I gratefully accepted. I hugged Beki good-bye, asking her to let us know when she and the others got home safely. She turned to catch up with the others, and then Sven and I walked hand in hand into my building.

I was so relieved to be back in my flat. It felt like a refuge after walking through the dark and barren streets of the city.

Sven and I prayed together, thanking the Lord for allowing us to arrive home safely, and then I flopped down on the couch, spent, and called my parents. They picked up on the first ring. They'd obviously been sitting by the phone, waiting for the call.

I recounted everything that had happened. The events were still so fresh, yet in the retelling, I felt like a third party or a spectator at a movie. As I spoke to my parents, my two sisters, and my grandmother, I heard the fear and concern in their voices, and suddenly it hit me: *They were afraid for me!*

At that point, the news reports were still sketchy, and the facts about the night's events were still under investigation. My family had spent the last hours glued to the TV, watching things unfold in real time on CNN without knowing where I was or if I was okay.

Because it was so late and I was exhausted from the long trek home, we kept our conversation brief, but I assured them I would call in the morning and keep them updated. The last thing I heard on the phone that night was my father's voice, quavering with emotion: "You know I love you, Jazz. Please be careful."

I love you. They were words my family said often and easily, but I could tell they came from a deeper place that night. We'd all been dramatically jolted into remembering that our loved ones are gifts, not something to be taken for granted.

Though I didn't yet know the extent of the lives lost that night, I thought about everyone around the globe who would never again get to say "I love you" to their loved ones who were now gone.

After I hung up with my family, the tears that had been pooling in my eyes during the calls finally flowed. Sven had been calling his own family from the table, and he came over and sat next to me on the couch. He wrapped his arms around me, and I'm sure my tears soaked the shoulder of his shirt. I'm not sure how long we sat there, finally allowing our frayed nerves and frazzled emotions to be released. Eventually we realized that our job wasn't finished yet; there were other people who needed to know we were okay.

I contacted my GEM colleagues via text to let them know I was safe. Then Sven and I looked up the German, French, and world news reports on our phones to find out exactly what had happened that night. That's when the extent of the tragedy hit us. When we read about the simultaneous terrorist attacks and the increasing death toll, we were shocked and heartbroken. As we reflected back on the confusing reports coming in while we were at the stadium, it all started to make sense. The reason we were hearing several different stories was because there had been more than one attack.

Sometime after 2:30 a.m., we could no longer keep our eyes open. I brought blankets and a pillow out for Sven, and he made his bed on the couch. With a kiss and an embrace that perhaps meant more that night than it ever had, we said good night. Then I went to my room and collapsed into bed, where exhaustion and adrenaline fought a small war in my mind and body. I was beyond tired from the stress of the night, the long walk home, and the late hour. Yet images from the evening's events raced through my mind and adrenaline coursed through my veins, keeping my system revved. Falling asleep seemed impossible.

I lay in my bed staring at the ceiling, grateful to be alive but plagued by worst-case scenarios. I imagined people running through the streets outside my building and killing random people. Or someone getting through the coded doors of my building, coming up the stairwell, and breaking down my door. I lay there for a long time, straining to hear any unusual activity in the stairwell or in the narrow street outside my building.

I tried to calm my swirling thoughts, reminding myself that Sven was in the other room, until at last my body and mind gave in to sleep.

CHAPTER 5

THE AFTERMATH

THAT NIGHT WAS MARKED BY DREAMS AND NIGHTMARES. I awoke the next morning feeling as though I were waking from a fog, wishing the bombings from the night before had been just a bad dream. As I came to grips with reality, I wondered what this new day would hold.

After a late breakfast of cereal and coffee, Sven and I looked online for updated news on the attacks. We read that one of the two suicide bombers at the stadium had tried to enter but hadn't made it past security. Chills ran down my spine, realizing how close we'd come to being on the victim list. Suddenly I was grateful for the security guard who had so thoroughly searched our bags the night before. I felt tears on my face and was shocked to realize I was crying again. I hadn't processed the excess of emotions from the night before, and they were eager to seep out.

Sven and I stopped our news search and paused to thank God for the stadium security and the police in the city who had done their jobs to prevent an even larger-scale attack. Almost immediately after our prayer ended, both of our phones buzzed, alerting us to the breaking news: President Hollande had declared a state of emergency for the nation of France.

That afternoon I got a call from Charles Cross, the GEM leader in France.

"Hey, Jazz, Charles here. I'm just checking in with all our folks. So far everyone is okay and accounted for, but that was a crazy night," he said. "Bev told me you were at the stadium with some of your friends. Is everyone okay?"

I gave him a brief summary of our time at the stadium and our long journey home.

"Wow. You actually felt the explosions in the stadium?" Charles sounded stunned. "That's a lot closer to all this than any of the rest of our folks. How are you doing?"

"I'm not really sure," I confided. "Okay, I guess, but I can't stop thinking about it. I just can't get it out of my head that news reporters could be reading off *our* names today. And I can't stop checking the news feeds. It's what I've been doing most of the day."

"Yeah, me too. I can't help wondering if it is really over." Charles took in a big breath. "You sound pretty shaken up. Are you worried? Scared? How are you processing all of this?"

"It's probably going to take a little time to get over the initial shock of what happened," I said. "But I guess I'll eventually try to get back to my normal business." I paused, trying to sort through the thoughts swirling in my mind. "When I signed up to be a missionary in Paris, I never thought I'd be involved in anything like this. This stuff happens in Syria and Palestine, not Paris! Until yesterday, Paris felt like one of the safest places on the planet, if you don't count the pickpockets and scammers. Now, I just don't know."

I needed to go out to the store for groceries, but so far I hadn't been able to force myself to go. Everything seemed normal on the streets, but I knew it wasn't.

"I know what you mean," Charles agreed. "This isn't the first time GEM missionaries have been in the thick of things, but it's the first time it has hit so close to home for me, too."

"Other missionaries have been in terrorist attacks?" I didn't remember hearing about that before.

"Well, not terrorist attacks, that I know of," Charles said. "But we had missionaries in Ireland throughout all the troubles there. Some of our missionaries were in Yugoslavia during the war, and Kosovo, too. They stayed even as the bombs were falling, and it opened amazing ministry doors for them." Charles paused, as if flipping through the pages of history in his mind. "Our founder, Bob Evans, was in France during World War II. He saw all the despair and devastation after the war, and that's what led him to start Greater Europe Mission back in the '40s."

"I guess I do remember hearing about him during GEM's new staff orientation," I said. "But I never thought about what that time was really like in Europe."

"I'm really sorry for what you went through last night. For so many reasons, I wish it had never happened," Charles said.

"But you just joined an elite group of GEM missionaries who have lived through some close calls for the sake of the gospel."

I'd hadn't thought of it that way before. When I went to the soccer game with my friends, I certainly had no intention of joining the ranks of the brave men and women who had gone before me.

"These experiences come with a price, though," Charles continued. "GEM has a great Member Care department, and you may want to contact them and talk about what you went through."

"Okay, thanks," I said. "Do you know where I can get a copy of Bob Evans's story?" For the first time, I was intrigued by how the organization I serve with came to be.

"I'll send you a link to the history," Charles said, "and connect you with Member Care."

"Thanks. I think I'm fine—or will be as soon as I get back in a routine and stop focusing on what might have been."

"Well, may I pray for you before I go?" Charles offered.

"Of course! I keep thinking about all the folks who didn't make it, and their families, too. God's heart must be breaking over all this."

As we prayed, I could feel the emotions welling up inside me. I hung up the phone, looked at the front door, and considered going out for groceries.

I don't want to go, but I really should, I thought. Just then my computer chimed, alerting me to a new e-mail. True to his word, Charles had sent the link to Bob Evans's story.

Maybe the grocery store can wait . . .

St. Tropez, France
August 15, 1944

BOB EVANS

CHAPTER 6

UNLIKELY CHURCH PLANT

I WILL ALWAYS REMEMBER THE STARS that night as we rocked back and forth aboard our infantry ship, LCI-45, twenty miles from the Mediterranean shore. It was our last glimpse of the beauty of God's creation before the horrifying hours to come. I looked up in amazement, surrounded by the quiet sounds of men shuffling to keep the blood flowing in their aching limbs.

In a few hours, Operation Dragoon would begin and our landing craft would power up and advance toward the German-fortified beaches north of St. Tropez in southern France. The German troops knew we were coming, if not exactly when.

Two months earlier, the Allied forces had stormed the beaches of Normandy, striking what we hoped would be the first nail in the coffin of the German occupation of France. We had all heard the tales from that bloody affair—both the heroics and the horrors. Those stories raced through our heads as we stood there, shoulder to shoulder, with the hot Mediterranean breeze stirring the air and rocking our boat.

With anticipation building, my fellow soldiers didn't want to talk much. I didn't either. This night was a time for thinking, not talking. I was thinking about my young wife, Jeanette, and my new daughter, Alyce, barely a month old now. What did she look like? I wondered where she was and if I would ever get to meet her. I wondered if Jeanette still had that Wheaton College textbook I'd sold her the day we met. I always joked with her that marrying her was just my way of keeping my hands on a good book.

As the boat swayed, it seemed like more than miles separated us; it felt like a lifetime. In reality, it had been barely two years since I'd followed my conscience and signed up to do my part to serve our country. As it turned out, my training for the ministry had come into play, and I landed the role of chaplain. On nights like these, that title bore a heavy weight. Even though our boat wouldn't be among the first to hit the beach, we were still headed into the eye of the storm.

In moments like these, in the somber quiet before the chaos of war, the deeper questions about life—the ones we keep under lock and key most days—rise to the surface, unbidden. That's where I came in: a hand on the shoulder and a quiet prayer. A verse of Scripture to strengthen the faint of heart. A listening ear to help a man clear his conscience, knowing he might meet his Maker. A reminder amid the ugliness that a God of beauty and wonder still exists.

Over the course of that night, I prayed with almost every

man on the ship, from the righteous to the roughneck. Not too many spurn God in moments like these—just in case.

And that was the great irony, I realized. I was just as scared as these men I was supposed to offer hope and courage to. The butterflies swirling through my stomach were probably not so different from what the men around me were experiencing. I stood there, shifting my weight from one leg to the other in an attempt to fend off the stiffness that had begun to set in hours ago and was now a dull, shaky ache.

What in the world had I been thinking by signing on for this? I asked myself. *Brilliant idea, Evans.*

+ + +

When I had arrived in North Africa months earlier, I was surprised to find that chaplains were assigned only to the big ships, the ones that stayed in the relative safety of the sea, close enough to the fighting to lob shells at but impervious to the personal, bloody warfare of the infantry. In my naïveté, I complained to Captain White that I thought a chaplain would be of more use among the men on the beach.

A few days later, he came to me with this news: "Good idea, Evans. Guess what? You'll be the first one."

So I packed up my meager belongings and transferred to the Third Army Assault Division. That was two months ago. Now here I was, wondering if I'd make it. With each sway of the ship, I prayed that the God I'd worked hard to serve would be with me and protect me along with all the guys I ministered to.

As the faint light of dawn began to ripple across the sea, a nudge from behind brought me out of my thoughts. Ed, a mountain of a man, sidled up next to me.

"What do you think, Evans? Is God watching us?" His words were punctuated by the distant thuds of explosions on the northern horizon. The shore bombardment was beginning in earnest.

"Sure he is," I said. "I imagine he's watching and weeping over what's about to happen."

"I feel him too." Ed sighed. "Don't know if I could do this without him—without knowing how it ends for me."

"Yeah, it's always good to remember we're immortal," I whispered.

Ed was the reason I came. Or at least guys like Ed.

Ed grew up as the son of a mechanic in the Bronx. His parents were Catholic, as he explained to me when we met. However, the only time God came into the picture was Christmas Eve and Easter, when his dad would dust off his ill-fitting suit and take him and his mother to church. They would sit in the back and try to sing along to songs they didn't know, just like the other families in the neighborhood who showed up on those two occasions. According to Ed, most of his fellow churchgoers were more likely to be seen in the local pub on a Sunday than in church.

"Jesus was pretty popular in the garage, though," Ed quipped. "Any time one of the guys would smash his finger or drop a part on his foot, they were sure to talk about Jesus!"

In the weeks before we received our orders, I introduced

Ed to the Jesus I knew—the one who forgave sinners, performed miracles, and died on a cross for all of us ordinary people who desperately need him. I'll never forget the night Ed came to my tent in tears, his massive shoulders shaking with sobs as he confessed what a sinner he was. And I'll never forget the quiet confidence and unfiltered sincerity in his voice as he prayed the "sinner's prayer." My heart soared to be used by God in this miraculous moment—the salvation of another's soul.

The next day, as I emerged from the sick tent after doing my rounds, Ed came running up to me, practically dragging another guy by the arm.

"Bob, you have to talk to this guy. His parents were Baptists on Christmas and Easter, just like mine. Except mine were Catholic. Anyway, tell him what you told me!"

"Um, okay. Well, I'm Bob Evans, the chaplain here. What's your name?"

"This is Frank," Ed burst in.

"Hi, Frank." I offered my hand, a smile forming on my lips. "So, you have some questions about God?"

"He doesn't know anything about Jesus dying on the cross for us!" Ed couldn't hold himself back.

"Well, that is important, but let's start at the beginning." I chuckled inwardly, celebrating Ed's enthusiasm.

"I told him about all the things I'd done and how Jesus forgave me, and he asked if Jesus can forgive stealing too. I told him he could, but then I thought I should ask you about that. Tell him! You're the preacher man!"

"Ed, are you trying to take my job as chaplain?" I laughed. "Hey guys, it's chow time. Let's grab some lunch and talk about it."

So yes, I came for Ed and Frank and four other guys I'd been discipling. These were tough guys, men's men. They hadn't given God much thought until they were thrust into a role where tomorrow was not guaranteed. Since accepting Christ, they were as hungry for God's Word as they were for our meager K rations. Day after day, we started our mornings praying and reading God's Word before our required regimen of physical training, and we often ended the day praying for our families and thanking God that he'd brought us through again.

+ + +

I may never have pictured myself serving God on a military ship on the eve of an invasion, but ministry was in my blood—it was the only life I knew. I grew up on the mission field not far south of where I floated now. Mom and Pop were missionaries to the Cameroonian people, where they served God in the poor, French-speaking villages around Elat. Both had been teachers before hearing the call of God to serve him in Africa, and I suppose they were teachers there too.

My brother, Rowell Jr., and I had grown up surrounded by the gospel and the messiness of missions, where there was no separation between life and work. Villagers constantly stopped by our simple home to learn more about Jesus. Mom and Pop welcomed people in day and night—sometimes all night. I suppose that's what led me to Wheaton College when the time came: I wanted to prepare for a life of ministry.

And I was doing overseas ministry, all right—it's just that the people I was serving were fellow soldiers, not people in a remote village. But this was where God had called me, and I was eager to serve him, regardless of the butterflies in my stomach.

Suddenly, with a guttural rumble, the engines beneath me churned to life, and the time for reflection was over. Every eye looked north as we began to gain way. It was light enough now for us to make out the dark line of the beach ahead. I saw explosions tear up the ground as destroyers and bombers cleared a path for our vessel. Planes swarmed overhead, and even in the semidarkness, I glimpsed the occasional midair explosion or drifting parachute. This was not child's play. This was war.

"Jesus, please be with us," I breathed.

CHAPTER 7

WELCOME TO FRANCE

TIME SEEMED SUSPENDED as we prepared to make landfall on the beach northeast of St. Tropez, but after a day of waiting, I felt the front of our transport bump against the solid ground. As I surveyed the scene in front of me, beyond the crystal-blue waters, the soldiers on the beach looked like a swarm of ants attacking a spilled picnic basket.

The beachhead was quiet except for the growl of tanks and bulldozers that were trying to form a hasty defensive line. The air was peppered by the occasional chatter of a machine gun or a random explosion. Ready or not, we were here.

The front ramp of LCI-45 dropped with a crash, and we got our first unobstructed view of the devastated beach before us. It took my breath away. The twisted wreckage of burned-out tanks and other destroyed military equipment littered the white-sand beaches as far as the eye could see. The most striking sight, though, was the hundreds of thousands of craters scarring the beach, remnants of the bombardment and the forest of antitank mines the Germans had left to welcome us to France.

As I took my first hesitant steps onto land on legs that had lost all sensation hours ago, I couldn't help but think that this wasn't how I'd dreamed of coming to France. After my years growing up in francophone Africa, I'd dreamed of visiting France one day: strolling along the Champs-Élysées, seeing the great cathedrals, and basking in the culture and art. But those dreams were from earlier days—before the Anschluss and Pearl Harbor, before the whole world had gone crazy in fits of violence and rage. Like most Americans coming of age in the 1930s, I saw vacation as something from a bygone age. Instead, we vacationed in our minds; we dreamed of being home with the people we loved and sleeping in our own beds.

Two hours after we landed, my company pitched its tents along the tree line at the edge of the beach. We fell into an exhausted sleep, lulled by the sound of the surf in one of the most idyllic places on the planet. However, this poignant moment was lost on my spent limbs and frayed nerves. As my eyes drifted shut, I began to pray the Lord's Prayer, but I was pretty sure I wouldn't make it all the way to "Amen."

+ + +

When dawn arrived, we were surprised to discover that the German forces that had been defending the beach and the whole region were making a hasty retreat toward the more defensible Toulon and Marseille. At our location, resistance had all but disappeared. We received our orders: we would pack up our tents and march into La Croix-Valmer to form a more secure base camp and begin the push into mainland France. As we prepared to roll out, I saw something entirely unexpected.

First in ones and twos, then in droves, the locals began to appear along the road to the beach. By the time we made our departure, hundreds of French men and women lined the road. Some waved French flags; others held up American flags. The beleaguered masses looked like they were ready for a Fourth of July parade.

Shortly after we began our ascent up the steep road leading away from the beach, I saw a man standing off to the side of the road. He was staring blankly at the formation of soldiers and repeatedly making the sign of the cross. Given the massive number of craters and the need for our anti-mine teams to check every inch of the road, our column moved at a snail's pace, and I couldn't resist the opportunity to talk with a real Frenchman.

"*Bonjour, Monsieur,*" I said, dredging up the French of my youth. "Are you a religious man?"

"No, not really," he said. "But look at this." He pointed to the line of tanks and armored vehicles. "If this is not a sight that requires one to cross oneself, what is?"

I agreed that it was a formidable sight. "But, sir, are you thanking God that we have come or just that you have survived?"

"God! What does he have to do with this mess? No, son, I do not believe in God. Religion just causes things like this; it doesn't do anything good."

I had no answer to that. The war had driven me into the arms of my Savior, not separated me from him. I politely bid the man farewell, and he resumed crossing himself and staring at the American and French troops moving up from the sea. I walked on, feeling disturbed by our conversation.

I had no way of knowing at the time that this moment was a precursor of things to come. Through that encounter, God was ushering me into ministry in France and the plans he had for me there.

+ + +

Shortly after leaving the beach at St. Tropez, our little boatful of soldiers was soon dispersed among various elements of the Alpha and Delta Sector. We'd had some casualties at landing, and we were in need of reinforcements. This meant that my discipleship group was now spread out over thirteen miles, from north to south along the defensive front.

It wasn't long before the forces were entrenched and engaged in holding the beachhead, and at that point I was able to visit the soldiers and see to their spiritual needs again. This was not a job for the faint of heart. As the only chaplain with the invasion force, I found myself taking on the weighty responsibilities of praying with wounded soldiers in the medical tents at the end of their lives, in addition to encouraging my friends who had accepted Christ in recent days. Each night as I collapsed into bed, I felt both deeply fulfilled and utterly spent. I couldn't remember ever feeling God so tangibly or experiencing such a close walk with him.

On the fourth day after we landed, Ed showed up smiling from ear to ear. I could tell he was up to something.

"Lookin' pretty tired, Evans." Ed's smile widened into a mischievous grin. "Been putting in a lot of miles these days?"

"Yeah, yesterday I hitched a ride up to St. Tropez to see Frank, but after a quick service there, I had to walk back. That's about ten miles, I'd guess." I grinned back at Ed. "Just doing God's work."

"Yeah, I know. Heard you were down at Cavalaire the day before. Bill said he saw you."

"Yep, that's another five and a half clicks up and over from St. Tropez," I said. "A bit too far to walk, particularly the 'up' part, so I waited for a ride each way."

"Well, I know that you're a saint and all, and that Paul walked everywhere when he wasn't getting shipwrecked. But the guys and I thought you might need a hand, you being an out-of-shape preacher and all." He shot me a sideways glance. "We happened to be wandering through the Army supply depot over by Delta Sector and saw a motorcycle no one was using. We appropriated it and repainted it up real nice, and now it's been reallocated to the chaplaincy."

"Oh, that sounds like trouble to me," I said warily. "God doesn't approve of stealing. As I recall, we went over that with Frank a while back."

"No one said anything about stealing," Ed scoffed. "This

is just military equipment that was waiting for a good use, and you're it. We need to talk to you, and you can't walk twenty miles every day. Consider it your chariot from God. Besides, with so many different forces mixed together here, I'm not sure anyone knows who really owns it."

"Well, I do like motorcycles," I conceded. "Is it one of those new Indian 700 series I saw coming off the transport ships?"

"Sure is. Nothing but the best for the preacher man." Ed smiled. "Want to come see it?"

CHAPTER 8

BEACHHEAD

Dear Jeanette,

Sitting here on the cliffs overlooking the Bay of St. Tropez, I am struck by the contrast of God's beauty and man's sinfulness. Below me, the anti-mine crews are working the beach relentlessly. It seems like the Third Reich emptied its storehouses of anti-tank mines and placed them all here. No matter how thoroughly we search, somehow there is always one more.

Every day when I go through the medical tents, more men are there. Such young men, all missing a hand or a leg or worse. What I see every day is horrific. I could almost believe that God has turned his back on us all, except that every day I see miracles too.

The medical rounds are the hardest for me. There's no way to prepare myself for the blank eyes that stare hopelessly back into mine and the desperation of these young men whose future is now so bleak. They are alive, yes. But to them, that's little solace.

Jesus, have mercy on us; we are sinful people.

A bright spot in this dark place is that my "church" is growing. Ed is unstoppable. Every day he brings by another guy or two whom he has led to the Lord and wants me to disciple. I finally told him the other day that it is time for him to start discipling them. I'll help if he gets stuck, of course, but his unabashed love for Jesus is bringing guys to faith left and right. He doesn't need me. What a pity that it takes circumstances like this to bring men to understand their need for a Savior.

Well, I need to wrap up. You and Alyce are in my prayers daily. The hope of coming home to see you is what sustains me—that and the baby steps the guys here are taking toward Jesus. I know you won't like this, but the guys got me a motorcycle so I can move between the camps easier. It's practical, but it's also a good bit of fun. It's even a nice shade of navy blue. If you were here, I would take you for a ride along the beach.

Forever yours,

Bob

After I sealed up the envelope, I whispered a prayer from high on a cliff overlooking the beach: "Father, I never dreamed that this is how you would use me, but thank you that you are at work. Most days I feel so inadequate to the task, yet all around me you are bringing men to yourself. Protect me today so I can serve you tomorrow, too. Show me the next man who needs to hear about you. And be with Jeanette and Alyce. Amen."

Refreshed from connecting with Jeanette on paper and with God in prayer, it was time to begin the day. After heading to the medical tents for morning rounds, I was off to Bible study with Bill in Cavalaire. If all the buzz was true, he had a whole group of guys who wanted to hear the plan of salvation before we packed up and headed to Toulon the next day.

Walking down the steep trail from the cliff, I caught glimpses of St. Tropez through the trees across the bay, where the spire of the cathedral dominated the village. It reminded me that even in this chaos, God hadn't given up on France or the French people, even though it seemed like every Frenchman had given up on him.

As I entered the main camp, I saw Ed hard at work, packing up with his squad.

"Orders are in, Evans," he announced. "We're going to take the road to Toulon tomorrow morning. Sounds like the road is mostly clear, but the Germans have had a few days to hunker down in Toulon. I think we'll be in the thick of it this time."

"I'm going to try to make it around to see all the guys one last time before we head out," I told him. "I know they'll want to pray together, and I hope there will be some new guys to share the gospel with before we go into the fight. You never know; this could be their last chance to hear it."

"Hey, I heard the technicians from the Third Armored have cleared out another little road between St. Tropez and Cavalaire. It heads over the mountain and then drops down and runs right along the beach. It could take some time off the trip for you—you should check it out." Ed gave me a good-natured nudge. "By the way, when am I going to get a chance to take the test drive you offered me?"

"Maybe this evening. We can play a bit when I'm done with the Lord's work for today," I said with a grin.

"Sure thing, preacher man." Ed slapped my shoulder. "Be safe."

Safe. What a strange word in a place like this. I knew I was safe with Jesus, but anything else was up for grabs. Stowing my Bible and notebook in the saddlebag along with an extra ration, I fired up the motorcycle and started picking my way toward the edge of the encampment. Waving to friends as I passed, I felt the powerful engine beneath me yearning to open up.

Gliding along open roads and feeling the sea air caress my face was one of my few guilty pleasures. It felt like flying, and I could almost forget the ugliness and pain around me for a few minutes. Climbing up the winding road to the top of the cliff, I discovered the turnoff to the new road Ed mentioned.

Another day, another adventure—all in the service of Uncle Sam, I thought as I turned the big bike onto the gravel road and eased up on the throttle.

The "road" looked like nothing more than an extra-wide cow path. With the path practically to myself, I began the five-kilometer trip considering what to talk about with Bill and his friends. Ahead I could see that the road was blocked off and that an arrow pointed to the left, toward the ditch and onto the beach. I saw tire tracks where vehicles before mine had ventured, indicating that the detour was safe. I gently pulled off the paved road and onto the wet, packed sand.

Seems stable enough, I thought as I weaved along the path, careful to avoid rocks and ruts. *I should be there in just a few minutes.*

All at once I was blinded by a white light. *I'm flying. I'm burning. I'm falling . . .*

CHAPTER 9

RESCUE

WITH EVENING MESS OVER and the daily training regimen done, Ed sat on a log at the beach, watching the waves rhythmically erase signs of the earlier battle. He was reading his already well-worn Bible, open to the book of John.

He could hardly believe it had been only a few days since the landing, and already nature had smoothed away many of the craters. If it weren't for the tents and the row of tanks nestled in the shadow of the tree line, he could almost forget he was in a war.

Ed heard a low rumble from the hills above, and he glanced up to see a convoy of trucks and tanks descending the hill. It was the Cavalaire squadron, arriving for tomorrow's push. Ed returned to memorizing a passage from John—one that seemed applicable to the next day's events: "These things I have spoken unto you, that in me ye might have peace. In the world ye shall have tribulation: but be of good cheer; I have overcome the world" (KJV). Ed *had* found peace. And he'd found it, of all places, in the middle of a war. *Crazy,* he thought.

A little while later, Ed heard footsteps approaching through the sand. He looked up to see Bill and two other guys from Cavalaire.

"Well, Ed, you ready for this?" Bill asked.

"Major General Truscott is, so I guess it doesn't matter much whether I am," Ed said. "But the sooner we get the Germans back to Germany, the sooner we get to go home. Sounds like the northern force is making great progress." He gave his friends a hopeful look. "Do you think it might be close to over? I'd love to be home for Christmas. I'd take Mom and Pop back to that little church for Christmas Eve, and then I'd tell them the rest of the story. I haven't been able to say it very well in my letters."

"Hard to say, Ed," Bill mumbled. "There's a lot of road between here and there, and right now our worry is that stretch tomorrow. Let's not get ahead of ourselves."

"How was your time with the preacher man today?" Ed asked. "He was determined to get around to see everyone before we pulled out."

"Evans? Don't know. Haven't seen him for a couple days," Bill said.

"Really? He tore out of here this morning on that bike of his, headed your way. Left about nine. You didn't pull up stakes that early, did you?" A tinge of concern made its way into Ed's mind.

"No, we left at three this afternoon, but I didn't see him,"

Bill said. "Maybe he changed his mind and went to St. Pierre first. You know how he loves that bike. Maybe he took the scenic route and missed us."

"I doubt it. He was pretty committed to seeing you all." Ed frowned. "We'll check his tent when we go up and see if he's back. He should be busy getting ready to pull out too. In the meantime, take a look at this verse I'm memorizing. Tell me if I get it right."

+ + +

Ed, Bill, and the guys talked and prayed until the sun faded behind the western horizon, its last rays shining like a beacon from the direction of Toulon—tomorrow's goal. As they walked back into the camp, Ed was surprised to see Bob's tent right where it had been. All of his belongings were sitting neatly around it, even though the other tents and supplies were already packed and ready to roll out.

That's strange, he thought. *I can't imagine Bob deciding to stay the night in St. Pierre. It's not safe to be out alone this time of night. I guess I'll just check on him first thing tomorrow.*

After Ed made it to his bedroll, he breathed a prayer before drifting off to a fitful night of sleep. "Father, be with the preacher man, wherever he is."

Ed awoke in the pale predawn light to a distant rumble from the east, marking the arrival of the St. Pierre troops at the rally point. *God, be with us today,* he prayed silently as he rolled out of bed and packed his few belongings.

He glanced across the camp. There was Evans's tent,

unchanged from the night before. *This isn't right,* he thought as he jogged over to take a look.

"Evans, are you in there?" Ed hollered. "Rise and shine, preacher man." He looked in the tent, but it was empty. With a growing sense of unease, he jogged toward the vehicles arriving from the east. As he walked along the column searching for Bob and his motorcycle, he saw Frank sitting on the back of one of the trucks that was easing its way into the formation.

"Hey, Frank!" Ed shouted over the grumble of the big diesel engine. "Is Evans with you?"

"The preacher? Nope. Haven't seen him in days."

Ed stopped in his tracks.

"Frank, get down here. I think we've got a problem."

Frank hopped down, shouldered his pack, and grabbed his M1.

"Problem? What kind of problem?"

"I'm not sure yet," Ed said. "But no one has seen Evans since he headed out for Cavalaire yesterday morning. He was planning on running all over creation to see the guys one last time before the assault. But as far as I can tell, he didn't see any of you." Ed's voice was growing more urgent. "Stow your gear on your transport, and let's go find Bill and the guys. They're down by the mess tent. I'll swing by medical to see if he's there and meet you in five."

Afterward, as Ed trotted to the mess tent, he saw Frank and Bill discussing the situation, worry creasing their brows.

"When I was up at medical, I heard them say we'll roll at

11:00," Ed said. "The way I see it, that gives us four hours to find Bob. He was going to take that new shortcut from Tropez to Cavalaire, so I think that's where we should start looking."

"We don't have time to walk to St. Tropez and back," Frank said. "Besides, the military police are patrolling the perimeter, looking for guys who are thinking about sitting out today's festivities, if you know what I mean. I can't afford to be AWOL."

"I know, but we can't just leave him," Ed pleaded. "I've been in this mess for three years now. This is my fourth landing, and we've never had a chaplain before Bob. He volunteered to be here with us. That's sacrifice. And I, for one, am willing to get in trouble if that's what it takes to help him. Think of everything he's done for us." Ed looked each man square in the eyes. "I saw a couple of Jeeps from the St. Tropez force sitting over by the highway. I say we borrow one for a quick trip. You guys in?"

"I don't know. I doubt they just left the keys there for us to take," Bill said warily.

"Keys?" Ed scoffed. "I told you, I'm the best mechanic in the Bronx! I don't need keys! Let's go before it's too late."

A few minutes, some sparks, and a couple of curses later, Ed, Frank, and Bill were bouncing down the road to St. Tropez as quickly as Ed could negotiate the narrow road.

"There it is!" Bill shouted. "That's the turn off to Cavalaire!"

"Hold on!" Ed made a sharp turn and forced the Jeep off

the pavement onto the gravel road, barely slowing down. A few minutes later, they came to the roadblock and slowed to a stop.

"Huh," Ed said. "They told me this road was open. That's why I suggested it to Bob."

"Let's take a look." Frank and Bill hopped out and started for the barricade.

"Hey! Over here!" Bill shouted. "Looks like there's a detour that goes around the barricade down here. And wait . . . look at this."

A single tire track ran through the soft sand, directly down the middle of the detour. Someone had driven there on a motorcycle.

"Get in," Ed ordered. Then he eased the Jeep toward the road's edge. Slowly they descended into the ditch and onto the dirt track, maneuvering to avoid the rocks and debris littering the newly created lane. After a few minutes, the road emptied onto the beach, and that's when they saw it.

About fifty yards in front of them, the tire tracks disappeared into the mouth of a massive crater. Just beyond it lay the charred wreckage of a motorcycle. Halting, the three men sprang from the Jeep and sprinted toward the bike. When they got close, they saw small patches of blue paint amid the charred and mangled mess. This was Bob's bike all right, but Bob was nowhere to be seen.

"Spread out! We've got to find him!" Ed commanded. "If nothing else, look for footprints. Maybe he survived and is headed back to St. Tropez."

However, the grisly truth soon became obvious. Thirty feet past the bike, on the other side of a small dune, they discovered a mottled, half-naked form lying facedown. Fearing the worst, they approached the lifeless form. To their surprise, they heard a hoarse, rasping plea.

"Help me. Please help me."

Ed and Bill knelt down next to Bob, shocked by the sight of the bloody, sand-encrusted body of their friend.

"We're here, Bob. We're here. Hang in there," Ed implored. "Jesus, please don't let him die." Then Ed turned to the others. "Frank, get that Jeep as close as you can, but stay off the beach. We don't know if there are more mines. Bill, grab the board in the back of the Jeep. We can try to put him on that. I'm afraid to just pick him up."

"Help me. Please help me," Bob wheezed. He seemed oblivious to the fact that help had indeed arrived.

The men carefully rolled Bob's body onto the board. As they turned him over, fearing the worst, they were surprised to see that most of his injuries appeared to be severe burns and surface injuries. His only other wound appeared to be a nasty gash in his scalp that was now caked with dried blood and sand. The men slowly carried Bob to the Jeep, trying to keep his body as still as possible.

"Bill and Frank, you're going to have to hold him down while I drive," Ed cautioned. "I'll be careful, but we have no way of keeping him inside without your help."

Ed jumped behind the wheel and sparked the Jeep to life.

He dropped the gearshift into first, ready to head out, when Bill grabbed his shoulder.

"Wait a second," Bill said, "I'm not really sure how to do this, but I think we should pray for God to protect Bob right now."

Ed sat there for a second, torn between wanting to get back to camp and understanding that they needed Jesus a whole lot right then.

"You're right," Ed said over his shoulder. "If anyone can make a difference right now, it's God. But we don't have time to wait. You pray; I'll drive."

Without waiting for consent, Ed stepped on the accelerator and headed back to the main road.

Thirty painstaking minutes later, they stopped the Jeep in front of the medical tent and were surprised to see it buzzing with activity. Rushing in, Ed grabbed one of the doctors he knew.

"Hey, you've got to come now," Ed panted. "I've got Evans out here. He hit a mine, and he's in bad shape. What's going on here anyway?"

"Sorry, Ed, new orders," Dr. Martens said. "With the forces pulling out, it's not safe to leave the medical depot here. We're moving all the patients to the hospital in Draguignan."

"Can you at least take a look at him? He's barely alive," Ed pleaded.

"Okay. Let's take a look." The doctor followed Ed to the Jeep.

As soon as the doctor laid eyes on Bob, he took in a sharp breath. "How long has he been like this?"

"I'm not really sure," Ed replied. "I'd guess for about a day. He keeps asking for help, but I don't think he's aware that anyone is here."

The doctor gently peeled Bob's eyes open and looked at his blank stare. Then he checked his pulse. "His heart is good. That's a relief, but I'm not sure what we can do for him right now. We're going to have to load him up and hope he makes it to Draguignan." The doctor turned away from Bob for a moment to call out orders. "Medic! Get me a stretcher now! Get this guy on the truck. Someone go with him and see if you can clean him up a bit. Bring a blanket to cover him up too. We're not going to be able to get him undressed the rest of the way until we get there, and it's going to be tricky then. I think some of the fabric is burned into his flesh."

Ed stood there, dazed, as the medics lifted his unconscious friend off of the board and placed him on the stretcher. Seconds later, they loaded him into one of the big trucks with the Red Cross symbol on the side. That's when he became aware of someone tugging on his sleeve.

"Ed, we've got to go," Bill whispered. "The MPs are right over there, and I've got to get back to my squad. We've done everything we can. He's in God's hands now."

Ed nodded dumbly and allowed himself to be led away.

"This is not right, Jesus," Ed muttered. "Not Bob. Don't take him—we need him. I don't think I can do this without him."

Paris, France
November 14, 2015

JAZZ JONES

CHAPTER 10

TAKING BACK THE TOWN

I CLOSED DOWN THE COMPUTER, trying to take in everything I'd been reading about Bob Evans. It was now four in the afternoon, and I still needed to get some groceries. I looked at Sven, who was sitting on the couch checking on the ongoing search for the terrorists. According to the news reports, things in the city were still chaotic. Paris was under a curfew, the first since World War II. President Hollande had declared a state of emergency and closed the borders, and people were being urged to stay home unless they had a reason to go out.

"*Schatz*, I really need to get some things from the grocery store," I said, using my favorite German term of endearment for him. "Do you think it's safe to go?"

"I think it's safe for us to go out. Most stores and restaurants are open, and people are going about their business. It would be good to get some fresh air—and that way we can see what's going on firsthand."

I realized I'd been half hoping Sven would say we should

just stay in. *Was I crazy to even think of going outside the four walls of my home?* After a minute, I realized I'd been so lost in my thoughts that I hadn't responded to Sven—or even moved, for that matter. Looking up, I saw Sven watching me.

I got up from the table, which itself felt like an act of defiance. I didn't want my life to be controlled by terror. "I'm not going to live in fear, babe," I declared. "I'll grab the grocery bags, and let's go have a look."

A few minutes later, Sven and I headed downstairs and toward the front door of the apartment complex. Despite my bravado, it felt eerie to take those first few steps out onto the street. This place was the same, yet it also felt like I was setting foot in a foreign city for the first time.

At first glance, nothing looked different. People were out and about. My friends at the crêpe stand down the street were open for business. Had it all been a dream?

Sven put his arm around my waist, and we just stood on the sidewalk for a moment. I took in the details of my neighborhood—the young men across the street sitting on the steps to their apartment, the elderly lady pushing her walker with her small bag of groceries slung over the front.

After a moment, I broke the silence. "It really does look safe. Look over there." I motioned with my head. "That woman with the walker is on her way back from the grocery store, and if she made it, we should be okay too."

Sven smiled and reached for my hand, and we started the ten-minute walk to the store.

As we moved through the streets, I was surprised by—and

proud of—the Parisians. Though everyone had clearly been affected by the attacks, they refused to allow fear to prevent them from moving on with their lives. The cafés were open, and a steady stream of patrons flowed in and out. Other people were enjoying their customary strolls along the tree-lined boulevards. I felt comforted to see the city continue to buzz, unabated, everywhere I looked.

Sven and I walked through the neighborhood and aligned ourselves with the Parisians who were committed to taking back the city. We felt a strong sense of solidarity with the evening strollers, café goers, dog walkers, pram pushers, and grocery shoppers. Walking hand in hand with Sven in the unusually warm evening, I began to feel more at ease with being outside the security of my flat.

That growing sense of peace vanished in an instant when I heard a siren in the distance. The wailing intensified and was soon joined by the blaring of a siren from a second vehicle. As the emergency vehicles approached our street, the volume crescendoed. Suddenly, a police car followed closely by an ambulance careened around the corner and sped past us. I stood staring at the flashing lights, barely breathing. I squeezed Sven's hand.

"Are you okay?" Sven asked, his eyebrows raised.

"*Oui,*" I responded slowly. I didn't want to overreact, but I couldn't help but wonder if something was happening nearby.

We continued to wind our way through the now-quiet streets and bought the groceries. The walk back to my flat was uneventful, though my false sense of safety had waned with the sound of the sirens.

As we rode the tiny elevator to my fourth-floor flat, two emotions warred within me. The first was a sense of satisfaction over having faced my fears and ventured out. But at the same time, I felt a deep sense of sorrow that "my" Paris was different today—it had changed overnight. In the past, I might have only half noticed a siren. Now it caused a tremor of fear to run through my body. And I knew I wasn't alone in this reaction. As determined as people were to get back to business as usual, the simple wail of a police siren was proof of how quickly bravado can morph into fear.

CHAPTER 11

REFUGE

LIFE SLOWLY RETURNED TO NORMAL, though the ever-present news stories kept the events of November 13 in the forefront of everyone's mind. I continued taking French classes at the Sorbonne, and the intensity of the immersive language course was just the distraction I needed. The class gave me something to pour myself into to help me forget the attacks and the subsequent fears.

A few days after the attacks, I returned to my flat and made myself a cup of tea. I was just about to settle down to an evening of French homework when the phone rang. I heard Charles Cross's voice on the line.

"Hello, Jazz. How is class going?" he asked without preamble.

"Hi, Charles," I said. "Well, you know, class is class. It's good, and I'm learning a ton, but after a full morning in

French, I can barely think straight in any language. And then I have two or three hours of homework to do before the next day, when I'll do it all over again."

"Yes, I remember those days," Charles commiserated. "Amy and I took classes together, and afterward we barely talked to each other on the way home, we were so mentally tired. Well, I know you have a lot to do, but I wanted to check on you and see how things are going this week."

"I'm okay, but I can get pretty emotional if I let myself really think about it," I said. "A friend of mine asked if I was talking to anyone to process what happened. I hadn't thought about talking to a counselor before, but maybe I should." I looked into my cup of tea. "Part of it, I guess, is that it seems like everyone around me is just moving on with life, and I feel kind of silly that what happened still bothers me."

"Well, I'm pretty sure everyone else is not okay," Charles said. "People are probably thinking the same thing but don't have anyone to process with. Why don't you talk to Member Care? That's what they're there for!"

Our talk turned back to life, French class, and GEM. "Did you see the e-mail I sent about GEM's response to the refugee crisis?" Charles asked.

"No, I haven't had a chance to check e-mail yet today," I said. "What did it say?"

"Do you remember the news report from earlier this fall about three-year-old Alan, the boy whose body was found on the shore in Turkey? His family had been trying to escape to Europe from Syria," Charles explained. "That was in early

September, I think. The story was all over the news, and I'll never forget the pictures of his little body in a red T-shirt lying on the beach. That story really increased awareness of the refugee situation in Europe, and GEM's leaders decided we had to do something to specifically address the physical and spiritual needs of these people."

"Sounds timely," I said.

"Now a missionary family from Germany has moved to an island in Greece near where the boy died. GEM will host teams from Europe and the US to welcome the folks coming across by boat. Some of the pictures are heartbreaking—I can't imagine what it must take to drive people to risk their lives by crossing the sea in a little rubber raft."

"I think we got a little taste of what that kind of desperation feels like last weekend," I said. "I know what happened here is a drop in the bucket compared to what those people are experiencing in Syria, but it was close enough for me. I can't imagine living someplace where bombs go off regularly and hundreds of people are killed each week." I took a breath, trying to calm my fraying nerves. "They're saying that the guys who attacked the Bataclan nightclub and the stadium came into Europe as refugees. It sounds like Greece is a pretty dangerous place to send missionaries."

"You're right, I guess," Charles responded. "But I'm sure most of the people coming in are fleeing for their lives, and they need help. I'm proud of our missionaries who are going to help, even though it isn't safe. Then again, I don't have to tell you it isn't safe here, either. Anyway, GEM leaders are asking if anyone here would like to go there for a week or two to help. And some of our French field missionaries are thinking about going down for a bit."

"Seriously?" I said. "That sounds kind of intense."

"One of the churches that supports me in Texas is considering sending a team, and I could join them. I could help with the ministry and see my old pastor. I'm not sure yet, but I need to decide by Monday. Would you pray that I hear from God over the weekend?"

"Sure," I said. "In fact, we should pray tonight before you go."

"They also asked if we thought Paris could be what GEM is calling a 'destination city': a place where we could start a ministry for incoming refugees. That almost makes more sense to me, because if they're staying here, we'd have more of a chance to build a relationship with them. Has Bill ever taken you to the park over by Gare du Nord, where a number of immigrants live?"

"No, he hasn't." I thought about my team leader, Bill Campbell. I don't think the man has ever experienced the slightest bit of fear when it comes to evangelism. Technically, we're not supposed to be engaged in ministry yet, but so far I can't imagine how 'real' ministry would give me more opportunities to share the gospel than I've already had in language school."

"Yes, there are a lot of opportunities here in Paris, and it would be cool if it became one of the destination cities,"

Charles said. "But we'd need to get some more missionaries to focus on that."

I wasn't sure how I would feel about a ministry focused on the same people group that committed last weekend's atrocities. It sent a chill down my spine, but I didn't want to dampen Charles's enthusiasm. "Let's take some time to pray about your decision to go to Greece and for all the people who were affected by the attacks. Then I need to get to work on my French, or I'll be up all night."

We prayed, and then Charles said, "Remember, Member Care is only an e-mail away." I thanked him, and we said good-bye.

After our phone call, my mind was plagued by thoughts of terrorists, immigrants, and danger. I looked out my window, thinking about the continued search for those responsible for the attacks. For the moment, the suggestion of Member Care was pushed from my mind. Instead, I decided to read a bit more of Bob Evans's story. Something about it was comforting, and I felt a bit of a connection with him after reading about his run-in with explosives. What happened to him after that? I needed to know.

Draguignan, France
August 29, 1944

BOB EVANS

CHAPTER 12

YOU ARE ALIVE

SOMEWHERE IN THE DISTANCE, I heard a familiar chime. *Church bells.* This was my first conscious thought in as long as I could remember. I felt a warm breeze crawling across my raw flesh. I tried to open my eyes, but all I could see was a dim light. *Where am I? What happened? Am I dead? Is this heaven?*

Suddenly it all rushed back to me. The thrum of the motorcycle engine, the wind on my face, the explosion. I winced as sand and debris seared into my flesh. Panicked, I cried out. Or, at least, I tried to—my dry, cracked lips and parched throat wouldn't cooperate. The whispered gasps sounded pathetic even to my ears, yet in moments, gentle hands grasped my arm, and a soft voice whispered, *"Calmez-vous! Ne bougez pas! Vous êtes en sécurité. Nous sommes ici."* The foreign yet familiar language surprised and disoriented me further.

Quiet. . . . We are here. . . . My foggy brain struggled to translate.

"Aidez-moi." My brain dredged up the words from somewhere in my youth.

"You are alive," a woman's voice said in halting English. "You live."

Kind fingers touched my face, and after a slight pulling sensation, light suddenly hit my eyes. The bandages were off my face, but I still couldn't make out my surroundings.

"Relax. You are safe."

As I began to acclimate, I became aware of a pillow beneath my head and the light weight of sheets covering my body. I squinted in the direction of the reassuring voice, trying to brace myself against the glaring midday light.

"Where am I?" I rasped.

"Wait. Wait," the voice said. "Water first."

A hand lifted my head, and my stiff muscles moved for the first time in what felt like a century.

"Drink. Drink." I felt a straw being placed against my lips. "Slowly."

Cool liquid seeped into my parched mouth. With every painful swallow, I felt life flowing through me. I tried to open my eyes again and realized that someone had closed the blinds and the room was now dimmer. Slowly, I forced my eyelids open. Blurry images coalesced into indistinct shapes, and finally my eyes made out the form of a young nurse.

"Rest now. You are alive." The footsteps retreated, and I was left to sort out how I'd gotten here.

By the time the door creaked open again, I had reassembled most of the puzzle pieces. I was a chaplain with the US Navy, and I'd been headed to see some of my men in Cavalaire when I hit a mine. That's where lucidity ended and the questions began. Was that today? Yesterday? A week ago? Where was my squad? Where was I?

As the nurse approached, I asked the most important question: *"Où suis-je?"* I had to know where I was.

"You are in a Draguignan hospital. There are many soldiers here." The voice was gentle and soothing. "Relax. You live."

Draguignan. That was to the east. We'd been about to attack the cities to the west—Toulon and Marseille.

"Where is the army? Where are the US soldiers?" I asked.

"Gone," the nurse said. "They took Toulon two days ago. The injured are still coming in. So many." She sighed. "But that is not for you. You must rest. I am here with something for the burns. Remain calm. This will hurt."

Pain radiated through my side. *How can ice burn?* I wondered, wincing.

"I know, I know. Relax," she soothed. "The pain will fade."

I closed my eyes as a gentle hand spread the salve across my wounds. In seconds, a warmth seemed to radiate from my side, and I felt myself slipping into unconsciousness again.

+ + +

A few days later, three men arrived and lifted me from the bed, placing me in a wheelchair. One of the men wheeled me toward the door while another gathered my belongings.

"Sorry, pal," the man pushing the chair barked in gruff English, "but you're good enough to go into gen pop now. This room is needed for another guy."

I said nothing as they wheeled me down the hall into a large waiting area. There, I saw row upon row of men—so many it took my breath away. The quiet moans and groans rose like a symphony of pain from every corner of the room. The man pushed my wheelchair into a small exam room on the other side of the large hall, where he stopped at one of four exam tables. Strong hands lifted me from the chair and deposited me gently but unceremoniously onto the table.

"You can rest here until the doc has a minute to see you."

I closed my eyes, praying for sleep, but I couldn't close my ears against the incessant groans coming from every direction.

"Dear Jesus, please help these men," I whispered. The desperation in the room hit me like a punch to the stomach. I felt tears running down my cheeks, and I wasn't sure if I was crying for them or for me. I wasn't sure it mattered.

Not knowing what else to do, I closed my eyes and began to recite the prayers of my youth. At some point, my exhausted body gave out, and I slipped into merciful sleep.

+ + +

A slightly gruff voice startled me awake.

"Lieutenant Evans, is it? You're not going to like this, but you have to get up today."

As my eyes came into focus, I saw a burly man wearing

the uniform of an Army doctor standing at the foot of my bed.

"I guess it was too much to hope that I could nap here for the rest of the war, right?" I said. "Trust me. I'm ready."

"That's what you say now, but I'm pretty sure you're going to hate me by the time you go to sleep tonight. I'm Ben Harper." He extended his hand. "I'm the US Army surgeon assigned to the wounded here in Draguignan. Rotten mess that it is."

"Yeah, I can think of better ways to meet," I agreed. "I'm Bob. I was a chaplain with the landing forces at St. Tropez. Maybe I still am, but I have no idea how to catch up with them."

"Well, I wouldn't worry about that if I were you." Dr. Harper began to examine my wounds. "I think your part might be done, though a lot of your friends are showing up here every day. Bloody mess down there in Toulon. We're winning, but at a high cost. I've never seen anything like it. Why can't the Germans just give up and head out? They're suffering worse than we are. Do we have to kill all of them before they give up and go home? I tell you, Evans, I've seen enough mangled young men to last a lifetime. French, Americans, Germans—it doesn't matter. God's heart must be breaking over what's going on here."

As our eyes met, I saw the depth of sorrow reflected there. And it wasn't just the physical pain; it was young lives going into a Christless eternity. I nodded and turned away, my heart breaking over the unfolding tragedy.

Dr. Harper wasn't joking about how painful our short walk would be. My muscles and flesh screamed with each painful step. Every movement stretched and flexed the burned skin that had been immobile for days. *I do hate him,* I thought.

"Come on, Evans," the doctor urged. "Just a few more steps. I'm not going to carry your sorry rear back to bed. You've got to walk yourself. Now move that leg. I know it hurts, but you're not dead, so let's get this done with so we can both get some rest."

In my mind, I knew he was doing what he had to—what was best for me. *Yes, I definitely hate him,* I thought as I swung my right leg awkwardly forward while leaning on Dr. Harper's arm.

I could see the empty bed just a few steps away, but it might as well have been a mile. I gritted my teeth and took another step. After what seemed like hours, I fell into my bed, exhausted. I heard Dr. Harper's voice saying, "You done good, kid," as I faded from consciousness.

+ + +

Those were long and painful days, but in time, I no longer needed Dr. Harper to compel me out of bed, and I began to long for something other than the halls of the hospital. It felt like parole the day the nurse nodded and said, "*Oui,* you may go out into the village today, if you want."

Bandages still enveloped my head and the hand that was burned the worst, but I didn't care. I was free.

CHAPTER 13

VILLAGE LIFE

WELL, GOD, this isn't how I imagined I would get to France, but here I am, I thought as I walked out onto the steps of the hospital and surveyed the street in front of me.

The hospital was at the far end of the main street, near the edge of the village, so it didn't take me long to find my way toward the center of town. Late-summer flowers filled the flower boxes, and even now, in early fall, the simple French restaurants had their outdoor seating set up. If it weren't for all the military vehicles lining the streets, I wouldn't have thought anything was amiss in this typical French Riviera town. As I took in the scene before me, I wondered if this adherence to normal life was how the townspeople were coping with the crisis that had enveloped them.

As I ambled down the street with my ill-fitting clothes and bandages, I must have been a frightful sight. I felt like I'd come back from the dead, and I probably looked like it too. But I soon realized I wasn't the only patient walking the streets of Draguignan. Almost everywhere I looked, I saw men and a few women in various stages of recovery making their way down the streets. In fact, they almost outnumbered the French villagers who scurried past, alternately trying not to make eye contact and staring outright.

Another phase of the war had come to this idyllic village, and the locals were struggling to make peace with it. I was just another walking corpse to remind them of the price that had to be paid for their freedom.

As I opened the door to the first restaurant I came across, I was surprised to find it empty except for one man sitting at a table, sipping a small glass of wine.

"Bonsoir, monsieur, est-ce que le restaurant est ouvert?" I greeted him with my best French and as big a smile as I could muster.

Taken aback, the man asked, *"Parlez-vous français?"*

"Oui, j'ai grandi au Cameroun," I said, indicating that I had grown up in a French-speaking part of Africa.

"Ah, let me find you a table," he said in English. He was obviously pleased at my attempt to speak French, but he was also aware that I was more comfortable in my native tongue.

When I sat down, he presented me with the menu.

"Anything. Anything you want. No cost."

"Thank you," I said, "but I have francs."

"I will not take them." His face was stern. "Not from you. Not from any American. You are my guest."

Looking into his eyes, I knew this was an argument I would never win.

"Bless you, sir," I said. "I'm afraid I haven't done much to earn your generosity, though. I was in France only a few days before I ended up at the hospital." I reached out my hand and offered him a smile. "I won't take food from a stranger. I'm Bob Evans."

"Kristophe Roux," the restaurant owner replied, shaking my hand heartily.

"Is it always this quiet?"

"Lunch was over an hour ago," he said with a chuckle.

"Oh, I'm sorry." I rose to my feet. "I didn't know."

"*Non, non*, sit down." He gestured toward the chair. "I get little enough business as it is. I never thought I would be lonely as a restaurant owner, but war changes everything."

"It's been difficult?" I asked.

"Difficult is an understatement." It was impossible to miss the haunted look in his eyes. "During the occupation, our village was overrun by the Germans, and I didn't have a choice but to cook for them. They paid every once in a while. But when they drank, I just tried to stay in the kitchen." A faraway look came over Kristophe's face. "I knew what the soldiers had done to other shop owners and folks in town. We were entertainment to them—property, and nothing more. You never knew what might upset them. Of course, when they were here, none of the locals would come. So for three years, I served the enemy, and my only real payment is that I am still alive. That's something, I guess. There's no justice in this godforsaken world," he finished in a whisper.

"I'm sorry. I can't imagine what it's been like."

"Yeah, well, you guys are here now, and it looks like you've got them on the run. Maybe there will be an end to this before all the cemeteries are filled to overflowing. Saint Peter ought to be happy," Kristophe said with a tinge of bitterness. "His business is up."

"Well, God sees it all, and he cares," I offered. "Even in the direst of circumstances, he is with us."

Kristophe looked me directly in the eye, with a sadness I could barely fathom. "God left France a long time ago, and it doesn't seem like he's planning on coming back any-time soon," he said. "When all this started, we flocked to the church to pray, but no one was listening. Stop by the church now, and you'll find it emptier than my restaurant. No, if there ever was a God, he's gone now. He has given up on all of us."

I held Kristophe's gaze, my heart breaking. No words—French or English—came to me. My voice was silenced by the despair emanating from my new French acquaintance.

Rising to his feet, he said, "You look hungry, my friend. What would you like to eat? I can offer a good meal and I make my own wine, but unfortunately I cannot offer you coffee to finish. There is none to be had anymore."

Kristophe served me a delicious, hearty meal complete with good wine and warm, fresh bread. He sat with me while I ate, and the rest of our conversation was decidedly light. We talked about our families and foods we enjoyed. Yet as he gathered the dishes and I walked to the door to return to the hospital, I saw the haunted look return to his eyes.

Dear Jesus, I prayed silently, *please show Kristophe that you still exist. He's a good man, and he is desperate for you right now. I wish I could offer him some assurance of your love, but I don't know what to say.*

Thoughts of Kristophe stayed with me the whole evening. I also recalled the man on the beach who had crossed himself while watching the Army approach. "Jesus, please send your Spirit to France," I prayed. "Show people here that you are real."

After hours of tossing and turning, my prayers faltered, and sleep overtook me.

CHAPTER 14

BROTHERS

I WOKE WITH A START. My brain snapped to attention as if an alarm had sounded. "The church!" I blurted. "That's it! I'll go to the church!" Maybe all my training at Wheaton College would finally pay off. Even if the sole church in town was Catholic, surely I could do something to help the local priest encourage the people.

I got out of bed with a new purpose burning in my heart. In whatever way I could, I would help the people in this village find or renew their faith in God. I had no way of knowing it at the time, but that day marked another piece of God's call on my life.

I dressed quickly despite the pain from my wounds, hurried to the mess hall, and downed a cup of weak coffee and a bowl of oatmeal. For the first time since the accident, I had a mission. Looking at my empty cup, I was struck by the nugget of an idea: *Hmm. Coffee.*

As I hobbled out of the hospital's front door and started

to make my way up the hill toward the town square and the church, I saw a medical transport turning onto the street, bringing yet another load of pain and despair. Another day, another legion of lives tragically altered or snuffed out almost before they had begun.

Everywhere I looked, I saw reminders of the cost of this war in Europe. I couldn't help but think of the countless families around the world who would soon receive official notices concerning their loved ones, delivered by mail or by soldiers with downcast eyes. Whether by post or in person, the explanations rang hollow. *Father, we need an army of chaplains to keep up with the enemy's work. I know I can't do it all, but please help me to do something. These people desperately need hope.*

As I passed the restaurant, I spied Kristophe filling out the day's menu on his signboard.

"*Bonjour*, Kristophe! I have been advertising your great food among the guys in the hospital. I think you'll need to make a little more today! And here's my suggestion: only the first meal is free. You have to eat too! And remember, there are other currencies in the world besides gold."

"*Merci*, Bob! I will consider it, but you know I get by." Kristophe returned my wave. "Where are you going today? You seem to be moving with purpose."

"I am," I replied with a grin. "I will tell you about it later. In the meantime, I thought you might like this." I pulled a small canvas bag from my pocket and tossed him some coffee beans I'd "liberated" from the mess hall.

As his fingers closed around the bag, a look of complete astonishment and gratitude washed over his face. *"Merci!"* was all he could manage as I continued up the street.

+ + +

Kristophe was right that I had a purpose, but honestly, I had no idea what I was supposed to do specifically. Early that morning, I'd felt certain God had prompted me to go to the church. The impression was so clear that he might as well have spoken it aloud. But what was next?

I walked up the winding street, my body reminding me that I hadn't been doing much for weeks. As I made my way, I took in more of the village. Each step that echoed from the well-worn cobblestones whispered of a deep history. The stones had been trodden on since the time of the Romans, who had used this town as a station on their route to the sea. Over the course of countless generations, the bedrock of this street had seen wars, plagues, betrayals, weddings, children, joy, and sorrow. The street now led up to the church, whose steeple loomed over the city like a sentinel in a storm.

As I walked, I saw that for every open shop or inhabited home, two or three others stood abandoned. The broken windows, boarded-up doors, and *Fermé* signs left an empty feeling inside me, but they were nothing compared to the quiet. Some of the blocks I passed were entirely silent— the antithesis of the bustling French villages that lived in my mind from the literature I'd read and the few photos I'd seen.

I finally arrived at the square in front of the church. Its former beauty remained, but where there should have been vendor stalls and crêpe kiosks, I saw abandoned antiaircraft guns surrounded by razor wire. The dragon-topped fountain in the center of the old town square was dry, filled only with dust and debris. Even the front of the church seemed silent and foreboding as I made my way up the worn stairs to the massive wooden doors of l'Église St. Michel.

To my surprise, the heavy oak door was unlocked. When I pulled on the handle, the door swung outward on unforgiving hinges that groaned in protest. I slipped inside, my eyes taking time to adjust to the dim light.

When I was able to take in my surroundings, I was struck by how the church was both inviting in its architecture and disturbing in its emptiness. A few lonely candles flickered on a stand near the front of the church. In the sparse light that crept through the dusty stained-glass windows and candlelight, I saw a single, bowed form sitting on the front row of pews. Unfazed by the invasion of daylight streaming from the door, the figure remained as still as a statue. I suddenly felt awkward and out of place.

Perhaps this was a mistake, I thought as the giant doors closed behind me. But I couldn't leave without at least trying to carry out the call I'd heard that morning.

Gathering my resolve, I turned and quietly—or at least as quietly as an out-of-shape, injured man who had just made his way from the hospital could—approached the front of the church. As I reached the second row of pews, I heard a tired voice in heavily accented English: "I don't speak English. Please go away."

I stopped, uncertain. Was it because I was an American? Was it something else? Should I turn around and retreat to the hospital?

No, the Spirit within me prompted. Jesus' message was clear, and I was here to follow him.

"Bonjour, Père. Je parle un petit peu français," I said, letting him know that I could speak French, at least a bit.

"Ah, why have you come?" He still didn't look up. "I have no answers for soldiers here."

"I'm not a soldier. I'm a chaplain—a priest of sorts."

"A priest. Are you Catholic, then?" For the first time, I sensed a small amount of interest in his voice.

"No. I was raised a Protestant. But I've spent a lot of time with Catholics since I joined the Navy, and I grew up on the mission field, where godly people from all backgrounds of Christianity served God together."

I wanted to avoid drawing denominational boundaries with the only other spiritual leader in this town. If I'd learned anything since joining the military, it was that unexplored adhearence to denominational lines meant death to the ministry.

My words were met with silence. Perhaps the priest hadn't expected someone like me to walk through those ancient doors today. After an awkward moment, he slowly turned toward me, regarding me with sorrowful eyes that seemed far too old for his young face.

"So, Chaplain," he said wearily, "what can I help you with? If you've come here to find God or answers to why so many men are lying on those hospital beds down there, I'm sorry, but I fear God has left us Frenchmen to reap the harvest of our sinful lives. My prayers and answers ran out a while ago. I just stay here because I have nowhere else to go."

In that moment, my heart felt like it would collapse with sorrow. I'd imagined a variety of scenarios of what it might be like to meet the Catholic leader of this town, but this was beyond my worst imaginings. The priest's despair sucked the air from my lungs, and I stood there, pondering what, if anything, I could say. That's when God's Spirit prompted me to speak.

"I think God sent me here today because one of his faithful and beloved sons needs him as much as anyone in that hospital. I'd be lying if I said I understood any of this. The pain and suffering are beyond anything—" I faltered. "I don't even have words for it. All I know is that if I give up hope, hope will leave entirely. So for the sake of those men down there and for the folks I've met in town this week, I'm holding on to the hope that God is still good and that he still loves us mortals. That's why I came here today. I need someone to hope with me."

"Hope," the man said slowly, as if he were trying out an unfamiliar word. "Hope is in short supply these days. You may be disappointed."

"I know," I whispered. "I can only imagine the things you have seen. The horrors and tragedies. I feel it too. Some nights I just lie there in the hospital hearing the pain of the helpless souls around me and weep. Yet in the midst of this carnage, I have seen rebirth, too. Some of the most unlikely men have turned their lives over to God and are following him in places like Marseille and Toulon. They're facing death—or worse—every day, and yet they believe. This helps me to continue to believe." I took a deep breath and then plunged on. "What helps you? Perhaps in this mess, we can help each other hold on."

Again, there was only silence. His eyes searched me like a man dying of thirst who sees an oasis in the desert. *Is it real, or is it an illusion?* In his eyes, I saw the battle raging between hope and fear.

Slowly, the priest stood up and extended his hand to me. "I am Father Matthias." His voice was drenched in exhaustion.

Holding his gaze, I stepped forward and gripped his hand. I sensed that it had been a long time since someone had come to this place for anything other than taking. I gave his hand a reassuring squeeze. In that moment, it felt like I'd found another survivor on a battlefield, a brother in hope and despair. Together, with God's help, we might just make it until morning.

Father, I prayed silently as our hands remained locked, *let me offer life to this wounded soul.*

CHAPTER 15

A BITTER CUP

"COME," MATTHIAS URGED suddenly, "let's get out of this drafty hall. I have some coffee that I received from some of the soldiers." He turned and headed toward a small door hidden in the shadows of the cathedral's towering nave. Once inside, I followed him through a narrow warren of hallways to a small living space. It was cluttered and unkempt.

"Pardon the mess," Matthias said, clearing a stack of clothes from a chair next to a simple wooden table. "I never have guests."

Taken slightly aback, I wondered, *What changed that after our conversation?*

I sat on the newly vacated chair and looked around the cluttered but homey room as my host stoked the fire and began to fill the chamber of a small espresso kettle.

"I am sorry, but I have only coffee to offer you." Matthias looked up briefly from his preparations.

"No apology needed," I assured him. "A cup of non-Army-ration coffee is more than enough. You are too generous; I know what a cup of coffee means these days."

We waited in silent anticipation as the small brass kettle gurgled and hissed, periodically releasing small jets of steam. In a few moments, Matthias carried the kettle and two small cups to the table, where he deftly poured us the steaming espresso. The rich aroma filled the small room, and Matthias sat down in the chair opposite me.

"Are you from here?" I asked.

"Me? No," he said. "I was assigned to this parish by the bishop in Marseille six years ago. I moved here from my home in Arles. You would not have recognized the town that existed then by the husk of what you see today. It was a quaint town, full of life. There were always visitors coming through to escape the colder climate in Paris and up north. It was a magical retreat from the craziness of the rest of Europe." The priest's eyes took on a wistful, distant look. "On days like today, everyone in town would have either been recovering from the last harvest festival, preparing for the next one, or working in the fields to bring in this year's crops. I loved harvest days, and the church was right at the center of it all. No one understands gratefulness quite like a farmer who has had a good year and knows it was nothing of his doing," he said. "That was before the war, of course. Even after the war began, it took some time for the occupation forces to get here. For a time, I think we believed it would just pass us by."

"So you've been here through all of it, then?"

"Yes," he replied simply.

We sipped our coffee in silence for a moment before he went on.

"At first it was just the German officers who arrived in town to tell us what had happened and what we should expect. They set up offices in the town hall and began to catalog what Draguignan had to offer. Some of our strongest men and those with specific skills were taken away— God alone knows where. But as the war escalated and the Germans needed more resources, they began to send trucks to gather our food—and, of course, our wine. Those days were tough, but not too bad for most of the town. We kept our heads down, said *ja* when we were supposed to, and tried to go on with our lives. There were families who lost their men, and we tried to take care of them, but it was mostly okay. It was manageable."

He fell silent again. "Well, can I get you more coffee?" he asked.

"Yes, please." I handed him my cup.

After pouring our refills, he placed the kettle on an iron hook near the fireplace and returned to his chair. He stared off into the distance for a long moment, and I wondered if I had overstayed my welcome.

Then he spoke again, his voice somber. "When the soldiers came, everything changed. First it was the Italians. They began to arrive in early '42. Later that year, one Thursday morning, a force of German SS troops arrived with a convoy of empty trucks. They set up a tent in the square, right in front of the church. The next morning, before dawn, we awoke to screams and shouts. During the night, they had raided every home in the Jewish quarter and brought the families to the town square."

Matthias took a ragged breath. "Draguignan was a peaceful town. We all got along, regardless of our religion. But not that day. That day, I saw what men are capable of. Those men and women, people I knew, were no more than cattle to the German troops. Women were screaming. Families were separated into different lines and loaded onto different trucks. Their homes were ransacked, and I saw soldiers carrying off everything that wasn't nailed down. I watched it all from an upper window of the church, praying that I wouldn't be next, praying that it would stop, praying that God would do something. That wasn't the last time I said that prayer, but I no longer think God hears my voice."

The priest covered his face with his hands. "By Friday evening, it was all over. The trucks rolled away, and the tent was torn down. When we awoke on Saturday, we realized that every Jewish family in our town—hundreds of our friends and neighbors—were gone. We had all heard the rumors from the north, but I don't think we believed we were truly at war until that day."

I sat there, swept into the story, trying to comprehend the pain and the tragedy. I had heard rumors of the work camps, but this was the first time I'd heard a firsthand account of the havoc that had been wreaked on innocent townspeople.

After a few moments, he began again. "When the Italian

forces moved in en masse, we began to experience what it was really like to be occupied. In general, the Italians weren't too bad. Italians and French both appreciate the finer things of life, and we found ways to live together. Some of the soldiers even came to Mass. However, it was not a good time to be a young woman in our town. Mostly, it was just men drinking too much and getting a bit out of control, but every so often, it was something worse. We did what we could to keep our girls safe and make sure they didn't leave their homes unless they had to. During that time, I filled my days by going around to families whose men had been taken away to offer them food. That was an uneasy summer and fall. Little did we know a day would come when we would look back fondly on the Italian occupation." Matthias shot me an ominous look.

Mass kidnapping. Abuse. Theft. Foreign occupation. "It got worse?" I asked.

"Worse, more complicated—I don't know. Perhaps *insane* is a better word." Matthias's voice was tinged with sarcasm. "In November of '42, the Germans took over the occupation. That's when you Allies were pushing them out of Africa. The soldiers who arrived then were different. They weren't the raw recruits who had come here from Italy; they were seasoned soldiers, men who had seen action. They had taken towns before, and death haunted their eyes. To make things worse, the news that was arriving wasn't good for them, and it made them desperate. These were young men with authority—and the guns to back it up. They never came to Mass, and soon the locals didn't either." Matthias looked me in the eye. "Bob, that's when God left this place. I don't know what we did to anger him, but he is no longer here."

I waited silently. I knew that tragedy like this broke the heart of the God I served; it didn't send him away in exile. But I wasn't sure how to say this to the clergyman in front of me.

"What little we had left was theirs for the taking," Matthias continued. "Nothing was safe. They didn't wait for the women to come out; they forced their way into people's homes and took them if they wanted them. If anyone resisted, a swift death awaited—if a person was lucky. If not, a brutal, gradual death was in store. You can't imagine how many broken people I have prayed with or prayed over. The cemetery is running out of plots, and even so, we're not allowed to bury all the dead. This town I love, these people I came to serve—we are the walking dead, the ones with no hope. Can you imagine living like that for a year? What would you say to redeem this God of love?" Matthias's question rang with accusation. "No, don't answer that," he muttered. "Let me finish this godforsaken tale."

I could see that he was reliving the horrors in his mind, and I was getting only glimpses, like a rock skipping across the surface of an ocean of tears.

"Have you seen the empty homes and shops in town?" he asked.

"Yes, I noticed them today on my way up here. Have the townsfolk fled?"

"Fled?" he retorted. "To where? No, each of those empty buildings represents another person—another husband, father, mother, sister, or brother—I had to bury. They aren't gone; they are dead, killed for one ridiculous reason or another in this crazy war. Perhaps they didn't do what they were asked. Perhaps they died of malnutrition. Perhaps they didn't show the right amount of deference. It doesn't matter—dead is dead."

And there it was. I saw it in his eyes. It was his job to keep hope alive, but no one could have done that in a place like this.

"And now here we are." There was no mistaking the resignation in his voice. "Our liberators have arrived. Soldiers are soldiers, and wine is still wine. What now? Will we win? Will we lose? Does it even matter? What is left for us? We are a generation of corpses. All that's left is empty homes, empty shops, and empty hearts.

"So, what words do you have for me, *Chaplain*? What verse from Scripture?" His voice was cynical, but I sensed that underneath the bitterness, he longed for a reason to hope again.

I breathed deeply. *This is all you, God,* I implored.

"Matthias, I have no verse. I'd guess you know the Bible better than I do. A person can't go through what you just described without looking to God's Word for every little scrap of hope he can find. I'm not here to preach. While the stories I could tell are different, they are no less tragic. Young men from a country far from here signed up, willingly or otherwise, for a war they don't understand. Patriotic fervor took them all the way to boot camp, but it was courage and resolve that took them the rest of the way. I signed up to help people—to preach the gospel to men who could be in God's presence at any moment. I barely got started before I hit a tank mine on the beach and ended up in the hospital. Suddenly, I was the patient instead of the doctor. I have the same questions you do. Why would God allow men to do this to each other? Why hasn't he stopped us?" I gulped, wondering if I'd said too much. "Did you see any of the fighting when we landed?"

"No, with the sirens going off, I was hunkered down in the church—the nearest place I could find with thick walls and a ceiling," Matthias said. "It doesn't matter, though. I have seen enough here to last me a lifetime. I don't need to see the bombs going off."

"Well, it's as awful as what you've described," I said. "Just all at once."

Looking at the floor, Matthias began hesitantly, "Growing up, I loved the church. It was a magical place: the candles, the beautiful windows, the singing. It seemed like everywhere I looked, God was there. I can't imagine a life where I didn't choose to serve him. But I never imagined this. I never imagined that he would leave us, that I would witness the end of all beauty, and that I would be left standing here in an empty building."

"He hasn't left us." My voice was quiet but firm.

He looked up, and I went on. I knew that if I didn't get

this out now, I never would. "Down on the beach, in the middle of all the death and chaos, do you know what was happening?" I paused. Before he had a chance to answer, I added, "God was saving people. Almost every week, I was praying with new guys who were accepting Jesus as their Savior and doing their best to learn how to follow him. I'm here today because some of the men I was discipling risked everything to come and find me. God is still here, even though the way he's working looks different than we'd have drawn it up." I waited until Matthias met my gaze. "I know how you feel. When I was lying in that hospital bed, all I could do was question what he was up to. I came here to serve with the men, and a few days into the action, I was lying there wounded, and they were out there dying. But do you know what he showed me? He showed me that there are more people who need to be reminded of the hope of heaven than just US soldiers."

"I hope you're right, Bob. But he has been silent toward me."

"No! He isn't," I said. "I'm here! Together, we need to find him again."

I saw tears about to overflow his red and swollen eyelids. In that moment, I felt like God gave me a glimpse into the depth of his soul, and what I saw there was hope.

"I pray you are right," Matthias said. "Our conversation today has been the closest I have felt to being in his presence since . . . I can't even remember when. Thank you for coming."

"Father, would you like to pray with me?" I knew it was a risk, but I felt compelled to ask.

"You're a Protestant, aren't you? Are you sure you want to pray with a Catholic?"

I smiled. "I'm a follower of Jesus. I think that's enough in the world we live in."

And so we prayed. It was perhaps one of the most honest prayers of my life. No pretense. No rehearsed words. Just my broken heart mingled with his, crying out to our Father.

As I walked back down the street toward the hospital, the empty windows and boarded doors took on new meaning. If I closed my eyes, I could almost see the faces of those who had suffered staring out at me.

My heart felt both heavy and alive. In that moment, I felt the Spirit whisper to me, *You are my ambassador of hope.* Those words marked my life forever.

CHAPTER 16

SECRETS

AND SO THE DAYS IN DRAGUIGNAN ROLLED ON. I had lunches with Kristophe and prayer meetings with Matthias. I met a shop owner, Samantha, who had two boys and whose husband had been taken during the early days of the war. I met Michel, an elderly farmer whose children were all either dead or missing. I helped him fix up his generations-old farm, which not only gave me some needed exercise but also allowed for some great spiritual conversations while we worked. I also met Leon, whose wife had been taken by soldiers, raped, and killed. Now he was raising his young son alone. The names went on and on.

I thought I'd heard it all until, one day, Kristophe asked me this question: "Can you keep a secret?"

"I think so," I replied, wondering what this was about.

"There's someone I think you should meet. I think she needs you."

"Needs me? Why?" I couldn't hide my curiosity.

"I honestly don't know," Kristophe said, "but there's something about you. When you come in for lunch, I can almost believe life can be different again. I think she needs that. Come back tonight at ten o'clock."

"Why at that hour?" I asked. "They may not let me leave the hospital so late."

"Come if you can."

I could think of little else the rest of the day. Who was I going to meet? Why was there so much mystery?

I waited until the hospital quieted down for the night and the sonorous snores of recovering soldiers began. I rose quietly and headed toward the latrine. Once there, I slipped around the back and into the shadows. I navigated the streets as quietly as I could and made my way to the door of the restaurant.

I tapped lightly on the door, and a moment later, I heard footsteps from within, followed by a creak as the door opened. The lamplight from inside spilled out onto the barren street.

"Come in, come in," Kristophe whispered.

As soon as I slipped through the door, he quickly bolted it behind me. Motioning for me to follow, he headed toward the back of the restaurant. I followed in silence, wondering again what I was getting myself into.

Once we arrived in the kitchen, Kristophe gestured for me to sit at a small table and pulled up a chair across from me.

"Bob, can I trust you?" I'd never heard him speak in such a serious tone.

Taken aback, I said, "Yes, of course. What's this about?" A twinge of fear fluttered in my stomach.

Looking intently into my eyes, he nodded once. "I don't know why exactly, but I do trust you." It seemed like he was more intent on convincing himself than convincing me.

"What I'm about to show you must be a secret. You can tell no one. Do you understand? No one."

I nodded solemnly.

With that, he got up and walked across the room, opened the door to the cellar, and disappeared inside. I heard the sound of something heavy being dragged across the floor and then the creak of hinges. Muffled voices floated toward me, and moments later, Kristophe reemerged, followed by a slight form in a hooded cowl. When they neared the lamplight, I saw the face of a young girl, perhaps in her late teens, peering out.

Kristophe offered her the chair opposite me and pulled up a small stool for himself.

"Bernadette, this is the man I told you about," he said. "You are safe with him. I want him to hear your story."

Bernadette regarded me silently, never fully meeting my gaze.

Turning to me, Kristophe said, "You need to know that Bernadette—she isn't what they say. She . . . she didn't go with them willingly. But some people would still kill her if they found her here."

I looked at Kristophe, confused, and saw tears forming in his eyes. "Who is she?"

"She's my niece. Her parents were killed when they wouldn't let the soldiers into their farmhouse. What could she do? She was only fifteen. They found her hiding under the bed and took her back to the hotel they'd taken over. They made a show of 'escorting' her and a few other girls into town and taking them to the restaurant or the pub. Everyone in town saw that she was always dressed in nice clothes and ate food with the soldiers when everyone else was starving. They also saw the soldiers' hands all over her." Kristophe's hands clenched.

"She didn't have a choice, but the rest of the town knows that she was with the Germans. I know some of the women went willingly with the soldiers just to survive. Others had no choice. But in the end, it makes no difference. No one would make a choice like that if our world weren't in the chaos it's in." Kristophe glanced at Bernadette, whose face registered no emotion.

"The day of the invasion a few weeks ago, the Germans had to leave quickly. When the townsmen entered the hotel, they found Bernadette and the other girls locked in a room. They also found the bodies of girls who had been beaten to death and left tied to beds. Since Bernadette was alive, the Frenchmen did to her what they do to all traitors: they shaved her, tattooed her head, and beat her. I think they would have killed her, but I persuaded them to throw her out of town. I followed, and when dusk fell, I brought her back and hid her below the restaurant. She hasn't spoken a word since I brought her here. I know you still believe in God . . ." His voice trailed off.

"You have to understand, the people here—they really aren't bad people, but they have suffered so much." He somehow sounded guilty, defensive, and angry all at the same time. "We have lived in fear for so long. It makes people angry to be impotent. I think they just need someone to blame in order to divert their own pain."

In the awkward silence, I managed to say, "I do believe in God, and I have seen what men can do."

Kristophe closed his eyes and lowered his head. "Can you help?" he said. "Will you pray for her? I don't know what to do." He hung his head, no longer able to contain his tears.

Once again, I found myself speechless. That had happened to me more in the past month than ever before in my life, and yet I sensed God in this moment.

"I would love to talk to her and pray with her." I looked at her face in the shadows of the hood, but there was no response. "Do you think she'll mind?"

Kristophe motioned for me to proceed.

"Bernadette, my name is Bob. I'm an American and a Christian." Not knowing what else to say, I breathed a prayer: *God, I need you to show up.* "I came here with the American Navy as a chaplain to try to encourage our soldiers. I have a young wife and a new daughter back home in America. My baby girl was born while I was here, and I haven't seen her yet. But even though I haven't held her or laid eyes on her, I already love her more than life itself. I would do anything to protect her. She is precious to me. The Bible tells us that's how God loves us—like his children. I can't even imagine what your life has been like. The things you've seen and the things that have been done to you—they break God's heart." I took a breath and forged on. "When I left my family to serve in the war, I thought I was coming here to minister to American soldiers, but now I believe God had other plans. I think he sent me for the people here, for you. He wanted someone to come to this town and tell you that God sees you and loves you."

On a sudden, Spirit-prompted impulse, I slowly reached across the table, clutched the hood in my hands, and pushed it back so it settled on Bernadette's shoulders. She didn't move a muscle. I wasn't sure she was even breathing. But as I sat down, I saw a glistening trail making its way down her cheek. Even though her eyes were still firmly fixed on the table, I saw that they were red-rimmed and brimming with tears. I could also see the tattoo of a swastika and the word *traître* circling her head.

Tears came unbidden to my own eyes as I looked at the young girl trembling across the table from me. How could anyone do this to someone so young? With the Holy Spirit swelling within me, I suddenly saw with Jesus' eyes the woman at the well in the girl before me. Exposed. Broken. Desperate.

A voice within me prompted, *Tell her she is forgiven.*

"Bernadette, God doesn't blame you for what happened," I said, emotion tripping my voice. "He died a long time ago to forgive all of your sins. It doesn't matter what the people here say. It doesn't even matter if you were glad you were alive when others were dead. Let it go. Jesus doesn't see you as a traitor. He sees you as his daughter, and he sent me here to tell you that he loves you. In his eyes, you are pure."

She blinked, and the trickle of tears became a flood. Out of the corner of my eye, I saw tears running from Kristophe's eyes too.

"Would you mind if I prayed for you? I think Jesus has more to say to you than I do right now."

For the briefest of moments, her eyes met mine. She gave a slight nod and quickly brushed the tears from her cheeks.

Trying to still my aching heart, I took a steadying breath. "Jesus, please speak to your daughter here. She is hurting, and her heart is breaking. She's beginning to think she deserves all the things others have said about her and all that has been done to her. She needs to see herself as you see her. She needs to know you love her with the same sacrificial love that her earthly father had for her. Her parents gave their lives trying to save her, but it wasn't enough. Please, dear Lord, what words do you have for your daughter?"

Suddenly my mind came alive with Scripture, with words of love and hope. *"Let the little children come to Me, and do not forbid them . . . Wash me, and I shall be whiter than snow . . . offered Himself without spot to God . . . sins may be blotted out . . . Then I will sprinkle clean water on you, and you shall be clean; I will cleanse you from all your filthiness . . . "* From this whirlwind of truth, one Scripture rose to the top. I recited it aloud: "Therefore, if anyone is in Christ, he is a new creation;

old things have passed away; behold, all things have become new." The verse hung in the air between us.

"Bernadette, you know about Easter, right?"

Surprised by the question, she looked up at me quizzically. Her tear-soaked eyes met mine, and she nodded.

"Jesus died on the cross for everything you have experienced—both what has been done to you and what you have done. Can you believe that?" I looked at her, but she cast her eyes down again. "Do you want to be remade, to be new again? To put your past behind you and start fresh?"

All at once, her body was racked with sobs, and she grasped the table in front of her. In a voice that was gravelly from disuse, she almost shouted, *"Oui, oui! S'il vous plaît, faites-moi propre de nouveau!"*

Make me clean. It was the cry of every person who had seen the horrors of this war. I reached across the small table and placed my hand on hers. *When was the last time anyone had touched her with benevolent love?* I wondered.

"Just ask him, Bernadette. He will forgive everything."

"God, please forgive me. I am so sorry I hid when the soldiers came to our house. I am so sorry for all the things I did when I was at the hotel. I am sorry I was happy to be alive. I am sorry I was happy when they took the other girls and not me. I am sorry that I liked the food. I am sorry that I liked my dress. I am sorry I did not always hate them. I am sorry I was a traitor to my town." Her confession went on and on, with words that had been pent up for months. Kristophe and I just sat there as this precious young woman bared her soul to God. Finally, her words wound down to quiet sobs, and I felt the Spirit nudge me to end our time together.

"Jesus, thank you for hearing the prayers of your daughter this night. Fill her with your peace, and let her know she is forgiven for all time. Amen."

The three of us sat there with tear-filled eyes, in awe of what had just happened. I had seen God at work before, and perhaps I was the least surprised. Kristophe had an unreadable expression on his face and a far-off gaze that spoke of someone lost in his own wrestling. Bernadette seemed both spent and at peace, like a marathon runner whose race was complete.

Suddenly, Kristophe roused himself and disappeared deeper into the kitchen, only to return seconds later with a bottle of wine and three glasses. "I think we all could use this," he said, pushing a glass toward each of us. "To God and new beginnings." He lifted his glass, and we responded in kind, gently clinking our glasses together.

Wheaton College wouldn't have approved, but I was a world away from fundamentalist America, and raising a glass seemed appropriate somehow. As the red liquid ran down my throat, I was suddenly aware of all that wine represents in Scripture, in terms of both past remembrance and hope of the coming day when Jesus will welcome us into a Kingdom that is far removed from the pain and suffering of our current world.

After saying my good-byes, I made my way toward the door. Kristophe grabbed my shoulder and turned me to face him. "I don't know if 'thank you' can cover what happened tonight, my friend, but thank you. I knew you would know what to do."

"Well, that made one of us." I chuckled. "Honestly, it wasn't me. God came to your home tonight. We were just privileged to be here too. I will pray for you both tonight, and we can talk again tomorrow if you want to. Oh, and don't worry. Your secret is safe with me. But I wonder, what would it take for the rest of the town to accept what God just did?"

"I think you may be right that God came here tonight, but he came here with you. I won't forget what you've done. You came here to be healed, but I think you may be the doctor this town needs." Kristophe shot me a meaningful look. "I will think about your question."

"Good night, Kristophe." I walked out into the silent night and made my way back to the hospital. "Thank you for showing up tonight, Jesus. Thank you for your love for broken people," I whispered. "After tonight, I think I understand how the Prodigal Son felt when he came home. Please keep the enemy from stealing her joy."

I quietly entered my section of the hospital and slithered, undetected, between the sheets of my bed. A riotous symphony of snoring men surrounded me. *Well, Jesus, it looks like I could use one more miracle tonight,* I prayed silently. *Make me deaf for the night!*

Suddenly my home in Hawaii felt a million miles away.

Paris, France
November 21, 2015

JAZZ JONES

CHAPTER 17

LOOKING BACK

ON A LAZY SATURDAY MORNING, I sat at my dining room table, sipping a cup of coffee and reminiscing about my family, who felt so far away at the moment, and my home in Hawaii—the last place my family was stationed and the place I considered home. As much as I loved Hawaii, the word *go* had reverberated within me for as long as I could remember.

The more I read in Scripture, the more convinced I became that I wasn't alone in this call. In Genesis 12, God told Abram, "Leave your native country, your relatives, and your father's family, and go to the land that I will show you" (verse 1, NLT). I felt God speaking to me every time I read that passage. For me, *go* meant leaving Hawaii when I was thirty-two in the hope that God would use me and stretch me in ways I couldn't imagine yet.

Despite the sense of urgency I felt to leave behind what was comfortable, I never thought I would live overseas as a missionary. I had always admired friends and other members of my church who left for missions overseas. And while I wanted to live abroad, I'd never thought about it in the context of ministry before.

In 2011, I was considering moving to one of four countries. In Japan and Brazil, I had the opportunity to teach English, and in the Czech Republic and France, I'd been offered an English-teaching certification course. My best friend, Leinani, suggested we each pray about these four countries for a week, not focusing on one more than another, to see how God would lead.

The end of the week brought an interesting surprise.

"I don't know about you, Jazz," Leinani told me, "but I felt God speak to me about two countries, not just one."

"No way!" I exclaimed. "God gave me two countries too! Which ones were they?"

"Well, Brazil stood out to me when I prayed."

"Same here!" I interjected.

"But an image of the Eiffel Tower kept coming to mind too," she continued. "Is France your second country?"

"Yes! Whoa, that is wild." I paused for a moment to let all this sink in. "Okay, so now how do I know which one it is?"

I decided to continue praying about Brazil and France, asking God to make his plan clear. Having gone on a mission trip to Brazil in 2009, I had always wanted to go back. I looked into the options for teaching English there, but despite the encouragement from my Brazilian friends, nothing seemed to fit. For one reason or another, the doors to Brazil kept closing.

Okay, it must be France then! I finally concluded. But even so, I didn't know how, when, or where God would use me in France.

Not long after I decided God wanted me to go to France, a friend on staff with Youth with a Mission in Honolulu told me about a tour of France that a staff member with YWAM was going on the next April. As soon as I heard her describe the tour, my heart leaped, and I sensed the Lord saying that was the trip for me. More quickly than I ever dreamed possible, God provided the money through family and friends, and it felt like an additional confirmation that I was headed in the right direction.

I tried to keep my expectations and desires in check, but the thought of being called back to the continent of my childhood excited me. Could God be so extravagant? I often found myself reminiscing about happy memories from growing up in Germany. I had felt important when my parents needed me to act as their translator with our German landlord when I was only five years old. I loved that I could easily pronounce *bügeleisen* (iron) and *löffel* (spoon)—words that my mother and father had a hard time pronouncing at first.

I thought back to my family's adventures of exploring Europe by car. The trips were always accompanied by my homeschooling homework, which included discovering useful travel phrases and facts about the places and cities ahead of time. God had instilled an adventurous spirit in me as a child, and now, in his grace, he was opening the door for me to live out a new adventure in Europe. But first things first: I needed to pray. I wanted to let God lead, not Jazz.

I contacted the leader of the trip, Edward, who was happy to have me join. Since I was going to visit some friends in Germany before our tour started, he arranged for me to stay with Chantal, a young woman in Paris he knew through YWAM. I would stay with her in her fifth-arrondissement flat in downtown Paris for a couple of days. I was beyond excited.

I went to France with my eyes open to see what God might be calling me to do. Yet I wasn't expecting God to give me the vision for full-time missionary work in Europe.

CHAPTER 18

A SPY IN THE LAND

I ARRIVED IN PARIS on the high-speed TGV at the Paris Est Station, west of the Seine River. I quickly spotted the signs for the #7 metro platform and headed to a kiosk to buy a ticket. Unfortunately, the first machine I waited in line for only took cash, so I had to wait for the next one to use my credit card. A man and a teenage girl from Germany were in line in front of me, but they had to leave to ask for help at the ticket counter. When they came back, I spoke to them in German, telling them to go ahead of me.

"Danke," the man said.

When it was my turn, I bought a pack of metro tickets. I saw a group of British people who were having trouble purchasing their tickets behind me in the line. Having five minutes of experience under my belt, I stayed to help them.

Finally, tickets in hand, I made my way to the #7 track, ready for my ride to the Latin Quarter. I glanced at my watch, realizing I was already behind schedule. When I got on the metro, I ended up standing next to the German man and girl. The girl sat down in an open seat, and the man offered me the other free one. We introduced ourselves in German and quickly discovered that we planned to get off at the same stop: Place Monge.

After several minutes on the train, I noticed that the doors were still open, even though they should have shut already. The metro loudspeaker finally came on, and I heard the words *"un accident."*

Not good! I thought, looking around for clues as to what was going on.

Stefan, my new German friend, asked a local what had been said on the announcement. It turned out there had been an accident right by Place Monge, so our metro was going to stop at Pont Neuf instead. *Fantastique,* I thought. *I only have the directions from the metro stop at Place Monge.*

When the train departed at last, we were delayed at every stop prior to Pont Neuf as workers cleared the way ahead. I started to feel anxious, knowing that Chantal was expecting me to be at her flat during her break from school.

When we finally arrived, Stefan suggested that I travel with him and Hannah to our final destinations. We decided to walk instead of taking a bus, and I was surprised to discover when we exited the station that it was raining. I was reminded of the movie *Midnight in Paris*, and to my delight, I found that the sentiment is true: "Paris is beautiful even when it rains."

As we crossed Pont Neuf, we saw the Eiffel Tower in the distance. *I'm in Paris!* The reality was finally starting to sink in. Thanks to Stefan's good sense of direction and the maps we'd found at the metro station, we felt confident we were headed in the right direction. I was in a rush to get to Chantal's place, but my pace was too fast for Hannah, whose shorter legs couldn't carry her so quickly and who was taking pictures as if the famous sites would no longer be there tomorrow.

Half an hour later, Stefan suggested I continue on alone, as he didn't want to slow me down. We said our adieus, and I thanked him for his help. *God is so good!* I thought, grateful for help with this part of my journey.

About two hours after I was due to arrive at Place Monge, I found Chantal's street. I walked down the narrow cobblestone lane lined with buildings about four stories high. Most of them had restaurants, cafés, and pubs on the street level with apartments above. Once I found Chantal's building, I schlepped my suitcase and backpack up four flights of stairs and found a note taped to the door. Chantal said that she wouldn't be back until nine and that I should hang out at a café until she came home. Back down the stairs I went, luggage in tow.

I spent the next two hours in a crêperie across the street and struck up a conversation with the crêpe man. When he realized I was American, he spoke a little English to me, although, when he started speaking rapidly, he randomly threw in words in French. I smiled, happy to feel like I was already experiencing French culture firsthand.

I was still warm from my trek, so I sat outside and ordered a *crêpe sucrée avec jus de citron*—a crêpe with sugar and lemon juice. I savored it, trying to make it last as long as I could. When it got chilly, I moved inside the small restaurant and ordered a cappuccino. I still had an hour to kill before Chantal got home. French songs were playing inside, and the crêpe man often sang along. *So French!* I thought.

I walked back to the apartment and waited about ten minutes until Chantal got home.

"I'm so glad you're here!" she said. "I was worried when you didn't get here when you thought you would. But you're here now!"

I don't think I'd ever been so happy to see someone I'd never met before. Right then, I made a mental note to get an international calling plan.

After talking to Chantal over a cup of tea about France and her ministry there, I felt excitement welling up inside me in spite of my exhaustion. I couldn't wait to see how God would move in my heart during this discovery trip.

+ + +

Since I was in Paris for a couple of days before meeting up with the YWAM group, I had a chance to wander around the city and get a feel for life there in a non-touristy way. Staying in Chantal's flat gave me a small taste of what it would be like to live in Paris—and, so far, I was captivated by what I was experiencing.

One of the mornings of my stay, I stopped at a small

boulangerie to pick up something for breakfast. As I stepped into the shop, the smell of freshly baked croissants and baguettes transported me back in time to my year of kindergarten in Germany. I had been best friends with the principal's daughter, and we'd often played together at her house. Every once in a while, her mother would give us a few deutschmarks to walk down to the little *bäckerei* close to their home to pick up fresh bread for the meal. Now, breathing in the smell of European delicacies, I felt a sense of coming home.

But what I loved most about wandering the streets and squares of Paris was being able to look at it with the eyes of Jesus—seeing both the beauty and the need of the city.

One afternoon, I headed to the base of the Eiffel Tower. According to my mother, when we'd visited there when I was three years old, I escaped her grasp and ran across the forbidden grass. I was laughing, but the policemen who were chasing me were not.

My happy memory was quickly dispelled by the plethora of Gypsies and beggars there pleading for money. Scammers lurked in the subway entrances looking for naive visitors. "Excuse me, do you have change for a twenty?" "Do you need help translating the ticket machines?" At the famed Parisian restaurants, people sat alone, sipping their wine with distant looks in their eyes. Yes, there was beauty, but there was also suffering, and God was breaking my heart for these people.

When the rest of the YWAM group arrived, we spent a few days in Paris, listening to history lessons about the city from our leader, Edward. Then we made our way south to spend time in Avignon, Marseille, and the YWAM base at Saint-Paul-Trois-Châteaux. Our schedule was leisurely, allowing us to spend a few days at each location and get a feel for the local atmosphere and the ministry opportunities there.

Not long into the trip, it became clear to me that God was planting a seed of love in my heart for France and the French people. I had a strong sense that my future home would be in France. My only question now was which part of France?

I had never been to the south of France before, and I was interested to see if my place would be there. I figured the warm climate would agree with me, having grown accustomed to the weather in Hawaii. In each of the three southern towns, I asked God, "Is this where you want me to be?" God responded to my heart with a no each time.

Then, one day before leaving Paris, I sensed God speaking to me in an unmistakable way. The rest of the group had already left for the States, leaving me to take in more of the beautiful city. Looking up to admire the puffy white clouds against the background of bright blue, I paused for a few seconds. I felt an overwhelming sense of peace and God's pleasure. In my spirit, I heard him whisper, *Yes, Jazz, this is for you.*

I didn't want to live in Paris because *I* wanted to. I wanted it to be a "God thing," not a "Jazz thinks this is a good idea, so it must be right" thing. My prayers for God's direction became more intense. *Perhaps if I pray more, God will direct me to the south of France,* I thought. *I am an island girl, after all!* When I offered those prayers, God was silent. But whenever I thought about Paris, a feeling of contentment washed over me and lingered the entire trip home.

+ + +

The morning after I returned home to Hawaii, I searched online for mission agencies that worked in Europe and came across Greater Europe Mission. GEM mobilizer Rick Bravine responded to my web inquiry within a day, and as it turned out, he and his family had been missionaries in Paris for many years. He was elated to answer my questions and put me in touch with the field leader, Charles Cross, who described how GEM would help me minster effectively in France.

Between the vision he cast for what God was doing and my recent experience there, I was hooked. That week I filled out my application to GEM and was invited to Colorado in November for final testing and training for new missionaries. Charles also virtually introduced me to Bill Campbell, the leader of the Paris team. After talking to him, I was encouraged to hear about what God was doing through him and his family in the Paris area. The same week, the possibility I'd heard about to work with a team in southern France disappeared almost as quickly as it had come up.

When Bill heard this, he responded, "See! God wants you to work with us in Paris!"

"So it seems!" I realized that God had closed one door but opened another. *God, I trust you with my life. If you want me in Paris, I'm ready to go.*

131

CHAPTER 19

THE FIRST DAY OF ADVENT

NOW, A YEAR LATER, I found myself wondering what God had been thinking.

The city that had seemed so wonderful and full of life now had a cloud of death and worry hanging over it. Even though people were trying to put on a brave face, I could see the fear in their eyes as they scanned the streets and hurried about their business. In the two weeks since the attacks, we kept hearing news of the investigation. Some of the perpetrators had been captured, and others had been traced to Brussels. The country remained in a state of national emergency, as evidenced by heightened security and an increased police presence at public places such as train stations and shopping malls. To make things worse, it was late November, and almost every day dawned gray and drizzly. I was a long way from the bright, sunny, hopeful days of my vision trip.

As the city struggled to return to life as usual, I decided that the first day of Advent was as good a reason as any to try to find some normalcy myself. France's Catholic roots still echoed in the city's culture in the form of the Marchés de Noël, traditional Christmas street markets. In many city squares, workers had been busily assembling small wooden booths that would become home to a plethora of home-made crafts, Christmas decorations, and Advent candles, as well as cheeses, sausages, desserts, and, of course, *vin chaud*, the French version of hot mulled wine. These markets were something I'd loved as a child when we'd visited the similar German Christmas markets as a family, and I hoped they would magically transport me back to quieter, simpler days.

This year, because of the attacks, many of the markets had been delayed in opening. Most of them were ready now, though, so Sven and I made plans to go to the markets the following day.

One of the things I love about Europe is the simplicity of Christmas. People still exchange gifts and observe traditions, but without the same frenzy of materialism we see in the States. In Europe, Christmas is muted, and strangely, for a place with such a small Christian population, sacred. I was looking forward to experiencing the markets, being with Sven, and taking my mind off the state of France after the attacks.

By the time Sven buzzed my doorbell the next day, I had already been up for a few hours, eager to enjoy the day together. I smiled as I looked forward to sampling one or two of the French delicacies that came out only at this time of year, and I could already taste the soul-warming *vin chaud*.

Today would be a turning point—I could feel it. Maybe this would mark a return to the Paris I'd arrived in a year ago. "God, please give us a special day today," I prayed.

I opened the door for Sven and greeted him with a quick kiss and a tight embrace. Through my south-facing windows, the sun was just breaking through, and it looked like it might be a semi-warm day. Still, like all good Europeans, I tucked my umbrella into my purse.

"Which market do you want to go to today—the big market in the business district or Champs-Élysées? Or the closest one on Place Saint-Germain-des-Prés?" Sven asked.

"How about the one in the square at la Défense? I hear it's the biggest Christmas market in the Paris region, and I didn't get a chance to go last year. But I'll go to any of them, as long as you're with me. Most of my homework is done— let's make a day of it!"

"That makes one of us!" Sven laughed. "But I can do it when I get home. La Défense it is." Sven took my hand and we headed toward the Luxembourg metro station.

When we came up from the metro near the square, glowing Christmas lights greeted us, and we entered the flow of people meandering toward the market. I also saw something I didn't expect to see: police vans and cars lined the street leading to the square, and police tape funneled visitors to security checkpoints on each side of the market. As we joined the line, a now-familiar sense of unease encroached on our perfect day. I didn't say anything to Sven, not wanting to ruin our outing by talking about the terrorists again. But I decided that the next day I would contact Member Care. *I think this is bothering me more than it should,* I thought.

Ten minutes later, after our bags had been thoroughly checked, I shrugged off the feeling of fear and strolled through the market, delighting in the vendors' wares and pondering which Christmas delicacy to sample first.

+ + +

Later that evening, when I arrived home, I turned on my computer, found the e-mail with the Member Care information in it, and wrote a reminder on a sticky note. I closed the computer, stuck the note on top so I would see it in the morning, and retired for the evening.

Advent: the season of hopeful anticipation. I wasn't sure I was ready to hope again, but maybe with a little help, I could get there.

CHAPTER 20

BEING GOOD NEIGHBORS

SINCE THE ATTACKS, I'd been wanting to connect with my neighbors. I'd actually been hoping to do so for the past several months, but somehow the threat of terrorism made that desire all the more urgent.

Like most people in Paris, my neighbors were busy, and that meant I'd only seen them once or twice in the hallway or by the elevator since I moved in. But the day after our outing to the Christmas market, I was struck by an inspiration about how to reach out to them. My first stop was the grocery store—to get the ingredients I'd need to make shortbread cookies.

Back at the apartment, I set Spotify to Christmas music and started mixing a batch of cookies. While the cookies were in the oven, I pulled out some Christmas cards, wrote a note introducing myself, and wished their family God's blessings in the coming year. After arranging the cookies on plates, I wrapped them up and attached the card with some ribbon.

"Father, please bless these simple plates of cookies and allow them to open doors with my neighbors. And please use me to bless them and show them who you are," I prayed. Then I took a deep breath and headed for the hallway.

When I knocked on the first door—the one directly across from mine—there was no answer. I knocked on the middle door but was met with the same result. Disappointed, I returned to my flat.

I tried a few more times that evening to no avail, and finally I decided to leave the cookies outside their doors, praying they'd get them. A few hours later, I poked my head into the hallway, and both plates were gone.

"Yes!" I proclaimed with a smile. Then I closed my door and returned to my French studies.

+ + +

Several weeks after Christmas, I still hadn't heard anything about the cookies. *What happened?* I wondered. It was odd to me that no one had acknowledged them. Did my neighbors think it was a strange gesture? Or had someone else taken the cookies?

The answer came one day in the form of a postcard on my doormat. It was from the couple next door, Jean-Claude and Brigitte, who thanked me for the cookies and wished me a belated *joyeux Noël et bonne année. Well, at least one family got them,* I thought.

A few days later, there was a knock on my door. When I answered, Jean-Claude and Brigitte stood there, wanting to introduce themselves in person. We chatted for a while, and then came a confession. With a sheepish grin, Jean-Claude admitted that since our other neighbor spent most of the year in South America, they had eaten his share too. They thought the cookies were too good to go to waste.

What do you know? I thought. *A compliment from the French on my baking!*

I told my neighbors about studying French at the Sorbonne and the work I'd eventually be doing. As our conversation drew to a close, we bid each other *bonne soirée*.

As I closed the door, a smile crept across my face. *Thank you, Jesus! That feels like progress.*

CHAPTER 21

MEMBER CARE

THE MORE I THOUGHT about talking with Member Care, the more I realized I needed to talk to someone. I hoped that processing the attack—and my life after—with a counselor would help me find ways to combat my fears and get to the heart of some of the feelings that lingered from that night. Sven agreed.

"You know, you can also always talk with me about this," Sven assured me. "I'm here for you, and I want to help you however I can. But the Member Care people have dealt with things like this in the past, and they probably can help more than I can."

"Thanks, *chéri*," I told him. "That means a lot to me."

I e-mailed Bev, one of my colleagues with GEM, to ask her about setting up a meeting with a Member Care counselor. She gave me the name of Michelle, who lived in another town in France. I wasted no time in contacting Michelle. In my message to her, I filled her in on my situation, including a link to the newsletter I'd written five days after the attacks, in which I shared with my family, friends, and supporters what I'd experienced on November 13.

Michelle responded that evening, and we set up a Skype meeting for the following week. Even though we hadn't talked yet, the last line of her e-mail made me feel better already. "I've already been praying for healing and comfort for you," she said. It's a powerful thing to know that people are praying for you and that God is hearing about you from another person.

+ + +

My Skype sessions with Michelle were eye opening and instructive. There were times when I was answering one of Michelle's questions or when she was sharing a Spirit-given insight and I would immediately tear up. I wasn't always able to figure out what was going on under the surface, but she asked just the right questions to help me get to the root of why certain topics made me emotional. Through Michelle, God disclosed deep-rooted feelings I'd been unaware of. When I was able to identify those feelings, it helped me confront and resolve them.

As I met with Michelle, I also shared with Sven what I was learning.

"Thanks for your support through all this, *chéri*," I told him. "Michelle has helped me see that I shouldn't minimize my experience or assume I am alone in this. When I used to think about the people who lost their lives that night, I would push what we went through aside, trying to convince myself that it wasn't that bad. What were my fears compared to what they went through? But I know God loves us as much as he loves each one of them. I'm not sure why I thought God cared about their experiences more than he did about mine. It was like I didn't see the value of my own life in God's eyes." I paused, searching for the right words. "You know how I said I was worried about my family, friends, supporters, and ministry during the attacks?"

"Yes, I remember," Sven said.

"Well, Michelle helped me see that I was feeling guilty," I admitted.

"Guilty? What do you mean? Guilty for what?" Sven asked.

"I know," I said. "I didn't understand it at first either. I felt guilty that if something had happened to me, it would have caused pain for all my loved ones. I hated to think they would be sad. Michelle pointed out that if I had died that night, God would have been brokenhearted too. I also felt guilty that if something happened to me, I wouldn't have been able to start my work, and I wouldn't have been able to fulfill what God had planned for me to do in Paris. My ministry partners who invested in me, prayed for me, and cared for me would have been robbed of seeing any results. You know how hard I worked to get here, and it would have all been for nothing just because I was at a soccer match before my ministry even started."

"Oh, honey," Sven sympathized. "I can't believe you felt

that way. I'm so sorry you were carrying all of that. God isn't the only one who sees who you are and the value of your life, not just of the ministry you can do. I care about you too. I love you, Jazz."

"I love you too, darling," I said, letting out a breath. "It's crazy that all of that was going through my mind in those few minutes we were running up and down the stairs and trying to get home. It's strange what you think of in chaotic moments like that."

"I've been worried about you," Sven said. "Thanks for letting me know what you've been thinking about."

"You know, my pastor in Hawaii often says that suffering ceases to be suffering when it finds purpose and meaning," I said. "After the attacks, I know more than ever that God loves me and values me. I think he can use pain to take us to deeper places and heal things that have been hidden for a long time. Who would have thought that all the awful things going on could spark something beautiful as well?

"I'm blown away by how people are coming together in support of Paris. I'm not sure I've ever seen so much solidarity and care for those who are hurting. I just hope that somehow people can hold on to the good and move past the pain."

"That reminds me, did you ever read any more about that guy who started GEM?" Sven asked.

"It's funny that you would mention that," I said. "I just read more about him the other day."

Draguignan, France
October 23, 1944

BOB EVANS

CHAPTER 22

REUNION

ROLLING OUT OF BED, I grabbed my clothes and towel and headed
for the makeshift showers set up behind the hospital. The
facility had been built with bathrooms and showers, just not
nearly enough for the number of men housed here.

I returned minutes later, dressed, shaved, and thankful for
hot water today. Then I stopped by my cot to grab my coat
and Bible before heading out of the hospital toward the edge
of town, where I found a small park overlooking the sea. This
was where I met God every day in his Word and prayed for
the growing list of new believers he was bringing into my life.
Today I added a new name to that list: Bernadette.

I settled onto the bench, which was damp with the tropical dew that moistened every surface at night before being
sucked back into the heavy air each morning. I wasn't fazed
by the momentary discomfort, knowing that within an hour
or two, the humidity would soak all my clothing.

Staring out at the crystal-blue waves and the sun coming up over the horizon, I was once again struck by the inherent contrasts of this place—unbelievable beauty mixed with unbelievable pain and suffering. Then I sensed God's voice within saying, *The sea isn't the only beautiful thing here, is it, Bob?* The words echoed through my heart like a gunshot bouncing off the walls of a canyon. He was right, of course. There was beauty in the people here too. Even in their brokenness. *Bernadette, Kristophe, and Matthias aren't the only ones I love here, Bob. Every village, town, and city in France is full of them,* I sensed him whisper.

"I know, Father," I said aloud, tears blurring the beautiful scenery in front of me. "Every day, it seems like I meet another one." My voice choked with emotion. "But I am only one person. And what about Ed, Frank, and the guys? I have to catch up with them. Who will be here when I leave?"

Silence.

Who, indeed?

I opened my Bible at random, somewhat distracted from my reading this morning. I was already thinking about how to encourage Matthias and wondering if I would see Bernadette again today. After a few more moments, I prayed, "God, give me something to encourage the hearts of all those I meet today."

I finally glanced down to the pages of my worn Bible, and my eyes focused on 2 Kings 17. I wished I'd opened the Bible more toward the back—something in the Gospels, maybe. But I began to read anyway.

And suddenly, there it was, leaping up from the page as if the words had been written in fire.

> Then the king of Assyria commanded, saying, "Send there one of the priests whom you brought from there; let him go and dwell there, and let him teach them the rituals of the God of the land." Then one of the priests whom they had carried away from Samaria came and dwelt in Bethel, and taught them how they should fear the LORD.

I quickly closed the Bible, not bothering to read any further. "The priests whom they had carried away . . ."

"God, that's ridiculous," I said. "That can't be you!" I stood up and brushed as much water as I could from my pants.

I was met with silence—the kind that's impossible to ignore. *What if . . . ? No, that's ridiculous. You can't mean that for me, can you?*

Stuffing the Bible into my pack, I took one more look at the beautiful sea and set off down the trail to meet with Matthias. As I walked, my mind turned to the task at hand. I pushed the strange encounter with God from my thoughts and began to focus on where I'd left off in my discipleship discussion with Matthias the day before.

+ + +

At the church later that morning, I met Matthias for coffee. He had been memorizing the Gospel of Mark, and we talked about Jesus rejecting the Pharisees and welcoming people like the demoniac in chapter 5. Then I made a quick stop at Samantha's shop to spend what little I had to give her some business. My visit inevitably led to a short game of boules with the boys. The game was their sole passion in life, and the boys had already marked out the pitch when I arrived.

I ate lunch with Kristophe, who told me that Bernadette had awoken early and prepared breakfast for them—something she'd never done before, preferring to stay hidden in the cellar. According to Kristophe, she had talked almost the whole meal, explaining all that was going on inside her and asking if Kristophe would ask me to come back that night to answer some questions.

"Bob, I've been thinking about the question you asked last night," Kristophe went on. "Do you think people in town would accept Bernadette if she went to the church to confess and receive Father Matthias's forgiveness? To me, it seems like God already did all the forgiving she needed, but sometimes other people need to see it too. Going to the church for forgiveness is just a part of life here. Do you think Father Matthias would do that?"

"I'm sure he would," I said. "I think you may be on to something. It would be hard for people to hold her past against her if she had been forgiven by a priest. I think you should go talk to him."

The afternoon shadows lay long on the streets as I made my way back to the hospital for supper and my physical therapy session. I passed the military ambulance parked on the street in front of the hospital almost without seeing it. Its presence was so common that it would have been more remarkable if it weren't there at all.

I walked into the reception hall and saw Dr. Harper wearing a concerned expression.

"Evans, hold up a sec," he said. After giving some final instructions to the nurse, he walked across the room to greet me.

"There's someone here asking for you, but we need to talk first." His voice was somber. "His name is Kowalski. Ed Kowalski. He came in on the last truck."

"Ed?" My brain registered alarm, and I immediately found my legs moving toward the door to the receiving room. "Where is he? What happened?"

"Hold on, son." Ben held out a hand to restrain me. "I said we needed to talk. He's in bad shape, and we're getting ready to operate. To begin, I'm going to have to take what's left of his leg, but that's not the worst of it. There's shrapnel from a grenade all throughout his chest. I'm not sure if I can get it all, or how bad it is yet." Dr. Harper took in a breath. "As soon as he arrived, he asked for you. He shouldn't have even been talking, but I couldn't get him to stop asking for you. I'm going to let you see him, but I need you to help me calm him down. He's in shock, and I don't think the ride down here helped at all. The situation is not good."

Heart pounding, I nodded. "Sure, Doc. I'll do anything I can. Take me to him."

"Not Ed, God," I muttered in a nearly incoherent prayer. "Don't take Ed. Help me. I don't know if I can do this."

Ben headed for the receiving room door and I followed, reeling. Moments later, I was standing at the side of the bed, looking down at the mangled body of my friend. His eyes were squeezed shut in pain, and his rattling breaths came out in sporadic gasps. I'd seen a lot since coming to the hospital, but even so, nothing prepared me to see the body of my friend wrapped in blood-soaked sheets as he barely clung to life.

God, give me the strength to do this.

"I'm here, Ed," I said. "You haven't been riding motorcycles, have you? I thought you would have learned better from me." I hoped levity would help keep my raging emotions at bay.

Ed opened one eye and focused on me. "Bob? No motorcycles, just a dirty grenade," he sputtered. "I hoped you would be here. You have to help me."

"Sure, Ed, anything." I took his bloody hand.

"I don't think I'm going to get out of this one. In my stuff is a letter . . ." He faltered, trying to take in another breath. "It's for my family. Explains about Jesus and everything. If I don't make it, you gotta get that to them."

"I will, Ed," I vowed. "Don't worry about it now. Besides,

you're going to be able to tell them yourself." I willed confidence into my words. "For now, you just need to relax. The doc said he'll have you patched up in no time." It wasn't the whole truth, but I knew Dr. Harper was counting on me to calm Ed down.

"Yeah, well, I don't know about that," he gasped.

The nurse rolled a small cart over to Ed's bedside. She picked up a needle and a small vial as she prepared to sedate Ed for surgery.

"Pray with me, Bob," Ed implored, gripping my hand. "I'm really scared, and it hurts so bad."

"I'm going to inject you now," the nurse told Ed matter-of-factly. "I know it hurts, but I need you to hold still."

Reaching across the bed, I gripped his shoulder and helped to steady him. As I did, I prayed aloud, "Jesus, you can do anything. Please heal Ed. Please heal him. Guide the doctors' hands like only you can. And whatever comes, help Ed to remember that you love him and will never leave him."

The nurse inserted the needle and depressed the plunger. Staring into Ed's eyes, I watched the fast-acting medicine roll over him and pull him toward unconsciousness.

"Thanks, Bob," Ed slurred. "I know he won't leave me." And then he was lost to the medicine.

"Thank you, Lieutenant Evans," the nurse said. "We are going to take him now. I'll let you know how it goes."

I released Ed's hand as the gurney was rolled away. I stood there staring as the double doors swung closed and my friend disappeared. Then the tears came. "God, I hate this war."

Eventually, reality returned to me. *Well, no PT today, I guess. I wonder if there's any food left lying around.* Knowing there was nothing else I could do, I walked numbly through the hospital toward the mess hall.

"God, I feel like I've asked a lot of you lately," I prayed wearily. "But please don't take Ed. It feels like I'm losing a brother, and I don't know if I can take it. There have to be some good stories left, right?"

Of course I knew that Ed's story was already a good story, but in the moment, it felt like defeat.

CHAPTER 23

QUESTIONS

AS I ATE the few pieces of bread left over in the kitchen, it suddenly dawned on me that I'd promised Kristophe I would see Bernadette that evening. My spirit deflated like a week-old balloon. I had nothing left to give. *I should stay here for Ed,* I thought. But I couldn't abandon Bernadette, not now. Or Kristophe. "Jesus, please help me."

I'll check on Ed first, I decided. *Then I'll sneak out to see Kristophe and Bernadette.*

Exhaustion, both emotional and physical, pulled at me, but as I was reminded today, our tomorrows are not promised. *Use me if you can, Lord. But I'm not sure what I have left to give.*

+ + +

When I arrived at the restaurant, Kristophe quickly ushered me in and closed the door. Back in the kitchen, I found the table set and waiting for me. Bernadette was sitting there wearing normal clothing, and there was a large tray filled with cheese and an apple on the table. In that moment, it looked better than any steak I'd ever seen.

Kristophe poured a glass of wine as I sat down, and without preamble, he said, "Bob, we have some questions about God."

After several hours of probing questions about topics from what I thought God's view on the war was to God's ability to forgive a laundry list of specific sins to God's requirement that we forgive those who hurt us, both my stomach and my spirit were full to overflowing. I was getting ready to step out into the night when Kristophe grabbed my arm. "I talked to Father Matthias, and he is happy to help," he said. "He asked me to bring Bernadette to Mass on Sunday, and he will forgive her publicly. You seem to be connected to God . . . will you pray about that?"

"I will," I assured him. "Will you pray about something too?" I briefly explained Ed's circumstances.

"I guess," Kristophe responded hesitantly. "Do you think he'll hear me?"

"He will," I assured him. "Remember that everything I told Bernadette about how God sees us is true for you, too."

"I suppose," Kristophe said doubtfully. "But I haven't spent much time talking to him these past few years. I think he's probably pretty disappointed in me."

"That's the beauty of the Good News, Kristophe," I said.

"Yesterday doesn't matter if you reach out to him *today*. I can't think of a better time to start again."

He nodded, and I headed out to return to the hospital.

There is no ordination process in the world that could have prepared me for this kind of questioning, I thought with a smile. *I can't think of anything more beautiful than a heart that truly wants to know more about God.* I couldn't help but wonder what our churches back home would be like if new believers tested our leaders this way.

I wandered back to the hospital, alive with the feeling of being used by my Creator for his work. Looking up at the brilliant display of stars in the clear night sky, I felt a closeness to Jesus that transcended words. This was what I was made for.

+ + +

As I reached out to open the door of the hospital, the rest of life suddenly flooded back in. *Ed.* Quietly closing the door behind me, I headed through the darkened entryway toward the operating and recovery rooms, hoping to find someone who could tell me how he was doing. I found Nurse Simmons, who seemed to be floating somewhere between wakefulness and sleep, seated at a small desk. Her face mirrored the exhaustion that was hitting me again.

Almost afraid to utter the question, I asked, "Did Ed make it?"

Looking up wearily, she nodded. "Yes. He's stabilized, but I'm not sure if we got him in time. We'll have to wait and see. I think you should keep praying; God seems to hear you more than the rest of us."

"Thanks," I said, relief rushing through me. "When can I see him?"

"He should be recovered enough for you to see him in the morning, although I'm not sure you'll be able to talk to him just yet."

I suddenly felt so tired I wasn't sure I could remain upright much longer. "Thank you," I said, ready to head toward my bed. But before I went through the door, I turned back. "He hears all of our prayers, you know," I said. "I'm no closer to him than you are."

The nurse looked up, surprised, but said nothing. I bid her good night and crawled into my welcoming bed.

Sleep was long in coming, however. I wasn't sure if I'd ever prayed for anything as earnestly as I did that night. There were so many lives. So many souls. And, somehow, God was allowing me to be a part of their story.

Before sleep overcame me, I wondered if this was what it had been like for my parents when they were missionaries years earlier. Did they feel the joy and sorrow of ministry like this when they lay down in exhaustion after their new disciples finally left our home in the evening?

At last, sleep came, thanks to pure physical exhaustion infused with a distant sense of God's pleasure.

CHAPTER 24

HEADACHE

AS MORNING BEGAN TO STREAM IN through the windows, my mind awakened before my body complied. Often in those moments, suspended between sleep and wakefulness, I could hear God most clearly. This morning was no exception, though what I heard was both comforting and puzzling.

I will be with you today, Bob, I felt the Spirit within me say.

Unsure what to make of the message, I rolled out of my cot, grabbed my clothes, and headed for the shower. My stiff muscles communicated their displeasure with my movement, and my head was pounding. *I missed PT,* I thought, *but I'm probably sorer than if I hadn't. All this ministry is wearing me out!*

Minutes later, I was as presentable as I was going to get, so I headed for the recovery room to try to talk with, or at least see, Ed. When I arrived, the head nurse saw me coming and shook her head slowly. Nurse Edmonds was a stout bulldog of a woman, and she was as much door warden as healer.

"Not yet. Everyone in there is still asleep, and I'm not going to let you wake them." She was wearing a slight smile, but her look assured me that she would brook no nonsense. "Go get yourself some breakfast," she said. "Remember, you're a patient, too, and honestly, you don't look that great today. Maybe you should still be in bed." She looked at me more closely. "Are you feeling okay?"

"Never better. How could I not be when I'm staying here in such luxurious accommodations with such a loving staff?" There was a note of mischief in my voice, and it was probably clear to both of us that I was trying to convince myself as much as I was trying to convince her.

"Well, you can come back in an hour or two and see him," she said before turning her attention back to the paperwork on the desk in front of her.

I waved in thanks and started for the mess hall. Lingering over my bowl of porridge gave me the time I needed to pray for the growing list of people God had brought into my life. Praying for each of them by name and asking God to show me what to do next felt almost overwhelming in times like this. There was so much need and opportunity, and so little time. As I came to the end of the list and began to pray for Jeanette and Alyce, a building headache interrupted my prayers. *God, please give me supernatural strength to make the most of the time I have here,* I implored. *And please take this headache away. I have too much to do today.*

While I wasn't sure which of my prayers God would choose to bless, it became obvious as I made my way back to the recovery room that he was in no hurry to answer my prayer for headache relief. I considered asking the nurse for some medicine but decided I would wait until after I saw Ed.

As I approached the door, Nurse Edmonds looked up from a pile of paperwork, which didn't seem to have diminished since I was last there. When she saw me, she smiled. "You can go in now for a bit. He's awake and was asking for you," she said. "But be as quiet as possible, and don't let him get excited. He's in a lot of pain, and I don't want to replace stitches today."

I nodded and slipped into the room, spotting Ed at the far end. His eyes were closed and he appeared to be sleeping, but as I approached, he blearily opened one eye. In a raspy voice, he said, "I think I'm going to have to take a pass on that bike ride you keep promising. I'm pretty sure you need two legs to ride one of those things, and, well . . ." His voice trailed off. "Weirdest thing, I can still feel it. When I woke up, I didn't believe the doc until he pulled back the sheets."

I had to look away from him to hold back the tears. For such a large and otherwise-healthy man, he seemed shrunken somehow as he lay there in a mass of stained bandages.

I will be with you today. The words echoed in my mind and spirit.

"Well, maybe I can 'borrow' a sidecar," I said, trying to match his levity, not yet ready to deal with the harder questions.

"We'll see." He chuckled and then winced. "Oof, no jokes. Laughing is way too painful." Suddenly, he shot me a serious look. "Do you remember what I asked you last night? That's important."

"I remember. How could I forget?" I assured him. "But as I said last night, it won't matter, because you're going home and can tell them yourself. Now, stop worrying. How did you end up here?"

"Yeah, that." He sighed. "We were going house to house in Toulon, and it was going okay. There were lots of Germans there, but they kept pulling back, so we were making good progress. There was a little café on the corner, and Frank and I went in to clear it. We hadn't seen anyone in a couple of hours, so we weren't too concerned. When we walked in, it looked empty, but you know you have to be sure. Frank started to go around behind the counter, and I headed for the door in back—the kitchen, I'm guessing. But as Frank got to the end of the counter, someone behind it chucked one of those potatoes at him. It bounced off one of the chairs and fell on the floor right in front of me. Instinct or training must have kicked in, because I dove for it, wanting to grab it and throw it out of the room. But the dirty rat must have cooked it a bit before tossing it, because as soon as I reached it, it exploded. Five seconds—yeah, right. That's the last thing I remember until I woke up in the back of a truck."

"Wow. Did Frank make it?"

"I think so. I'm not sure, but it seemed like I heard him firing his gun just as the grenade went off," he said. "I sure hope he did."

I pulled up a chair, and we talked and prayed for a bit. I

was cognizant of the nurse's warning not to wear him out, so before long, I started to wind down the conversation. "I'll come back and see you later, Ed. You should probably get some more rest. I don't want to rile you up and get on the bad side of the nurse, or we'll be back in the US before I get to see you again."

"Hold on," Ed said seriously, leaning forward in the bed. "There's something I have to say before you go. I don't even know how to start, but I've got to say it. I owe my life to you, Bob. I'm not sure what in the world possessed you to come into the thick of this mess as a chaplain. I'm pretty sure if I had had the opportunity for a safer job, I would have taken it, but you didn't. Do you know there are twenty-seven guys who are now meeting to study the Bible? Well, twenty-six, I guess. We may not make it home, but we are guaranteed to make it *home* now, if you get my meaning." Tears welled in his eyes. "I just wanted you to know. Thank you for caring more about us than . . ." Suddenly, seized by a body-wracking cough, Ed could no longer speak. A look of wide-eyed panic crossed his face as he gasped for breath, and then, with another enormous cough, blood appeared on his chin.

I reached out to steady and help him lay back. "It's okay, Ed. I know. Just rest."

He continued to cough, and more blood appeared. The nurse rushed to the bed and shot me a stern look. "You're going to have to leave now. You can come back later." Turning away from me, she yelled, "Simmons, get the doctor!"

I stepped back, stunned, but Ed grabbed my hand. "Thanks, Bob. Don't forget what I asked you."

"No problem," I stammered. "I'll see you later. You rest now."

Immediately, Ed was surrounded by scurrying medical personnel. After one last shooing motion from the nurse, I turned to leave.

As I moved toward the door, the intrusive pain in my head reminded me to resume the hunt for medicine. Looking over my shoulder, I realized that none of the staff there could help me, as they were all focused on Ed. *Perhaps there are still some nurses on morning rounds in the main hall,* I thought.

I arrived in the main hall and found a couple of nurses pushing their carts down the rows of beds. "Don't suppose you have a couple of extra aspirin on that cart, do you?"

The nurse turned toward me with a smile that abruptly turned into a frown when she saw my face. "You don't look too well this morning. Are you feeling okay?"

Hoping to avoid the poking and prodding that nurses the world over seem so fond of, I responded as nonchalantly as possible, "I'm feeling all right. Just a bit of a headache. Probably overdid it yesterday."

"Hmm." Her tone was noncommittal, but her eyes betrayed that she wasn't buying a word of it. "Unfortunately, all the medicine I have with me is for specific patients. If you're tired, I suggest you head back to your bed and get some rest. As soon as I finish here, I'll see what I can do for you."

"Well, maybe I'll step outside for a minute and see what the weather is like. I'll come back in a bit."

"The weather's just fine today. We're in Draguignan! I don't even have to stick my head out to know it's hot and humid," she said. "I suggest you head to your bed so I'll know where you are. I have a busy day and no time to waste trying to find you."

Not wanting to jeopardize my chances of getting the aspirin, I held up my hands in surrender. "No, you're probably right. A little more rest is exactly what I need. I'll be waiting for you there."

As I made my way through the rows to my cot, I thought, *Well, I guess I could catch up on my Bible memorization.* I'd been trying to memorize a number of the parables so I could tell them without using the Bible. I'd found that pulling out a Bible in the middle of a conversation with someone who is far from God could be a bit intimidating.

After settling onto my cot and trying rather unsuccessfully to fold my meager pillow into a backrest, I grabbed my well-worn Bible and flipped to Mark 5—the story about Jesus with the naked, demon-possessed guy. It was a favorite of mine for illustrating God's power to change us. No matter what most of the guys I ministered to had done, they usually still had their clothes on, so this account gave them hope.

Chuckling to myself, I remembered the time I'd gone through this passage with Ed, Frank, and Bill. Bill's family was Jewish by heritage, and we got a bit hung up on the pigs in the passage. *If there was a rabbit trail to find, Bill would be the first to find it,* I thought, wondering where he was at that moment and if he was safe, or even alive.

"Father, be with Bill and Frank and the guys today," I prayed. "Keep them safe, and keep them close to your heart and your Word." Then I turned my attention back to my memorization. However, I found that no matter what I tried, I couldn't quite get my eyes to focus on the text. *Crazy,* I thought. *It must just be a trick of the light in here.* With a sigh of resignation, I set my Bible on the little table next to my bed and tried to follow the nurse's orders to get some sleep. I closed my eyes, but I soon realized that I wasn't nearly tired enough to overcome the pulsing pain in my temples. I lay there with images of Ed's broken body shaking as he coughed, blood running down his sturdy jaw.

I was still thinking and praying about Ed when I heard the sound of purposeful steps. I turned my head toward the sound, but to my surprise, the person striding in my direction wasn't the nurse. Rather, it was Dr. Harper.

"Hey, Evans. Nurse Thompson tells me you need someone to take a look at you. How are you feeling?"

"Betrayed," I mumbled. "I should have known she wouldn't simply give me the medicine." Forcing a grin, I said, "Well, I just asked for a couple of aspirin. I had no idea she'd pull out the big guns. I'm sure you have better things to do than dole out pills for a simple headache."

"Simple headache, is it?" he said, grabbing the chart at the end of my bed and flipping through the pages. "That's not exactly the picture Nurse Thompson painted when she came to see me. When did this 'simple headache' begin?"

"I woke up with it this morning," I said, feeling a little foolish to be mentioning something so trivial in a room full of guys with life-threatening injuries. "It's really not that big of a deal. I just wanted something to dampen the pain a bit."

"Sit here on the end of the bed," he directed. Then, with expert hands, he grabbed my head and began to twist it this way and that. He pried open my eyelids, depressed my tongue, and inspected my ears. Then, stepping back, he pulled a small flashlight from his coat pocket and said, "Follow the light with your eyes."

Yeesh, I thought, *I'm not asking for morphine, for Pete's sake.*

My eyes followed the small light. Up. Down. Right. Left . . . Turning my head slightly, I tracked the light to the left.

"No, don't move your head," Dr. Harper instructed. "Just follow it with your eyes."

Up. Down. Right. Left . . . The light disappeared. He could tell from the startled expression on my face what had happened.

"Are you having a hard time seeing today? Having trouble focusing?" He was trying to put me at ease, but he couldn't keep the concern from seeping into his voice.

"Well, I tried to read my Bible a bit and couldn't focus on the words," I admitted. "I just thought I was overtired."

"When is your birthday, Bob?"

"February 21," I said confidently.

"Rank and service number?"

"Lieutenant Evans, 231144," I said by rote.

"Home address?"

"It's . . . umm . . . in Illinois," I stammered. *Come on, Evans, you write the silly thing every other day on your letters to Jeanette,* I told myself. "I'm sorry. I really must be tired. I can't remember it."

He stared at me, considering. "Evans, that mine you hit really did a number on you. Ever since you came, I've been a bit concerned that there may have been more damage than we initially discovered. Even with that old helmet, it's clear you hit your head really hard. I want to give you some tests tomorrow morning. Come to my office at 10:30. In the meantime, here are four strong aspirin. Take two now and two a bit later with some food. And try to take it easy today. I know you're out to save the whole town, but that can wait 'til tomorrow." He shot me a friendly grin.

"I'm not trying to save the whole town, Doc." My face flushed at his words. "I'm just doing what I can to remind people that there's still a reason to have hope, even in this mess. People need hope to survive."

He looked directly at me. "Yeah, I guess that's about right. I tell you, if I could have ten more guys just like you, I'd take them. I may be the doctor in this hospital, but I sometimes think *you* are the one who's healing them. Take care of yourself; you are needed here." With that, he turned and strode toward the door, leaving me somewhat stunned.

Needed. The word echoed in my soul.

Grabbing two of the pills, I ambled to the sink, still pondering the ramifications of our conversation. One thought grabbed hold of my mind and wouldn't let go: *He's more concerned about me than he's letting on.*

CHAPTER 25

WHEN THE SPIRIT MOVES

HAVING INGESTED THE PRECIOUS MEDICINE, it was time for part two of my prescription: food. Although I was sure Dr. Harper's intention was for me to grab a quick meal in the mess hall and return to bed, I was more interested in what the *soupe du jour* might be at Kristophe's.

After swallowing the pills, I peeked out to see if both the doctor and Nurse Thompson were within eyeshot. The coast was clear, so I quickly headed toward the door. *Well,* I told myself, *he didn't specifically say where the food had to come from. I'm obeying . . . kind of.*

Not waiting for anyone to correct my self-imposed misconceptions, I descended the steps of the hospital and headed up the street toward Kristophe's.

It was nearing the end of the French lunchtime when I opened the door. I entered the café and saw Kristophe seated near the back with a group of townspeople, enjoying some cheese and wine. Seeing me come through the door, he stood and motioned me back to their table.

"Bob, you already know Father Matthias and Samantha, of course. I'd like you to meet Jean-Denis and Christabel. As it is, we have just been discussing some of the things you've been talking to us about. So now that you're here, you can clarify everything."

Bracing myself for the awkward European greeting that would undoubtedly happen next, my mind reeled. *Is it left cheek first, or right?* Thankfully, Jean-Denis extended his hand for a firm handshake, but just when I thought I was in the clear, Christabel rose and said, "Shall we *faire la bise*?" as she leaned forward in the traditional greeting of friendship.

Left. Start with the left. I leaned in, and the cheeks of our faces touched briefly as we made the appropriate kissing sound. *Success!* As I pulled back, relieved, I saw the slight conspiratorial smiles of Samantha and Kristophe out of the corner of my eye. *Why does "hello" have to be so complicated?* I wondered.

I pulled up a chair and squeezed around the table as Kristophe disappeared to get another plate and silverware. Either the aspirin or the fresh air seemed to have worked; my headache had diminished significantly. However, the jumble of thoughts and emotions running through my mind and heart had not. The confusion must have been written clearly on my face, because before Kristophe returned, Samantha asked, "Are you all right, Bob?"

My first thought was to dismiss the question. After all,

Kristophe said the group wanted to talk over some things. However, something in my spirit rebelled at the idea. Before I knew what was happening, I found myself telling this band of survivors about Ed, my headache, and the men I'd discipled—and how I wondered whether they were still alive or not. I told them about the daughter I'd never seen and, finally, about my fear that my headache might be something more. And that was when something miraculous happened.

"You can't give up hope," Matthias said. "The Bible tells us Jesus is the great healer. Ed is in good hands, both here on earth and in the realms above."

"Yes," Samantha chimed in. "We all understand more than you know what it feels like to wonder where someone is and whether or not he's alive. I doubt there's a person in this town who doesn't live with that every day."

"Do you have a picture of your daughter?" Christabel asked. "What can you tell us about her?"

Fishing a worn photo from my wallet, I passed my prized possession across the table. It was a picture of Jeanette and Alyce taken when Alyce was one week old. I'd stared at it so long that I almost expected it to burst into color or come to life.

By the time Kristophe returned, the concerned questions and reassurances slowly began to lift my eyes from my problems and worries.

Finally, Kristophe said, "Folks, I can't even believe I am saying this, but I think we should pray for Ed and Bob.

Maybe Father Matthias could do that, even though we aren't in the church."

I was stunned. Was this the same Kristophe I'd met that first day in the village—the one who held so much anger toward God? In the next moment, I felt the Spirit's nudge to speak up.

"Kristophe, that's a great idea. And of course Father Matthias can pray. But I want you to know that you can too—all of you. When it comes to God hearing us, there's nothing more sacred about the church than there is about this restaurant. In fact, I think if Jesus came to Draguignan, this would be one of his favorite places. I'm not saying anything against the church building—it's beautiful and worshipful—but Jesus likes to be where the people are. And if you read Matthew, Mark, Luke, and John, you'll see he spent more time among the townsfolk than in the Temple. Jesus is closer to us than you think."

And so began one of the most honest, heartfelt, and God-honoring prayer times I ever experienced, either before or after, and I did not utter a single word of it.

When Matthias finished praying, he surprised me by saying, "Bob is right, you know. Since he came here, I've been reading the Bible with new eyes. I've been around the church my whole life, but it wasn't until we started talking that I really began to understand who Jesus is and what he cares about. He loves people. All people. I've been waiting in the church, feeling sorry for myself that not many people were coming there to see me anymore. But I'm finding God these days more outside the church than in it."

"That's just it," Kristophe interjected. "It seems like God is with you, Bob, and we were wondering if you could tell us how to experience Jesus like you do. It's like he's alive to you."

Astonished, I exclaimed the first thing that came to my mind: "Well, he is! That's the whole point of the Bible! Jesus died on the cross for our sins, he rose again, and he still lives today. It's not about church or religion. It's about a person who is alive and with me—with us—every day! I can tell you for sure that I wouldn't be here with you today if I were just trying to convince people to join a religion. I'm here because Jesus saved my life and gives me everything I need to live for him. I joined the war to help those guys realize that, and I believe he sent me to this town to share that with all of you as well."

"If it weren't for all I've seen since you came here, I'd say you were crazy," Kristophe said. "But there's something about your life and your hope in the face of despair that makes me believe you're telling the truth. It's not just me, either. Samantha told us the same thing over lunch, and Matthias has a new lease on life thanks to your 'coffee talks.' I was a little upset, by the way, when I found out our town priest has been holding out on the coffee supply!" He shot Matthias a wry smile.

Matthias held up his hands in mock guilt. "I had to have something to keep Bob coming back! I couldn't risk my supply."

When the laughter died down, I said, "Jesus is right here with us. And the only thing he requires of you is your belief that he is who he claims he is, that he really did die for your sins. He is only waiting for you to say yes to him so you can begin a personal relationship with him. Then you can agree to live your life in a way that shows others what he means to you."

"I told them about Bernadette," Kristophe said. "About how you prayed with her the other night. We all discussed it, and we want you to pray with us, too. We've all seen things and done things that we know God is against. But if God will forgive us, we're ready."

Dumbfounded, I thought back to all my classes at Wheaton and all the Sundays I'd spent in church. It wasn't until I remembered my parents' simple kitchen in Cameroon that I could picture a scene like this—of people hungry for the life God offers. In that moment, I was proud to be my parents' son. Proud to be Jesus' son.

This was, indeed, what I was made for.

+   +   +

The sun had long since set when I made my way back to the hospital, a tinge of my headache slowly returning. Grateful that I had two more aspirin to take, I snuck back into the hospital, thankful no one had noticed my absence. *It's too late to bother Ed,* I thought as I headed for my own cot. *I'll go to see him first thing in the morning.*

As I lay in bed that night, I could hardly remember the

specifics of our conversations that day, but I remembered the tears, the joy, and the hope. I remembered the feeling of Jesus being tangibly in our midst as hearts and lives and eternity were altered. That feeling would haunt me and drive me and, ultimately, chart the course of my life.

CHAPTER 26

ETERNITY

A STRONG HAND on my shoulder drew me up from the depths of sleep. It was firm and insistent, yet gentle. As my eyelids creaked open, I was surprised to find Ben seated on the edge of my bed, wearing a concerned expression. As the last vestiges of sleep left me, I mumbled, "Morning, Doc."

"Evans, there's no easy way of saying this, so I'm just going to tell you. Ed didn't make it. We did everything we could, but some of the grenade that we couldn't find perforated his stomach. I know he was a close friend of yours, and I'm sorry to tell you this news. There was nothing we could have done. It was just a matter of time."

Ed. Gone. I understood the words. But I couldn't accept them. I had nothing to say; I just stared at the doctor as unbidden tears began their slow trek down my cheeks.

Inside, I screamed at God, *Do you hear any of my prayers? Are you even there?*

In my spirit, I sensed Jesus respond, and I was shocked by what he said. *You asked me to heal him. I did. He is with me now. You will see him again one day.*

"Ed wanted me to mail a letter he had in his stuff," I said through choked-back tears. Somehow, I couldn't think of anything more meaningful to say.

"I know," Ben said with a chuckle. "So does every nurse who works here. He reminded all of us about it incessantly. It's there on your table. Someday you're going to need to tell me what you guys went through together. He trusted you with his life—that's for sure."

"Ed is the guy who found me after the accident," I said, knowing immediately how inadequate that explanation was. "He was also the first guy I led to the Lord as a chaplain."

Those words also rang hollow. He was so much more than that. We gave each other hope of something better in the midst of a world that sought to remind us every minute of every day how evil men can be to each other. In a sense, we were each other's anchor in the storm. He was my "Timothy," and I couldn't plumb the depths of all that meant to me.

"I'm sorry," Dr. Harper said. "We did everything we could, but you've been in the hospital long enough to know that isn't saying much. We save a few—too few. That brings me to my other reason for coming to see you. I still need to see you in a few hours for those tests. I wanted to tell you about Ed as soon as I could so you could process it for a bit before we start the tests. I'll leave you now and see you in a little while. I'm so sorry I couldn't be here telling you Ed was fine."

"It's okay, Doc," I said. The next perfunctory phrase rolled off my tongue before I could even think about it. "He's in a better place now."

"He is, Evans. Thanks to you."

CHAPTER 27

THE END OF MY WAR

I SAT ON THE EDGE of my bed in stunned silence, unaware of time and my surroundings. The loss was so palpable that it was hard to breathe, and any time I focused on what I was feeling, my heart retreated as if it were too close to a candle's flame. Was it really possible that Ed was gone?

Ed was more than just one of my disciples; he was the first one who had responded to the gospel during my time in the military. We had a symbiotic relationship of sorts. We drew courage from one another; we drew life from one another. Each of us was what the other needed to keep pressing on and keep daring greatly for the gospel. Whenever I felt inadequate, Ed would burst in with his newest crazy act of obedience to Christ, and the fact that I had chosen to sacrifice to be with him and the other men made him want to keep going too.

And just like that, he was gone.

He was with Jesus, though, undoubtedly causing mischief

(or the sinless equivalent) in heaven. There's no doubt he wasn't the only one of my men to precede me into eternity; it's just that it had happened right there in front of me. It was a visceral kind of pain, and I found myself repeatedly rubbing my hands as though his blood were still on them.

I will be with you today, a voice whispered within my spirit, like a sturdy rock in the middle of a white-water rapid of emotion. Solid. Immovable.

"I trust you, Jesus," I said, more to affirm myself than to assure him. "I just didn't expect this."

Suddenly, I was aware of another presence and a light hand on my shoulder. Looking up, I saw Nurse Simmons staring at me, sorrow in her eyes. "I'm sorry about your friend, Bob," she offered quietly. "Normally, I'd send you to talk with someone. But you're the only chaplain here. I don't know what to say to you other than I'm sorry. And perhaps your God knows how you feel."

"Thank you," I said, not trusting myself to say anything further without crying again.

"I came to get you for your tests. Do you think you're up for it?"

Taking a deep breath, I forced my thoughts to focus on this issue. "Yes, I'll be okay. I know the doc is busy, so I don't want to waste his time. Besides, I want to know whether there's anything to worry about or if I just need more sleep and a couple of aspirin. Do I have time to go get cleaned up a bit first?"

"Sure, just be quick," she said. "We're prepping one of the

new arrivals for surgery in an hour or so, and the doc wants to get your tests done before then."

She gave my shoulder a squeeze. "Have faith."

Grabbing my clothes, I headed to the latrine to wash my face and put on fresh clothes, along with my best "I'm doing okay" countenance.

A few minutes later, refreshed by the icy water, which seemed to be the only kind they had in the hospital, I knocked quietly on the door to the doctor's office.

"Come in, Bob. How are you doing?" The empathy was evident in his voice.

"Well, it depends on what you mean by that," I said. "In the past twenty-four hours, I've seen a number of my French friends come to faith in Christ, lost my best friend, and been told by a doctor that I may have some vague but serious problem with my head. I honestly have no idea how I'm doing."

"Fair enough." He sounded relieved that I was ready to address the medical concerns. "I don't want you to be alarmed about these tests, but I do need you to be as honest and forthright as possible. I know you have a lot going on, but your answers are very important—they may mean the difference between life and death. I know you well enough to know that you'd do just about anything for the sake of someone else, but for the next hour, I want you to set that aside and do what is right for you and your family."

The frankness of his comments hit me like a blast of cold

air, and suddenly he had my full attention. Jeanette and Alyce deserved no less. They were, after all, my first priority.

Looking him firmly in the eye, I said in my best imitation of military solemnity, "I understand, sir. I will do my best."

"Good. The headaches could be nothing, or they could be something quite serious. My ability to diagnose the problem here in the field is limited, so any little thing you can tell me will help. The other day when we talked, you were having a problem remembering your address and following the light in the eye test. Both of those things can—and I emphasize *can*—be indicators of brain trauma. Since the accident, have you had other instances when you struggled to remember things?"

"It has happened once or twice," I admitted, not wanting to make too much of it. "In particular, there was a time or two when I couldn't remember Scripture references I've known all my life. I just figured that all the activity and stress pushed them out of my head. I can't say I've thought about it much, and most days I'm just fine. Does that mean anything?"

"Again, I'm not sure," Ben said. "Without consistent symptoms, it's hard to diagnose things like this with certainty. How about your vision? The other day, you had a hard time looking to the left without moving your head. Has that happened before? Or anything else with your eyes?"

"I haven't noticed that issue much," I said. "The only thing I've noticed is that sometimes I can't get my eyes to focus on the text to read something. I just figured it was a trick of the light. The hospital isn't exactly lit like a library, you know," I added with an attempt at humor, though inside I was beginning to worry. "What exactly does all this point to?"

"I can't say conclusively yet, but what I'm looking for is evidence of brain trauma—like a concussion," he said.

His last word brought with it a sense of relief. A concussion was something I'd heard of, at least. I remembered a guy in college who got a concussion while playing football, and he'd been fine after a few days. "I have a series of tests to do, so let's get started. Hopefully then we'll find some answers."

And so the poking and prodding began. Dr. Harper gave me the preemptory tests for pulse and blood pressure before he began a series of exercises designed to test my hearing, eyesight, memory, and depth perception. The tests went smoothly at first, and my confidence was growing. Then he returned to the part of the test that required me to follow the flashlight. Again, I couldn't see the light when he moved it to the left. I also wasn't able to complete simple depth-perception tests without mistakes.

Seeing my growing concern, he tried to reassure me. "Evans, you know you're lucky to be alive after hitting that mine," he said. "It's not uncommon after something like that to experience a few problems like this. Keep your chin up, and I'll do a little more reading on this in my medical journals. Hopefully I can give you some recommendations by tomorrow. In the meantime, try not to focus on this too much; stress won't help you. Try to take it easier than normal, and we'll just see what God has in store."

CHAPTER 28

THREE DAYS

I WAS TYING UP MY BOOTS and getting ready to head out to my favorite cliff when I saw Nurse Simmons approaching from across the room.

"Morning, Bob," she said cheerily. "The doctor wants to see you in his office as soon as you can get there."

A little alarmed, I asked, "Should I be worried?"

"No, I don't think so," she said. "He has some news for you. He didn't seem worried to me."

"Thanks for letting me know." Grabbing my Bible for later, I headed to Dr. Harper's office.

That morning I'd woken up surprisingly full of energy, despite all that was weighing down my mind and heart. I glanced out the window to see another beautiful day in Provence. There were no remnants of my headache from the day before, and although I hadn't truly grieved the loss of Ed yet, the reassurance that he was with Jesus buoyed my spirits.

I knocked on Ben's door. When he saw me, he waved me

in and pulled out a file from his drawer. "Take a seat, Evans," he said. "I have some news for you." I was startled to note that he was skipping over the normal pleasantries. "I spent some time yesterday reading the information I have here on brain trauma, and you'll be glad to know it doesn't look like you're in any immediate danger. However, you clearly have some of the symptoms of brain injury. The problem is that I don't have the right equipment to determine much more than that. Yesterday, I spoke with your commanding officer in the Navy, and given the nature of the injury and what you experienced on the beach, plus the fact that you have a young family at home, he approved your transfer back stateside. You are going home, Bob."

Home. The word hung in the air between us. How many times had I prayed and dreamed about just that?

Home, because my brain might be damaged. *Home*, because of a freak accident on an empty beach while my friends were fighting and dying to remain here.

How could so many emotions and thoughts be captured by such a small word?

The doctor's voice broke through my whirling thoughts: "Did you hear me, Bob? You're headed home to see that daughter of yours. I would guess you'll be holding her, and not just that picture, in a couple of weeks. There's a transport ship leaving from St. Tropez in three days, and you have a berth on it."

With a distracted shake of my head, I said, "Home . . ."

In a cascade of conflicting emotions and chaotic thoughts, tears began to roll unheeded down my cheeks.

For the life of me, I couldn't form a coherent thought until one realization, like the first ray of sunlight, broke through. *Alyce. I will get to see Alyce. And Jeanette.* With that, I could feel a grin rerouting the tears as they fell.

"You all right?" Ben sounded worried. "I thought you'd be excited."

"I am," I managed to say. "It's just shocking, that's all. And there's so much to do here. How am I going to tell my new French friends? I don't want them to feel abandoned one more time."

"I know," Ben assured me. "We can sort all that out. I know how much you've done here in the village and in the hospital. Trust me when I say I will hate to see you go. However, this is about you and your health. It's not just a fickle military decision. I asked to send you home because I can't serve you well enough here. You need to take that seriously. When we're done here, you need to go to Nurse Simmons to fill out some paperwork so you can make it on that ship."

I stood and reached out to shake Ben's hand. "Thank you. Thank you for everything."

Placing a hand on my shoulder and looking me in the eye, he said, "No thanks are needed. I'm just doing my job. Thank you for doing yours as well. Ever since you woke up, you've been a symbol of hope to the guys here. I've asked the nurses to make arrangements for you to speak to the whole group one last time. I know they'll want to say good-bye."

A little surprised, I pumped his hand one last time and turned toward the door. People came and went here all the time, and I couldn't remember ever having a going-away party.

+ + +

An hour later, I walked up the street toward the cliffs overlooking the Bay of St. Tropez. It was surreal to think about all the relationships I'd formed in this beautiful town in such a short time.

When I arrived at the bench, I looked out over the bay and wondered which of the ships moored there would be the one to take us home. *Us.* The sad thought intruded into my mind as I thought about Ed's body being prepared for transport.

This isn't how Ed and I envisioned returning home, I thought.

From the moment I'd woken up in the hospital in Draguignan, I'd been living each day in the moment—walking through the doors God opened with no clear thought about the day I would leave. These past few weeks felt suspended in time. In retrospect, it was like being trapped in paradise. Each new day held surprises and victories, and I felt alive in Christ as he used me in the lives of those around me. This had been like nothing else I'd experienced. I felt like I was smack in the middle of God's will for my life, and I loved every minute of it.

And yet the end had come, and suddenly I was over-whelmed by the responsibility of all that I'd begun here. Matthias. Kristophe. Bernadette. Samantha and her sons. Jean-Denis and Christabel. All the men I'd spoken with daily at the hospital. And now, I felt like God was asking me to abandon them.

As I sat there staring at the relentless rows of waves sliding toward the beach, I prayed. "God, what am I supposed to do? How can I leave all these people right now?"

Silence was the only answer to my frantic thoughts.

"I need to hear from you today, God," I whispered. "This is more than I can handle."

Settling onto the perpetually damp bench, I felt the famil-iar coolness of the morning dew and was reminded of all the days God had met me here through his Word and through the beauty of his creation. I needed to remember that. He hadn't left me, nor was he leaving Draguignan. *I* was leaving.

"Jesus," I prayed, "you know how much I've wanted to go home to see my new daughter and my wife. I've longed for that—prayed for it. And yet now that the moment is here, I'm not sure. How am I going to tell my new friends that I have to leave? Will they understand, or will they think one more person is abandoning them? Please, Father, don't aban-don them. Show me what to do, and I will do it."

Suddenly, God brought to my mind the image from his Word of the newly clothed man experiencing his first hours of freedom after Jesus cast a demon out of him. The man begged to go with Jesus, yet Jesus insisted he stay behind. In my spirit, I felt God say, *You are free. Remember how I stayed with that man even after Jesus went on ahead without him? I will stay with Matthias, Kristophe, and the rest. I love them more than you do.*

This was the reminder I needed. God didn't need me to accomplish his ends, though it had been amazing to be right in the midst of it these past few weeks.

Somehow released, I sat there looking out at the beautiful scene before me. "I know I'm usually here to pray for others, but today *I* need you, Jesus. So much has happened these past two days. Help me to make sense of it. What do you want me to do?"

But there were no lightning bolts, no burning bushes. "I've followed you, Jesus, even though I rarely knew what you were up to," I said.

I just sat there for a while, with my mind in overdrive, my emotions scrambled. There, in the humid morning air, I felt the drain of the past few days dragging my eyelids downward. Somewhere deep inside, a familiar echo began to bubble toward the surface: *This is who you are. This is what you were made for.*

I sensed that God wasn't done with me here. I felt sure, somehow, that I would return to Europe. What a strange thought! I'd never intended to go to Europe. I just wanted to serve my country. And yet here I was in France, a place that truly brought my spirit alive.

Maybe when this crazy war is over, I'll bring Jeanette and Alyce here, I thought. But as soon as the thought was complete, I recognized that it was a shallow echo of what God was saying. This was not about a vacation.

Does he really want me to come back? It seemed crazy and unlikely, yet my spirit resonated with the rightness of it.

In the damp heat of that French morning, God was planting a seed in me that would take years to germinate. When it did, I would be immediately transported back to this simple scene of feeling God's pleasure at using me to serve him.

In that moment, I had little to offer beyond a willing, obedient heart. But perhaps that was exactly what God wanted from me.

CHAPTER 29

THERE ARE NO GOOD-BYES IN THE KINGDOM OF GOD

WITH THE GOLDEN GLOW of the late-afternoon sun reflecting off the buildings in the village, I made my way with leaden feet down the street toward the café. I had no idea what I was going to say—how I was going to tell my friends I was leaving. With each step, my anxiety grew, and so did my feelings of inadequacy. The reassurance I'd had that morning of being in God's will now seemed like a distant memory.

I knew God could shepherd these people spiritually without me, but how would he do it? It wasn't so much about me as the fact there seemed to be no one else. "God, please send your next missionary to Draguignan," I prayed as I raised my hand to open the door.

Well, here I go, I thought.

When my eyes adjusted to the dim light in the restaurant, I was taken aback to see Ben Harper seated at a table with

Kristophe, Matthias, and Samantha. Dr. Harper? I couldn't remember ever seeing him without scrubs on, let alone outside the hospital.

"Hey, Bob. *Venez ici et asseyez-vous. Nous avons tout juste ouvert une bouteille de vin,*" Ben said in competent French, holding up a bottle of wine.

Ben speaks French? I just stared at him for a moment. "Have you met Kristophe before?"

"*Oui,*" Ben said mischievously. "He runs the restaurant you are always raving about at the hospital. Did you think none of us heard you?"

"Well, I suppose I did mention it once or twice," I admitted.

"I know you think none of us spoke to a Frenchman before you showed up, but I've known Kristophe for almost a year and a half. Though I have to say that it wasn't until you came that I spoke with him about God. I've also met most of the rest of the town in my medical role."

"Oh," I said sheepishly. "I suppose that makes sense."

"Don't get me wrong, Evans." Ben chuckled and looked around the table. "I've *met* these people; you *know* them. There's a difference. I came here today so they would know how important it is for you to go home and also to let them know how hard it is for you to leave."

Looking at the floor, I nodded my head. "Yeah, I've been worried about that all afternoon."

"I've never met a foreigner in my life I would want to stay

here more than you," Kristophe declared. "But not if it's a risk to you. We understand, even if we will miss you greatly."

"Did he tell you I have to leave on Friday?" I asked quietly, still afraid to meet their eyes.

"Yes," Kristophe said. "In fact, Ben came to help us plan a party for you."

That's the second time today, I marveled.

"You need to be at the church tomorrow evening at six. We'll arrange everything," Matthias said.

The church?

"Are you excited about seeing Alyce?" Samantha asked, clearly changing the subject.

Before long, it was time for Ben and me to return to the hospital. As I made the walk back for one of the last times, I was struck by the feeling of being known and loved. That reality transcended my ability to speak French or even the short time I'd been friends with these dear people. God had knit us together in his Kingdom in ways that went beyond words.

+ + +

The next day, shortly after 5 p.m., I began to make my way up the hill toward the church. The first thing I noticed was how silent the streets were for this time of day. I was even more shocked to see the *"Fermé"* sign in the restaurant window as I passed. The restaurant, the store—everything was closed. That seemed a bit odd, but as I approached the main square, I caught the whisper of voices and laughter and snatches of music on the soft evening breeze.

Rounding the last corner before the town square, I finally saw the source of the music—and the merriment. The street in front of the church had been transformed by an array of small tables. A string of lights and paper streamers had been hastily hung, turning the normally somber church facade into a festive place that felt both foreign and somehow normal. All around me, I saw locals and friends milling about with plates and wineglasses.

Taking in the scene, I realized that everyone was there—everyone! Kristophe, Samantha and her boys, Matthias, Jean-Denis and Christabel, Michel, Ben, even Nurse Simmons. I spotted Matthias carrying a tray of food through the crowd. Some of the men from the hospital were in the crowd as well.

Bernadette arrived wearing a pretty dress and a bandanna around her shorn head. Kids I'd never seen before were running to and fro, playing with Samantha's boys. All around me, I heard ripples of laughter and conversation. I couldn't help but remember the first time I'd approached the foreboding church amid the ruins of the destroyed square. *This moment is as close to actual resurrection as I think I'll ever experience here on earth,* I thought. *God has truly brought dead things to life.*

Matthias spotted me from across the crowd and hurried over, narrowly avoiding a brigade of young boys darting through the crowd, playing some form of tag. "Welcome, my friend," Matthias said, grabbing my shoulders for a quick kiss of greeting. "We were going to wait, but the children—"

He waved his hands at the gathered crowd, most of whom had already started in on a drink or a plate of food.

"No problem," I assured him with a laugh. "I was slow getting here. I'm glad to see the party has started. But I have to admit, this is a surprise. How did you do all of this since last night?"

"When the occasion calls for it, no one does a party like the French." Matthias winked. "This is almost like old times. Come, let's get you some food and a glass of wine." With that, he took me by the shoulder and led me toward a small table overflowing with food. Though it wasn't far away, I had to run a gauntlet of handshakes, embraces, and greetings to get there, and by the time I picked up a small plate, the grin on my face was threatening to blossom into full-blown, joyful laughter.

How fitting a location for a party like this, I thought. *The doorsteps of a church is where a party should start.*

Inside, my spirit was singing. I loved these people. My only regret was that Jeanette and Alyce weren't there to experience it with me. *Someday.*

Matthias filled my plate to overflowing and handed me a glass of wine. Raising his refilled glass, he said in mock solemnity, *"À votre santé,"* before clinking his glass against mine.

Was this really the same man I'd met inside the darkened church a few weeks ago? But then it struck me: *Why should I be amazed? This is one of the Lord's servants who has rediscovered hope.*

A passage from the fifteenth chapter of the book of Romans resonated in my mind as I saw it lived out in front of me: "Now may the God of hope fill you with all joy and peace in believing, that you may abound in hope by the power of the Holy Spirit." Hope had returned to Draguignan, and it was alive and well in the hearts of these men and women who only weeks before had been lost in despair. Not for the first time, I was amazed by the dramatic changes that came from the smallest degree of hope in something greater.

I probably looked foolish as I stood there holding my food while tears formed in my eyes. But it somehow felt like Communion: a celebration of Christ at work in people's hearts and in our world.

+ + +

All around me, the party continued. Matthias was talking with Jean-Denis, and even as we ate, more food continued to appear from within the church. The music stopped only briefly as the musicians ate a few bites and washed it down before people pressed them to start playing again. I soon gathered my emotions and began making the rounds to talk with all my friends. It was rich. It was life.

I was many things: soldier, missionary, chaplain, husband, father, disciple. One thing I was decidedly *not*: a dancer. Thankfully, Wheaton College, in its good wisdom, had kept us from that. But in this place, in this moment, I couldn't help myself. Was the wedding in John 2 like this evening? This was what the Kingdom should feel like.

As the shadows grew long, the music slowed and people stood around talking in small clusters. One after the other, they came to say their good-byes and wish me well. After an endless line of hugs and handshakes, just a few of us remained—the people I wanted to say good-bye to the least.

Ben approached and, gripping my hand in a strong embrace, confided, "In all my days in this town, I have never seen something like this. You will be missed more than you will ever know. Enjoy this night—you deserve it. I need to head back, but I'll see you in the morning. Come by my office around ten."

With that, he waved to the dwindling crowd and bid them *bonsoir*.

I noticed that Matthias was balancing a large stack of dirty plates and teetering toward the door to the church, so I collected more plates from the table and followed him as he made his way to his apartment at the rear of the church.

As we entered, I was surprised to find the area cleaned and orderly, even bright. We set down our stacks of dishes by the sink, and I mentioned the changes. "I love what you've done with the place, Matthias. What's the occasion?"

"Well, more and more people come to visit these days, and I decided it was time that it didn't look like the home of a depressed bachelor."

"Who's visiting?" I asked, surprised.

"I took your example, and I now meet with people from

town to talk about the Bible and faith. I was shocked at how many people really were interested, even though not many people come to Mass on Sundays anymore. Of course, some of them may just meet with me for the coffee, but that's okay," he said with a conspiratorial smile. "God can work with that, too."

"I'm proud of you, Matthias," I said sincerely. "You're becoming the man of God this town needs. You always had the job, but now you're truly living it out. The party tonight was amazing. I saw more joy tonight than I've seen in my entire stay in Draguignan. And to think it all happened at the church."

"I know," he said. "I should have been doing it all along, but I'm afraid I was too self-focused."

"Nonsense!" I grabbed his shoulder and looked him in the eye. "Do you remember what I said that first day I came? I think all we needed was someone to hope with. I can't tell you how many days our talks and prayers together gave me the strength to go back to the hospital and give just a little more. We all need hope, and we need each other. I firmly believe you are one of the main reasons God brought me here."

"I think you may be right," he confided. "I don't know if I could have held on much longer if you hadn't come. Tonight I glimpsed what the church could be—should be—a beacon of hope and life amid the tragedy. I want more of it. Thank you for coming to the church that day despite all the reasons you could have stayed away. You rescued me . . . no, God rescued me; he just used an American to do it. I'll miss our meetings more than words can say. I hope that when all this madness is over, you will bring your family back here. Then we'll have another party, like only the French can, to welcome you back."

"This place, these people . . ." I paused for a moment to find the right words. "God has infected me with this place. I don't think I could stay away even if I wanted to. I would give anything for Jeanette and Alyce to enjoy this with me."

Grabbing me in a spontaneous embrace, Matthias squeezed me tightly, tears welling in his eyes. "It's a plan, then! And I'll hold you to it."

I stood there looking at him. He was the unlikeliest of partners, I realized, and I felt the smile of the Holy Spirit as if he were having a private chuckle at our expense.

This is the Kingdom, I thought. *This is exactly the kind of group the God who made a winning team out of fishermen and tax collectors would put together.*

In that moment, the truth that I really was at the center of his will nearly overwhelmed me. All I could think to say was, "Thank you, Jesus, for using simple, ordinary people like us for your Kingdom purposes."

Suddenly feeling serious, I declared, "Matthias, even if I don't come back, everything we have experienced here is true. This is the Kingdom of God at work. No matter what happens, hold on to this. This town needs you desperately. It won't be easy, but it will be worth it. Don't lose faith, my brother."

"I won't. You needn't fear," he responded just as solemnly.

"But right now, we need to get the rest of this cleaned up, or none of us will ever get to bed."

As I went to gather more plates, I saw Kristophe cleaning up glasses with Jean-Denis, and Samantha was folding tablecloths. But the band and most of the rest of the folks were now gone. I was disappointed that Bernadette had gone before I had a chance to say good-bye. Folding and stacking some chairs, I contemplated what it would mean to leave this place.

When the work was finally done, Kristophe called us over to the stairs in front of the church and produced a small bottle covered in wood from his coat. "Now, Bob, I know that having an occasional glass of wine is a stretch for you American Christians, but tonight is a special night. I've been saving this for a number of years to celebrate the end of the war. It's a regional specialty called Élixir Végétal de la Grande-Chartreuse. It's made by monks, so you should be safe."

Passing small cups to Matthias, Jean-Denis, and me, he uncorked the bottle, lifted it to his nose, and breathed in the fruity aroma. Starting with Matthias, he poured a small amount of the bright-green liqueur into the cups before recorking the bottle and returning it to his coat.

Holding out his cup, he said, "Men, I don't know if and when the war will end, but I pray every day that this day will be the last. That day will be amazing. But tonight, right now, is amazing as well. Life and God have come back to Draguignan, and they came in on the coattails of this unlikely American. Whatever the future holds, I don't think it will be any more amazing than what I saw here tonight or what I witnessed in the past few weeks and months. To that, I lift my glass and toast with you. *À la vie et gloire à Dieu!*"

To life, and thanks be to God.

Lifting our glasses high, we raised a toast. I had never experienced anything like that flavorful green liquid. It warmed and burned all the way down.

"That, my friend, is how we celebrate amazing things in Draguignan," Kristophe said. "And tonight, you are the amazing thing God has brought to us all. There aren't enough words to express our gratitude for you and to you. But because of you—if I understand the Bible correctly—we will have all of eternity to figure it out. This town and I have cried too many tears already to let this be a sad night. Did you see the people laughing and dancing tonight? I wasn't sure I would ever see something like that again in my life, and yet I did. It will be a long time before Draguignan forgets the wounded American preacher who nearly blew himself up to bring us the Good News. You are welcome here any day. You must bring your family to visit so I can tell your dear wife what a bad dancer you are and make her a proper French meal."

We talked and laughed and tried not to cry for a while longer until they saw I was having a hard time keeping my eyes open. "It looks like we have worn out the star of the party, friends," Matthias said. "I know we don't want to, but I think we need to say *bonsoir*."

As the finality of that pronouncement settled in, there were heartfelt hugs and handshakes all around, and before

I knew it, I was making my way back toward the hospital for the last time. I was full to overflowing with joy, sorrow, and longing. *Will I ever see these dear men again? Yes, of course I will.*

I crept into the hospital, trying not to waken other patients as I slipped into my bed.

Tomorrow morning I'm leaving. I am going home to my family. It seemed like a dream, though I hadn't fallen asleep yet.

Paris, France
January 26, 2016

JAZZ JONES

CHAPTER 30

THE FIRST DAYS OF "REAL" MINISTRY

I SPENT MUCH OF MY FIRST YEAR after arriving in Paris learning about the culture and language of my new country. Like many ministries, GEM has procedures in place to help new missionaries acclimate to their surroundings, learn the language, and process culture shock.

Now, as the dreary days of January were drawing to a close, language school was mostly behind me, and I was eager to begin "real" ministry. And as our trainers frequently said, "Ministry means relationships." I had already begun developing informal friendships with language-school classmates and other people in the community, and while I always made an effort to bring spiritual topics into our conversations, I hadn't fully pursued this aspect of my life as a missionary yet.

One of my most meaningful relationships from those early days on the field was with Margot, a seventy-three-year-old Parisian woman I met with regularly for a language and conversation exchange. When we got together, we spent half the time talking in French and the other half talking in English.

When I first began looking for a language partner in early 2015, I felt hesitant about meeting people, so when I saw her ad in an online site dedicated to helping people find language partners, I figured a woman in her seventies would make a safe, albeit interesting, language partner.

I could tell from the moment I met Margot that she was truly lovely. We met in a café in her neighborhood in the eleventh arrondissement, just across the river from my flat. While we sipped espressos, we took turns speaking in either French or English about life, our past, and whatever else came up. She had been a German teacher for forty years, so it was nice to have one language as a common connection. It was also a joy for me to learn about Paris and French culture from her perspective and to be around someone who was still eager to learn and grow at her age.

In the process of getting to know about each other, the conversation eventually turned to what I did for a job. Although she described herself as an *athée*, or atheist, she respected what I stood for. She did, however, have trouble comprehending that my job was a "real job." I felt free to talk with her about spiritual things, and her curiosity about what would bring a young person halfway around the globe to be a missionary in one of the world's elite cities periodically brought us back to conversations about God and faith.

Of course, being a missionary wasn't the only significant thing happening in my life. When I invited her to the wedding-celebration dinner Sven and I were planning for our Paris friends, she was eager to attend. She also told me that she would love to meet my family when they were in Paris after my wedding. Building close relationships with the French isn't usually immediate or easy, so that felt like a significant milestone in our friendship.

Margot was one of the first people in Paris I added to my list of people to pray for. I wasn't surprised when she proclaimed she didn't believe in God; in almost a year of being in France, I had yet to meet another believer outside of a church context. Still, I felt a pang of sadness on her behalf. Here was such a lovely, vivacious French lady who had yet to experience the love of God.

Margot wasn't the only person God put in my path. Another was a young man who worked in the corner convenience store on the bottom floor of my building. We exchanged our first *"bonjour"* within a day or two of my moving into the flat. He told me he was Moroccan but had lived in France for several years. From the beginning, he was easy to talk to and eager to help me practice my French. Our conversations grew over time as my vocabulary expanded. We discussed weather, life, holidays, my upcoming marriage, and what I was doing in Paris. He was intrigued by my work, and whenever possible, I tried to include some spiritual or life-related topics, just to see where God would take the conversation.

I'd been talking with him for several months when it dawned on me that, after all this time, I didn't know his name. French culture is a polite culture, and, like Germany, it's common for people to know each other for years before losing some of the formality and exchanging names. It's even possible for some friendships to never go beyond "Madame" and "Monsieur."

However, in the Kingdom of God, we are invited to be on a first-name basis. It's all about community and belonging. So after our next conversation, I introduced myself by name, and he gave me his name in return: Ilias. Another name for the prayer list! It was also a step forward in my friendship with him. I smiled to myself as I walked out of the store that day. *God, let Ilias experience just a little bit of you through me,* I prayed.

+ + +

One day when I was talking to Ilias, the subject of my upcoming marriage came up. "Why doesn't Sven live with you?" Ilias asked.

I explained that sexual purity was one of my Christian values. "Sven and I have prayed a lot to make sure our marriage is God's will," I added.

"You mean God will confirm whom you should marry?" There was a hint of amazement in his voice.

"Yes," I replied. "God cares about all aspects of our lives, and we want to make sure we're doing things his way."

"I've never thought about that," Ilias said. "But if God can help you with such things, it really seems like you're doing this the right way. Not many people take so much time and thought before making an important life step. I wish you the best."

"Thank you, Ilias." I said, struck by the sincerity of his reply.

As I said good-bye and walked toward the entrance to my building, I half wondered, half prayed, *How can I bring Jesus into this relationship more effectively?*

Norfolk, Virginia
Back in the USA.

Draguignan, France
December 4, 1944

BOB EVANS

DEPARTURE

IT SEEMED LIKE I HAD BEEN ASLEEP for only moments when I felt a gentle hand shaking my shoulder. "Lieutenant Evans, it's time to get up. Your Jeep will be here soon to take you to the docks. The doctor will be here to see you and give you some instructions."

Rubbing sleep from my eyes, I focused enough to see that the voice belonged to Nurse Simmons. She remained standing at the foot of my bed as I swung my feet from under the covers and reached for my pants. "Thanks for waking me," I said awkwardly, pulling up my pants as quickly as I could.

"I asked if I could," she confessed. "You once told me that you thought God heard my prayers just like he hears yours. How do you know that? I'm not the best person sometimes."

"I said that because it's the truth." I barely remembered the conversation she was referring to, but that didn't really matter. "Jesus came to die for all of us, and frankly, I'm not that good of a person either. I have lots of issues. But that's the Good News. Jesus offers all of us the same opportunity to have a relationship with him, and when we pray in his name, he promises that his Father will hear us." I stuffed the few belongings I had into my duffel bag.

"I know you have to go and you don't have time to talk about this," she apologized. "I'm sorry I waited so long to ask. I felt a bit foolish, to tell the truth." She looked down at her shoes. "Is there someone here I could talk to about it? I see you with lots of the guys."

It hit me for the first time: *There are people she can talk to here!* "Well, if you know some French, you could talk with Kristophe, who owns the restaurant, or Samantha, who owns the store, or Father Matthias up at the church. That would be a good start. You might also try Dr. Harper. He tends to keep quiet about matters of faith because of his position, but he believes in Jesus too. And don't worry about your questions—that's how we all learn. I have all kinds of questions myself."

"Thanks," she responded brightly, noticeably relieved. "That's more than I expected. I've met Samantha a few times—maybe I'll start there." Impulsively, she gave me a quick hug. "Thanks for all you've done here. You will really be missed. Not many patients brighten the room the way you do." With that, she turned and walked away, just as Dr. Harper entered the room from the other side.

"All packed up, Evans?" he asked.

I nodded. "Kind of surreal to think I'm going home today—actually going home. I'll get to hold my new daughter for the first time in just a couple of weeks."

"I hope you have a smooth voyage. I heard a while back that sub activity in the Atlantic slowed down after the Germans retreated to continental Europe." He seemed lost in thought for a moment. Then, coming back to the present, he declared, "Well, I don't have a lot of instructions for you, but the ones I have are important. First, if you haven't already told your wife about your head injuries, tell her as soon as you can. It's important, and if something happens, that will help her know what to do. Second, here's a little journal I got at the shop in town. I need you to keep a record of anything out of the ordinary with your head, hearing, and vision. If you have a headache, write it down, and note the date. If you have problems with your vision, write it down. That will give the doctors some good data to work with in the future. And as soon as you get on board the ship, report to the medical bay to let them know what you are dealing with. That way, if something happens, they won't have to guess. Other than that, keep eating and take care not to overdo it."

Throughout his speech, I nodded where I was supposed to, letting him know I was taking this seriously.

"Doc, do you really think there's a problem?" I asked.

"It's hard to say for sure," he said. "There's a lot we don't know about head injuries and the brain. The tests show you have some issues, but I've also read about a number of situations where the brain seems to heal itself naturally. I wouldn't recommend playing football or anything else that requires a helmet anytime soon. Your injury could be nothing, or it could be quite significant. That's why you have to pay attention and report anything out of the ordinary. And frankly, I would pray daily that God would heal your brain. God probably has a better chance of doing that than any doctor right now."

"Thanks. That's helpful," I said. "By the way, Nurse Simmons was asking about prayer and God today. I think she's just about ready, if you want to walk her into the Kingdom."

"Really?" Ben looked at me, surprised. "I've never done that before. Do you think I could?"

"Sure. If you're saved, you're the right guy," I said. "You know what you believe, right? You can answer her questions about the Bible. I think she understands the sin part already. Just show her how Jesus paid the price, how she can accept that as truth and begin to live like Jesus. Jesus has always used guys who weren't sure they could do it because he's the one doing it through us. If you're a believer, God wants you to be a disciple and make more disciples. This could be your first chance."

"I have to admit, watching you around here has shown me there's a lot more I could do to make God known here," Ben said. "The things you've done are all things I could do—I'm just not sure why I never have."

"Today is a new day, Ben." I clapped him on the shoulder. "That's part of the beauty of God's mercy and grace: every day is a new day. This hospital needs a pastor and a healer, and I don't think I could leave it in any better hands."

Smiling broadly, he nodded his head. "Just keep an eye on

your mailbox. If I really get stuck, the hospital has a telegraph machine."

"I have a better idea," I said. "Just talk to Kristophe, Samantha, Matthias, and the folks at the party last night—figure it out together. It's all in here." I held up my Bible before returning it to the top of my duffel bag.

"If you can run over a mine, almost die, and do all this while recovering from a brain injury, I guess I don't have a lot of excuses. Thanks for showing me how to live out the gospel and for being such an example of what a disciple-maker looks like. I'm going to miss having you around here, and I know everyone else will too. You need to get out to your ride, but I wanted to tell you myself. You make me want to be a better Christian, and I hope that someone will say that about me one day too." He shook my hand vigorously and then skipped the formality to embrace me tightly. "Godspeed, Bob. Draguignan may never be the same because of what you did here."

I hugged him back and then decided to lighten the moment. "Well, one good turn deserves another," I said. "You sewed me back together, after all. Although I can't tell you how many times I wanted to kick you in the shins for making me walk that first day." I gave him one last hand-shake, and then it was time to go.

As I approached the door, the gray light of predawn was just beginning to seep through the front windows into the foyer. When I opened the door, I was surprised to find Bernadette sitting on the front steps.

Looking up with obvious relief, she scampered to the top of the steps and gave me a tight hug. "I was so worried you were gone. I needed to see you. I just couldn't bring myself to say good-bye last night."

Prying her off me so I could see her, I said, "I'm glad to get to see you too. I had something I wanted to say to you before I left—a message I heard from God just for you."

Surprised, she stepped back. "He does that?"

"Well, yes, he does," I said, chuckling. "Though a lot of what he has to say to us he already wrote down in the Bible. Sometimes he speaks to us in visions and dreams, or a quiet voice in our heart. We just have to learn to listen."

"Well, what did he say?"

"He told me you are his trophy in Draguignan. You represent everything he cares about—hope for the hopeless, beauty from ashes. He wants to display your life as an example of what forgiveness looks like in the flesh. He loves you deeply, Bernadette. Never forget that long before you were unjustly beaten, so was he."

Her tears had begun with my first word and then flowed in an unabated river as I continued. In that moment, I sensed God was doing something deep and healing in Bernadette's heart. It was sacred.

The Jeep's driver, who had been waiting patiently up to this point, gave the horn a quick bump. My time in Draguignan, France, had come to an end.

Quickly embracing Bernadette, I prayed, "Father, this amazing child of yours has a pure heart and wants to experience your love so she can show others what love really looks like. Bless her and protect her as only you can. In Jesus' name, I declare this to be so."

I hoisted my bag onto my shoulder, and then, through tears—hers and mine—I heard her whisper, "*Merci.* I will be brave."

+   +   +

The Jeep bounced down the road toward the beach—the same beach where all this had begun. How amazing to think that God used a German land mine to accomplish his purposes in Draguignan. Though I could feel the scars in many places on my body, I sensed God had also brought healing that was far more profound and lasting.

Twenty minutes later, as we passed the exact spot where the Delta Sector camp had stood mere months ago, I was amazed to see only pristine white-sand beach with crystal-blue waves lapping against it. It was a reminder to me that the ugliness of this war would, in time, be washed away, and God's beauty would return.

I rode in silence as I passed through the tropical beauty of Provence for the last time. I hadn't gotten here the way I expected or dreamed, and now I was leaving. It still felt too soon, too abrupt. *God, what was this all about?*

CHAPTER 32

ABOARD THE *SANTA PAULA*

I WAS PULLED OUT of my pondering when the driver pulled up in front of the gangway of the USAT *Santa Paula*, a 1930s-era US cruise liner pressed into military service during the war. I grabbed my bag and joined the queue of people waiting to board.

An hour later, after heading up the gangway in the hot Mediterranean sun, I was met by a Navy ensign who asked for my transfer papers. Checking my paperwork against his list, he finally mumbled, "Ah, Evans. Here it is. You'll be in berth 9A-137 on lower deck three. Please follow Ensign Sampson here, and he'll show you to your spot. Then he'll show you how to get to medical aid if you need it. We should be weighing anchor in about two hours. Have you spent any time on a ship before?"

"Yes, Ensign. I've been assigned to the Third Armored

Division since their Italian landing. So I was there when they took southern France. This ship looks a little more stable than the one I was on as we assaulted the beach," I said with a lopsided grin.

"Welcome aboard, Lieutenant Evans," he said with a nod.

Hoisting my bag, I followed Sampson through the bowels of the ship until he pointed to a small outer cabin with six bunks. "Here's your new home, Lieutenant Evans. Drop your stuff in an open locker, and I'll show you where medical and the mess hall are located."

As we made our way aft, I asked, "So, how long have you been aboard, Sampson? Have you seen any action?"

"Not really," he answered. "There are always subs at the crossing, especially around Gibraltar where it narrows, but we're usually part of a larger convoy. It gets your attention when you know an enemy is there but you can't see him. I've seen some smaller escort ships hit—that's about it. How about you? You said you were part of the Third Armored. You infantry?"

Hmm, I guess, in a way, I'm a foot soldier, I thought. "Well, if you can believe it, I'm a Navy chaplain. I volunteered to go with the invasion force because I thought they might need God more than the other guys."

"Seriously?" He looked over his shoulder to study me. "You *chose* to hit the beach?"

"Yeah, now that you mention it, it was a little crazy," I agreed. "As it turned out, I really did hit the beach—about thirty feet after my motorcycle hit one of those Teller mines the Germans are so fond of putting out to welcome us. That's why I'm here now. The doc thinks I might have damaged what little brains I have, so no more war for me."

"Still, going in on the boats—that's the real deal. Glad you made it." I could hear a hint of respect in his voice.

"Yeah, my friends—the ones with the guns—are amazing guys. I've never seen courage like that before." I thought back to those early days in France. "But as courageous and crazy as they are, they still have fears and doubts, and knowing God was with them really seemed to help."

"Courageous and crazy. That sounds about right," Sampson agreed. "Every time we head back to the States, we have a couple hundred of them in the hold in pine boxes. It seems like a real waste to me. I'm not so sure our guys should be sacrificing their lives for France. We drove the Germans back to Europe—maybe they should deal with them now."

Our conversation halted as we climbed down a ladder to the deck below. Then we continued winding our way aft.

"I know what you mean," I said. "There has been way too much death all around. German, French, English, and American lives, all snuffed out too early. And yet if you saw all that happened in some of those French towns and villages, you might feel different. I think what our boys are doing is an echo of the Good News—people sacrificing their lives for the innocent and abused who can't stand up for themselves."

"Guess I never thought of it like that," he said.

"Don't mind me, Sampson. I'll take any opportunity to preach. So what's your first name?"

He offered a hand. "George."

"I'm Bob."

"Glad to have you aboard, Bob. Maybe I'll see you around. Well, here we are. Second deck, far aft. The mess hall is on the right, though you'll soon realize this used to be a cruise liner, so it's a little nicer than most ships. Medical is just behind it. Chow is served three times a day for two hours at a time, unless we're in action. Just listen for the three quick bells—that means it's open and ready. However, if the bells keep ringing and red lights flash, get back to your berth quick as you can. That means we're going into action. As for medical, there should always be someone there, although you might have to wake them up. Things are pretty slow on the *Paula*. Usually, it's just your typical Navy injuries—rope burns, falls, and the like. Depends on how heavy the seas get."

"Thanks, George. I'll let you get back now. I think I can find my way back to my berth. Up one level and about three-quarters of the way forward starboard, I think."

George nodded. "See you around, Evans. I want to hear more about France, if you have some time."

+ + +

I looked at the mess hall and checked in with medical, letting them know about my condition and symptoms. By the time I was back at my berth, I could hear a low, constant rumble, and I felt a barely perceptible roll as the anchor was weighed.

I wanted to get a final view of France, so I headed up

to the deck and found a place along the crowded sides of the ship. As the giant moorings were cast, the *Santa Paula* coaxed her giant engines to life and began steaming out of St. Tropez. We cleared the harbor, and I saw a convoy of five or six other transport ships plus seven smaller frigates forming a protective ring about ten miles offshore.

Turning back, I could still see a dwindling image of the white beaches across from St. Tropez glowing in the late-afternoon sun. *Will I ever see the Delta Sector beach again?* I wondered. I was surprised how hard it was to leave.

Somewhere over that first line of hills lay Draguignan, the unlikely mission field God had brought me to. A part of me was still there now, and I was pretty sure a piece of France was going home inside of me. I felt confused by how those painful weeks of recovery, even with all of the relationships I'd formed, could even register against the pure joy I felt about heading home to my wife and daughter, but they did. *God, what happened there?*

But I heard no immediate answer, only the thrum of the engines and the mournful call of the sea birds circling in our wake.

+ + +

I occupied myself on the voyage by reading Scripture and talking with some of the men I met about the war, the hope of peace, and what things were like in France. George, in particular, showed a keen interest in the people I'd met in France and how they responded to the idea of hope and forgiveness. I discovered on day two that George had lost two brothers in the invasion of Normandy, and suddenly his feelings about American lives being "wasted" on France made more sense.

That's one thing I'd learned along the way: there is always a story.

We spoke a lot about forgiveness and how forgiving someone—even a nation of people—is more important for the forgiver than for the forgiven. When he heard the story of Bernadette, his eyes began to fill with tears, and he said he had to get back to work.

On day four, I found a quiet room on one of the upper decks that became my hideaway during the rest of the voyage. I was glad for a place that was protected from the cold North Atlantic wind, since the temperatures had dropped hourly since we rounded the Rock of Gibraltar.

Unlike my sleeping berth, this room had a large, forward-facing window that gave me a view of the endless sea in front of us. There were two tables where I could spread out some books and a cup of coffee for a few hours of reading and reflection. The view was particularly spectacular late at night, when the northern lights flickered in magical green hues. In those moments of beauty, I sensed God's presence most. It was also in those moments that I prayed that he would help me make sense of all I had experienced.

As I prayed and cried and thanked him for his grace, I was left with one clear, undeniable thought: *I was made for Europe—and Europe needs believers who feel burdened to tell everyone they can about God.* And yet here I was, steaming directly away from Europe back to suburban America, my family, and . . . *And what? What is next for me?*

On three occasions during the voyage, each time at night, the bells sounded and the red lights flashed. It took my breath away to be floating on the vast ocean in what suddenly seemed like a small dinghy, knowing that someone out there was intent on sinking us.

Those were long, tense hours, but in the end, nothing ever came of the threats. A few of our frigates would steam at high speed in one direction or another, and eventually the lights would turn off. Yet a sense of fear grew with each engagement, like being stalked by a wild animal that was just out of sight.

When I woke on day nine, the East Coast of America was visible. We were heading for the naval station docks at Norfolk.

CHAPTER 33

ROAD TRIP

I STOOD ALONG THE RAILING OF THE SHIP with the cold mist on my face, staring at the docks ahead. Suddenly, Ensign Sampson appeared at my shoulder. I hadn't seen him since our talk about forgiveness, and I worried I'd said too much.

"It's always an amazing sight to see home on the horizon," he offered. "Getting excited about seeing that daughter of yours?"

"Excited doesn't begin to touch it, George. I think a bunch of butterflies are doing the tango in my stomach, and I can hardly think of anything else. But I'm not sure how long it's going to take to get there. I am booked on a flight tomorrow from Norfolk to Chicago. Once the plane lands in Chicago, I have to catch a bus or a train to St. Louis, and then another one to Mount Vernon, Illinois, before getting a bus from there to Pinckneyville."

"Pinckneyville?" George exclaimed. "You're kidding! I'm from Cape Girardeau! Tell you what . . . I have leave, and my uncle is picking me up in Chicago. I'll give you a lift. We're headed to my grandparents' house in Mount Vernon for a couple of weeks. That's where my family is originally from. That will save you some hassle."

"Are you sure?" I asked. "That would be great, but Pinckneyville is a little out of the way for you."

"Sure. I would enjoy the company, and besides, I have a few questions for you. But just to give you a heads-up, my uncle isn't much of a talker."

"Ah, that's no problem. Thanks for the ride. I already have my stuff, so just tell me where to go."

+ + +

The following day, I was sitting in the backseat of Uncle Jerry's Buick Roadmaster as we cleared the outskirts of Chicago and drove south on Route 66 toward St. Louis. It wasn't long before George said, "I've been thinking a lot about what you said about forgiveness. The thing is, I don't even know who I'm mad at, but it seems apparent that I'm mad at someone. It's kind of silly to be mad at the French, particularly after all you told me they went through. Do you think I'm mad at God?"

Okay, here we go, God. I'd like to make it home; help me not say anything stupid. "I'm not sure," I said. "But I know how you feel. I haven't really talked about this with anyone, but I lost my brother too. He was shot down in a plane over Belgium. At least I think he's dead; I haven't heard for sure yet. I had a lot of the same questions you do. But the thing

I keep coming back to is that Rowland Jr. was a good man—he chose to join the service, just like I did. He knew what was at stake, but he went anyway because it was the right thing to do. I can't really blame the Germans without minimizing the sacrifice Rowland chose to make. I miss him, and it does make me mad sometimes—and sad. But in the end, I keep coming back to one thing: I'm proud of my brother and the sacrifice he was willing to make. I bet you joined the cause for the same reasons, and if the roles were reversed, you would have done what was needed regardless of the cost. And if you'd had to pay the ultimate price, you wouldn't want anyone to take that away from you—not even your brothers." I looked at George's face, and he seemed to be tracking with me. "Do you know what the Bible says about this in Romans 5? 'For when we were still without strength, in due time Christ died for the ungodly. For scarcely for a righteous man will one die; yet perhaps for a good man someone would even dare to die. But God demonstrates His own love toward us, in that while we were still sinners, Christ died for us.' I realize the point of those verses is that Jesus died for us, but I also think what it says about someone dying for a good man may apply to our brothers, too."

As the miles passed, I listened to George and encouraged him as he processed the idea of forgiving France, the French people, and the Germans. Eventually, we talked about how God forgives us through Jesus. Finally, through heartfelt tears, George accepted that he, too, needed to be forgiven.

Somewhere near Springfield, Illinois, before we stopped

for supper, George gave his life to Jesus. It was amazing, as it always is when someone comes to the Father. But it wasn't the most surprising thing that happened on the trip. That came just on the outskirts of Pinckneyville, when Jerry spoke up for the first time.

"You did a good job with that, Bob. Have you ever thought about working with a church? The young people at our church would really respond to a guy like you, I think. We've been working with a network of ministers in the Midwest, including some mentoring from Jack Wyrtzen, and it seems like every week more and more new young adults show up." Jerry never took his eyes off the road.

Silence hung inside the car for a good sixty seconds while George and I both stared at Jerry, our mouths hanging open. Then the questions came pouring out. As it turned out, Jerry was a deacon at his church—something he'd never discussed with his nephew.

"Sometimes family and religion don't mix well," he said. "So I'm always a little hesitant to bring it up. But, Bob, you don't have any qualms at all. I think that might be what God wants from all of us."

"You have to remember I've been sharing the love of Jesus in a war zone, where none of us were assured another day to talk about it," I said. "I just knew Jesus had some things he wanted to say to George here, so I said them for him."

We continued bumping along the rough, neglected streets of Pinckneyville, and then, at last, I was there.

Across the street stood the small, tan house of my wife's parents. For a long moment, I sat there, unmoving. *Home.*

Are they even inside? I wondered. I had had no way of letting them know when I'd arrive. I had sent a telegram two weeks earlier saying I was headed home, but I really had no way of knowing if they'd even received it.

And then it hit me: Jeanette and Alyce were likely just one hundred yards away from where I sat right then. What was I waiting for?

Shoving the car door open, I leaped out, leaned in to grab my satchel, and shook hands over the seat with Jerry and George. That's when I realized I didn't have a single US dollar to my name to offer them for gas.

Embarrassed, I said, "George and Jerry, I'd like to keep in touch with you. May I please get your addresses?"

While George rummaged through the car in search of a pencil and paper, Jerry reached into his wallet and pulled out a business card. "You can reach me at this company. I was serious about that church business. Come see me. But right now, you need to see your family. Why are you still standing here jawing with us? Get going!"

Glancing at the card, I read, *Jerry Richards, Unified Metal Works, Midwest Region Salesman* before stuffing it into my pocket.

CHAPTER 34

HOMECOMING

WHY INDEED? I thought, an unstoppable grin spreading across my weary face. Racing to the rear of the car, I opened the trunk and pulled out my duffel bag. I waved over my shoulder and trotted across the street and up the sidewalk toward the house that held the two people I loved most on earth.

As I bounded up the stairs onto the porch, concern washed over me. *Are they home?* The porch light wasn't on. *Were they already in bed?* As quickly as it came, the concern fled, and I reached for the door knocker and gave it three solid whacks.

For a moment, I heard no movement inside. But then, somewhere in the back of the home, I saw a light switch on, and footsteps approached the door. A man's face peered out from behind the lace curtain. Then he called excitedly to the other inhabitants of the house, and a flurry of footsteps ensued.

The lock thudded open, and he slid the safety chain free. In seconds, the door flew open, and my father-in-law stepped aside to make way for Jeanette. She burst through the open door and into my arms like a running back making the winning touchdown.

Tears of joy streamed down our cheeks as the moment we had been hoping and praying for finally arrived. We were together again. After alternating between crushing hugs and passionate kisses, we held each other at arm's length, absorbing the sight of each other. I wasn't sure how long we stood there or what Jeanette's parents thought, but we finally turned back toward the door, still holding hands. We were half-afraid that the moment was just a dream and we'd suddenly wake up separated if we let go.

Before we even stepped inside, the questions began.

"When did you get back to the States? How did you get here? Are you all right?"

I tried to answer the questions all at once, caught up in the excitement of the moment, but I couldn't keep up with the barrage of inquiries. Observing my growing confusion, Jeanette's mother finally interrupted.

"Dear, Bob must be famished," she said calmly, gently touching Jeanette's elbow. "Why don't we go into the kitchen and make a sandwich and let him take a breath? We don't have to have all our questions answered tonight—he isn't going anywhere. But we can continue talking inside instead of standing here on the porch for all the neighborhood to gawk at. It's almost ten o'clock, after all."

"With all due respect, ma'am," I said, "I could probably eat a horse. But as I recall, somewhere in this home is a daughter of mine whom I've never seen, and I don't think I can wait another minute to see her. It's almost all I've thought of since she was born."

"Well, I suppose there's no chance she has slept through all this racket anyway," she said. "You go have a look, and Harold and I will make the sandwiches."

Squeezing my hand, Jeanette pulled me along the hall toward the steps. "Bob, how could I not have thought to bring her? She's perfect. Wait 'til you see her chubby little cheeks! And I think she has your smile."

We stopped outside a bedroom door upstairs, and Jeanette put her finger over her lips. Then she slowly opened the door. And there was Alyce, wide awake in her crib, looking at us with an irresistible smile on her face.

There are many amazing moments in life, but I'm not sure any of them come close to the feeling a man has when he sees his daughter for the first time. Even though it took me a little longer than most to get to this moment, it was no less precious.

Jeanette crossed the room and picked Alyce up, crooning softly. "Guess what, little one? Your daddy's home."

As she walked toward me with Alyce in her arms, panic hit: *A baby! What do I do with a baby? How do you hold a baby without breaking her?*

My fears melted when we stood there, embracing each

other for the first time as a family. Tears streamed down my face, and I wanted this moment to last forever.

Finally, Jeanette asked, "Would you like to hold her? She should still be a little sleepy, so she won't be too wiggly."

Afraid to trust my voice, I nodded and reached out for her. For the first time, I held my beautiful, fragile daughter, thanking God as I realized that months and months of heartfelt prayers were being answered in this simple, quiet moment.

Not alarmed that an apparent stranger was holding her, Alyce stretched her small hand up to touch my rough, unshaven face. Then she smiled. *My daughter. Alyce.*

After a while, Jeanette took Alyce from me, placed her in the crib again, and motioned me toward the door.

"If she doesn't go back to sleep soon, I fear none of us will get any sleep tonight," she whispered. "And I'm guessing you could use a good night's sleep."

As if those words cast a spell over me, I was suddenly aware of how exhausted I was. "Yes, sleep will be good." I stifled a yawn. "I feel like I have been up for days."

In the kitchen, we found Jeanette's mother and father seated at the table across from a plate of chicken salad sandwiches. "I'm sorry it isn't much," her mother fussed. "If we'd known you were arriving today, we could have had something more ready."

"No problem, ma'am." I smiled and reached for the first sandwich. "This is more than enough, and it's much appreciated. They don't feed you homemade chicken salad in the

Navy. Do you mind if I say a blessing over it? There's so much I have to be thankful for right now, and I just feel the need to let God know."

An hour or so later, as I settled into a non-military-issue bed for the first time in more than a year, with my wife nestled into the crook of my arm, I was still thanking God for all the things I'd longed for and waited for that had come to pass.

I was home.

Paris, France
March 3, 2016

JAZZ JONES

CHAPTER 35

A PERSON OF PEACE

A FEW DAYS LATER, during a team meeting with Bill Campbell, my team leader, he asked me how things were going, and I shared with him the conversations I was having with Ilias.

"You know, Jazz, Ilias could be a 'person of peace' in your neighborhood," Bill said. "Working there in the shop, he must know almost everyone in your building and around the area."

Thinking back to my training, I recalled that a "person of peace" is from a reference in Luke 10. Jesus sent the seventy disciples to look for people who would welcome their message. GEM uses the term to refer to two kinds of people, both of whom are well known within a community. The first is a person who may or may not be a believer but is well connected, such as a bartender or a shop owner—someone almost everyone knows. Cornelius, the soldier in Acts 10 who gathered family and friends to hear the gospel, was an example of this type of "person of peace." The second is someone in the community everyone knows but not for good reasons—the town drunk, the bully, the drug dealer, or the guy people cross the street to avoid. When a person like this receives Christ and is transformed, it can have a radical effect on the community because God's power is revealed in a changed life. The apostle Paul and the demoniac in Mark 5 are examples of this type of person. *Ilias could be one of the first type,* I thought.

"Yes, I see what you mean," I replied. "But what could I do to develop that?"

"Well, what if you and Sven offered to do a Bible study with him?" Bill asked. "He lives in your building, right?"

"Yes!" I was getting excited about the possibility. "He seems to have a lot of friends all over Paris. Just think what could happen if he became a believer!"

"Exactly." Bill nodded. "Let's add that to the prayer list for the team. Be sure to keep us updated on what happens."

"Can I get your advice about my neighbors Jean-Claude and Brigitte, too?" I asked. "We talked briefly after I made them cookies, but I've only seen them in passing since then. Do you have any ideas on what my next steps should be?"

"I almost always assume that I'll need to be the initiator in new relationships like that," Bill said. "People lead busy lives, and most of them don't wake up one day thinking, *If I could only find an American who is just learning French to hang out with!* So even when it's not comfortable, we should take the initiative. Why don't you ask them to have coffee or drinks some evening, either at your place or at a café in the neighborhood? Just get together with them and get to know them. You don't need an agenda." Bill paused and then added, "One of the best things you can do is ask for their help. When you make people feel like the experts at something, it pushes value into them as people. You could ask their advice about Paris or where to buy certain things or what it's like living as a couple in Paris, since you'll be getting married soon."

"Wow, those are all good ideas!" I said. "I think they would go for it."

Walking home from the metro station after the meeting, I had an added spring in my step. I was starting to see more tangibly the ways God could use me here in Paris. I couldn't wait to discuss the idea with Sven when we talked next.

CHAPTER 36

NEIGHBORHOOD MIRACLES

MY CHURCH HOME in France was called Liberté, a gathering started by Bill and his family in their home in an eastern suburb of Paris. One Saturday, several of us from Liberté met at the Campbells' house to prepare to do a "person of peace" search in the neighborhood and town center. We began with prayer, worship, and training, and then we divided into pairs to begin our search.

We'd done things like this as a church before. In an attempt to start a conversation with people, we often asked the "miracle question": If God could do a miracle in your life, what would you want it to be? To the people who responded—and surprisingly, many did—we explained that as a small church and a part of the community, we cared for and loved the people in the neighborhood. Then, if they were interested, we asked how we could pray for them.

We talked to people on the streets, and we also went door to door in neighborhoods and apartment complexes. Some people asked us to leave, but others remained open to continuing the conversation. We tried to meet them where they were, always looking for an opportunity to share our testimonies or give a gospel presentation.

When I first heard this idea, I was pretty skeptical. I didn't think people would open up, and I thought it would be intrusive to ask strangers to pray for them. But over time, I found that many people, even those who didn't believe in God, wanted us to pray for them. Our hope was that these conversations would result in an invitation to their home, where we could continue discussing God and truths from the Bible.

That day we divided into pairs and headed to a nearby apartment building. A lunch and birthday celebration for the youngest Campbell was planned for the next day, so we had the opportunity to invite people to join us for the party. We hoped it would become a neighborhood celebration.

I was paired with Véronique, a woman from our church who exuded joy and was an easy conversationalist. She also had the ability to give biblical responses to people's questions on just about any topic. I still struggled with complex conversations in French, and I felt nervous. I was grateful to have Véronique with me. She did most of the talking, and I prayed during the conversations.

As we knocked on doors in two buildings in our neighborhood, we discovered that not many people were home. It was a beautiful spring afternoon, so we figured most people were out taking advantage of the lovely weather. A few people we met wanted to end the conversation as soon as they heard the words *God* and *prayer*—either because they didn't claim a faith at all or because they were Muslim. In the latter case, we attempted to explain that God loves Muslims, too, but we were often met with a frown and a closed door.

In the first building, we met a sweet couple who wanted us to pray with them. In another flat, a young woman was moved by the "miracle question." She immediately teared up while telling us that she wanted her son to come back. I didn't fully understand what she was saying, but it turned out that she was in a custody battle. She told us she was a Muslim, but she still wanted us to pray with her. Véronique asked me to start the prayer, so I prayed in English first and then in French. Véronique prayed after me. With tears in her eyes, the woman told us how grateful she was for our prayers. Those three people also said they might come to the Campbells' home for the lunch the following day. We might not have found our "person of peace" yet, but we were definitely making inroads.

After a snack break at the Campbells', we went to the nearby park and sports complex. Shortly after we arrived, Véronique stopped three young footballers who were leaving the area. They seemed a little surprised by her enthusiastic greeting, but two of them answered the "miracle question." The first one said he wanted to become a professional footballer, and the other said he'd ask for health. Véronique and I both prayed for them, and I was surprised that they took the time to listen to us and be prayed for. *You never know what God is up to,* I thought.

During our time at the park, we also prayed for two Muslim women who were sitting on the grass with their children. One of them was open to hearing what Véronique shared about Christ, while the other looked at us warily the whole time. We offered the interested women a booklet directed specifically to Muslims, and she took it gladly, despite her friend's warnings. We also talked with a woman who was a Catholic, and we prayed for her and her children.

+ + +

That evening during our debriefing time, I was amazed at the stories the other missionaries and church members shared. I left feeling like God was truly at work in the neighborhood, and I felt proud to finally be an active part of it. Not only was I pleased to be part of a church that was so intentional about reaching out to people, but I also felt fully a part of Greater Europe Mission, knowing I was carrying on the legacy Bob Evans had begun so many years ago.

Soldier Field: YFC Outreach, May 30, 1945

Pinckneyville, Illinois
January 7, 1945

BOB EVANS

CHAPTER 37

NEXT STEPS

THE NEXT FEW DAYS were a blur: playing with Alyce, answering questions about the war and my time in France, making arrangements to visit the local military hospital in St. Louis so I could be assigned a doctor, learning how to change a diaper, and taking long walks with Jeanette. The days were full and wonderful—and almost surreal after waiting for this for so long. In some ways it felt like I was in a dream, and I was afraid that at any moment I would wake up back on my small cot in Draguignan.

At some point, however, I felt a shift take place inside me. Now home began to feel like reality, and I started to wonder if my time in France had been the dream. If it was a dream, it was one that haunted me, and I spent hours thinking about the folks in Draguignan and the guys in the Third Armored.

During one of these times, Jeanette walked into the living

room and saw me sitting in a chair, staring out the window. She asked me a question I wasn't prepared for.

"Now that you're home, have you thought about what's next?" Jeanette was never one to beat around the bush. "My father said their church needs some help with its youth program. It's not a paid position, but if you serve for a while at the church, maybe there will be something for you there in the future. It's a good church, and Dad thinks they have the budget for another pastor."

As soon as Jeanette voiced the question, I realized I hadn't thought at all about what was next. The blank look on my face gave her all the answer she needed. She didn't push me any further; she just stood there, holding Alyce.

As I stared at my young wife and daughter, I realized how complicated that question was. Up until that point in my life, I had always just walked through the next door God had opened. I knew I wanted to be in full-time ministry, probably as a pastor, so Wheaton College and Eastern Baptist Seminary had been logical steps toward ordination. After I met Jeanette, I couldn't imagine life without her, so getting married had been an obvious decision. Then came the war. Joining the cause had also been an obvious decision to me, as it was to most men in those days. My chaplain's training at the College of William & Mary had been required. But now here we were. What was next?

"I haven't really thought about it," I stammered. "I didn't think that the war or my part in it would be over so quickly. I've just been living one day at a time—surviving and waiting to get back here. I think we need to spend some time praying about it before we make any decisions. I can't help feeling like we're standing at a significant crossroads, but I don't think I even understand what the options are." I paused as a realization dawned on me. "For the first time in my life, I don't think I'm meant to be a pastor, at least not a traditional one."

I could tell this declaration alarmed her, but to her credit, she simply agreed that we should pray about it and ask a few other people to pray with us as well. That was one of the things I loved about Jeanette: she was more concerned about following God than about living out her own plans.

+ + +

As we prayed over the next several days, I realized that Jeanette's question had flipped a switch in me. Inside my heart, a page was turning. A chapter was ending, and a new one was beginning.

Our first step was to do some informal research. After church meetings, I asked anyone who would answer what was going on in the Church in the States. I had been gone for only two years, but a lot had happened in that time. It seemed as though the war had sparked a revival in the North American Church. I suppose that having so many young men overseas and in danger reminded us all of our need for God.

There was one consistent thread that ran through the answers: an evangelistic movement was sweeping the continent, and it centered around large youth rallies. In many of the accounts I heard about, the names of two particular men kept coming up: Jack Wyrtzen and Torrey Johnson.

That's when I remembered Jerry and the business card he had given me. I went to our bedroom and started rifling through my things.

"Honey, have you seen a business card for Jerry Richards?" I asked. "I can't seem to find it."

From the baby's room, I heard Jeanette say, "I think I saw it when I was doing laundry. Check your sock drawer. I put a bunch of miscellaneous things you brought home in there."

"I already looked in there. Any other ideas?"

"Just a second." After putting the baby down, she strode into the bedroom and went directly to the dresser. Reaching into the top drawer, where I kept my socks and ties, she plucked out the card and handed it to me with one eyebrow raised.

"Thanks," I said sheepishly. "Must have been under something."

"Hmm," she muttered as she strode out of the bedroom.

I looked at the card. *Jerry Richards, Unified Metal Works, Midwest Region Salesman.* I saw there was a telephone number at the bottom.

Tapping the card, I prayed, "God, is this from you?"

Tucking the card into my shirt pocket, I headed for the front door and called to Jeanette, "I'm going down to the post office to make a call. I'll tell you about it when I get back."

Pulling my coat from the closet, I stepped out into the chilly afternoon, feeling a spark of purpose in my spirit for the first time in weeks. After paying the postal worker a nickel, I picked up the receiver and waited for the operator's assistance in connecting me with Jerry.

"Operator. How can I help you today?" A disembodied voice with a thick Chicago accent came across the line.

"I'd like to be connected to Unified Metal Works in St. Louis, please."

"Certainly, sir. One moment."

After a couple of clicks and buzzes, I heard the phone on the other end ring. I talked to a receptionist and waited for a few long minutes, aware of the people behind me waiting to use the phone, until I finally heard Jerry's voice on the other end.

"Jerry Richards here. I was beginning to think you had forgotten about me, Bob. How are Alyce and Jeanette? Did you have a good homecoming?"

I was surprised that he remembered so much of our conversation, given how little he'd said in the car. "It was wonderful," I said. "I still can't believe I'm home, but I am. You mentioned that your church is working with a network of youth workers and evangelists. I was wondering if you were serious about needing some help."

"I was hoping you'd call. We certainly could use some help. We're planning a big rally here this spring, and we will need some extra hands. Tell you what, I'm kind of busy today, but would you and Jeanette like to come to church this Sunday? Then you can see for yourself. Our service starts at 10:30, and I can pick you up at the station if you can get there by 9:45. After church, I can show you around and you can meet some of our folks. I know my wife would love to meet you and your wife."

Pleased by the unexpected offer, I grinned. *Maybe God really is in this.* "That sounds great," I said. "We'll be there before 9:45. Thanks, Jerry."

"Great. I'll see you then," Jerry said. "I hate to be short, but I need to get back to my meeting. We can talk more on Sunday. Good-bye for now."

With a click, the line went dead, and I stood there stunned, staring at the receiver in my hand. A gentle clearing of the throat behind me reminded me that I was using a public phone. Abashed, I quickly hung up and made for the door.

I shook my head as I thought about all the seeming coincidences that had connected me with Jerry in the first place. More and more, I was beginning to believe there are no coincidences in the Kingdom of God.

CHAPTER 38

THE YOUTH MOVEMENT

THAT SUNDAY MORNING dawned crisp and cold as only a Midwestern January day can. Our breath hung in the air as we stepped onto the front porch at 5 a.m. to make the drive to Mount Vernon, where we would catch the train into St. Louis.

Jeanette's father had agreed to drive us to the train station in his 1935 Ford Fordor sedan. It was a trusty car, but even so, he had to work feverishly to get it started on this frigid morning. Jeanette's mother had offered to watch Alyce, so in addition to spending time with Jerry and the church folks, we were looking forward to some extended one-on-one time together. We were giddy about the adventure and the possibilities of what the day ahead might hold—even the cold temperatures couldn't dampen our spirits.

Jeanette stood huddled on the porch, her smile warm as her father checked the spark plugs and I chipped away at the layer of frost and ice on the car windows.

Finally, with a belch of black exhaust, the trusty Ford turned over and churned to life. Jeanette's father shooed us into the house for one more cup of coffee while the car warmed up a bit. Still, when we climbed into the automobile, I was convinced that *only* the engine had warmed up; the car's interior still felt like a meat locker. But we had no complaints as we bounced along on the way to the train station.

We arrived with thirty minutes to spare before our departure, so we bought two steaming-hot cups of coffee, a copy of the morning paper, and a pastry to split. Then we ventured over to track 11 and found a bench where we could wait, sip, and read.

The headlines of the paper immediately caught our attention: "Factory of Death! Largest Concentration Camp to Date Discovered in Auschwitz, Poland!" We read in horror as the article described the heinous scene discovered by Russian soldiers as they marched into Auschwitz and the Birkenau camp nearby. *God, how could you permit something like this? Have mercy on us.*

+   +   +

Twenty minutes later, with a series of chugs and hisses, the venerable Baldwin 4-6-2 Pacific engine pulling twelve passenger cars slowed to a stop alongside the platform. After hearing the "all clear" bell, we climbed aboard. As we found our seats, we were still shaken, unable to fathom the level of evil described in the newspaper. And to think how close I'd been to the atrocities taking place in Europe just weeks before!

"I saw a lot of horrible things in France," I told Jeanette. "I saw men injured almost beyond recognition. But they were soldiers. This . . . this is something else. It's pure evil." I was unable to contain my revulsion.

She nodded silently, looking out the window.

We rode without speaking until the train slowed and the announcer indicated we were approaching Union Station in St. Louis. With the train's final jolt, Jeanette and I looked into each other's eyes. Even without saying a word, I sensed our unity: we were grieving for the suffering and dead, but for now, God wanted our attention to be focused on him and what he was about to do in our lives.

True to his word, Jerry picked us up at 9:45 in the familiar Buick, and soon we were seated in the third row of Calvary Baptist Church. The crowd of people flocking into the sanctuary was decidedly young—not the "typical" church crowd. Certainly some people wore suits and ties, but we also saw a number of men and women, mostly under the age of thirty, dressed in casual attire. I was struck by the contrast to most of the churches I had been in.

After a simple but unremarkable church service, we walked out to the foyer, where informal introductions were made and a small group of people began to talk about what God was doing in the church.

"I was amazed by the number of young people here, and many seem to be coming by themselves," I said to Jerry.

"Exactly. They began coming after we held a small youth rally in St. Louis last year," Jerry explained. "The response was pretty amazing, and we're one of the churches associated with a network of youth evangelists in the Midwest. A guy named Torrey Johnson, from Indiana, did a Sunday service with us about a year ago."

Impressed by the fruit of what God had been doing through the effort, I asked, "What do you think makes this youth movement so effective?"

"It's nothing special," Jerry said. "The speakers usually just make a compelling plea to receive the gospel, pure and simple. I think this new generation has been affected by the war and the turmoil in our world. They're asking different questions, and they're finding that Jesus is the answer to those questions. I've been going to church most of my life, but I've never seen anything like this. God is on the move."

"How is the church able to disciple so many new believers at once?" I asked.

"Well, that's the crux of the dilemma," Jerry said. "We can't. Or perhaps we don't. Many folks think it's enough just to have them come to church, but I think they forget that we grew up in this. Many of these new believers have never been to church before. The youth pastor and a couple of guys like me are trying to fill in the gap, but I have a full-time job and can only meet with one or two guys a week. That's why we need some guys like you. I saw how you handled George in the car, and I think that's exactly what we need—a man who will call it like he sees it and help get these young folks on the right path and into God's Word." He grinned at me. "But I'm getting ahead of myself. We've scheduled a major rally in

Kansas City, and Jack Wyrtzen and some of his friends are going to speak there. We're still trying to find a venue, but we're thinking of holding it at the State Fairgrounds."

"How can we help?" I sensed the Spirit of God confirming that this was part of the path ahead for Jeanette and me. "We're eager to get involved in something bigger than just going to church. I had some amazing ministry opportunities in Europe, both with soldiers and with Europeans, and I really miss the joy of discipling new believers. It's satisfying to help folks who don't know God begin to make changes in their lives and pursue him fully."

"A couple of us are meeting on Tuesday and Thursday evenings to plan for an event in Kansas City. We'll probably talk about the possibility of some smaller regional events leading up to it. I know it's four hours away, but if you could make at least one meeting a week, we could really use your help." He paused for a moment, as if deciding whether to say something or not. "I know we just met, but my wife and I would like to offer our basement to you and Jeanette. I have no idea what your work situation is, but we could really use a sharp young couple here to help us pull this off." I opened my mouth to respond, but he put a hand on my shoulder. "Don't answer right now. Let's just enjoy a nice lunch together to get to know each other. I'm in sales, and I rarely see any reason not to just come out and make the offer. But pray about everything you see today, and then you can give us an answer in a week or so. There's no rush—the event isn't scheduled to happen for another month and a half.

I have to see to a few things here at the church, so I am going to leave you for a bit. In the meantime, get to know some of the folks from the church, and I'll be back shortly."

That morning we met many people on the church's leadership team, including the pastor and a number of elders and deacons, all of whom were excited about the recent influx of young people.

An hour later, after most people had gone home, Jerry reappeared with his wife on his arm. "Bob and Jeanette, this is my wife, Patty. Patty, this is the young couple who is coming over for lunch today."

Shortly after the introductions were complete, Patty and Jeanette fell into conversation as we made our way to their home twelve blocks away. Their two-story house was pleasant and well cared for, even if the blue paint was faded and in need of a refresh. Any extra income people had these days went to support the war effort in one form or another. Plus, many of the supplies needed to complete home improvements were rationed, and everyone worked together to make sure the military had what was needed to succeed.

We spent a leisurely afternoon with the Richardses, enjoying homemade stew with fresh biscuits and bread pudding for dessert. Throughout the afternoon, we got to know Jerry and Patty, hearing how they came to faith and how they met. Jerry had grown up on a dairy farm in southeast Iowa near the town of Farmington, while Patty had grown up in St. Louis, the daughter of a well-known engineering professor.

Jerry had always loved mechanics, and growing up on

the farm had given him ample opportunity to learn how to fix things. All through high school he saved up his money to go to college. The costs for commuter students at Bradley University were still high at $50 a semester, but by the time he graduated from high school, he'd saved up enough for the first three years' tuition. He enrolled in the engineering program, where one of his first-year professors was Bob Owen.

Dr. Owen admired Jerry's drive to succeed and took an interest in him. When he invited Jerry over to the house for Sunday dinner, though, he likely didn't expect to one day become his father-in-law. For Jerry's part, he knew from that first dinner that he was in love with the lovely and intelligent Patty Owen. Jerry proposed to Patty during his senior year, and they married shortly after graduation. Jerry went on to become an engineer, but he and Patty had an even more driving passion: to serve the Lord.

The most memorable moment of our afternoon came when Jerry made this statement: "God is on the move, Bob. Did you know that what you saw this morning with all those young people at church is happening all over the country? Torrey Johnson is seeing in his church what you saw today— young people who are desperate for God. It's been a year since Jack Wyrtzen's big event at Madison Square Garden, where twenty thousand students packed the house. Now events like that are popping up all over."

Twenty thousand? Amazing, I thought. *It would be incredible to be part of a movement of God like that.*

Jerry and Patty were lovely hosts, and over numerous cups

of coffee and a second helping of bread pudding, they asked about my life as a child in Africa, Jeanette's work as a nurse, our time apart during the war, and a seemingly endless list of other topics. I was disappointed when I looked at my watch and realized that if we were going to make the evening train, we would need to leave soon.

All in all, it was one of the most pleasant afternoons Jeanette and I had spent together since my return, and I felt content as we found our seats on the 6:10 train back to Mount Vernon.

That's probably why I was so startled when, out of the blue, Jeanette asked, "Have you given any more thought to the opportunity to volunteer at my family's church? It could be a great start for us, and we could continue to live at home and save some money to buy or rent a place of our own. I bet our church would be interested in young people, too, if you asked them."

Truth be told, I hadn't given her earlier suggestion much thought. I stared out the window as I considered how to gently address the subject. Her folks' church was a nice church, full of nice people. The choir always sounded nice, and the sermons were nice, biblically based admonitions to live a better life. And yet it felt like the church was asleep, just going through the motions every Sunday and Wednesday because that's what they were supposed to do.

I couldn't think of a time there when I'd heard anyone talk about evangelism, missions, or discipleship. Thinking back to my time in France, I realized that in many ways my friends there were the reason I was so hesitant about this church. It wasn't the kind of place I would have wanted to take them. It wasn't the kind of place where they would have been able to find real spiritual life or been challenged to offer life to others.

Steeling myself for what I anticipated was going to be a difficult conversation, I asked, "Why do you think that would be a better choice than working with the church in St. Louis?"

CHAPTER 39

A DIFFERENT KIND OF SACRIFICE

"I'VE GROWN UP in this church, and I know the people," Jeanette said. "They're all good families. I'm not sure if you noticed, but some of the people in the church this morning looked a little rough."

Rough is relative, I thought, recalling the men of the Third Armored.

"Mom and Dad really want us to stay in Pinckneyville. They love Alyce, and my parents are all she's ever known," Jeanette continued. "I think it would be hard on her to live someplace else, even as close as St. Louis. Pinckneyville is a safe place to raise our daughter."

I hadn't really thought about that, I admitted to myself. *There are more things to consider today than just sharing the gospel and doing what I want.*

"Dad thinks their church will bring you on staff in just a few months if you get along with the other leaders, and he says the church pays their pastors a pretty good salary. Plus, with my job at the clinic, Alyce and I are covered by medical insurance. That's pretty good, given how unstable so much of the world is right now. Besides, I really don't want to leave Mom and Dad. They've made a nice home for us."

A tinge of frustration entered my thoughts as I recalled our wedding vows: "for better, for worse" and "leaving our mothers and fathers." *And yet,* I reminded myself, *I did leave her for two years to traipse around the world with Uncle Sam while she stayed home and had a child by herself.*

"Jeanette," I began carefully, "I'm not entirely sure what to do. A lot of things changed for me while I was in Africa and France. Not just the injury but my perspective on what effective ministry is. God used me almost every day with a whole host of people. The one common denominator among all of them is that I'm pretty sure they wouldn't be comfortable in your folks' church. The people I ministered to in the last two years look more like the people we saw this morning in St. Louis—young, disillusioned, and hungry for answers. And they were coming to Jesus. I don't think I could work at a place without people like that. Frankly, I really don't think the church in Pinckneyville even needs me—everyone there seems perfectly satisfied with life. What would I do?"

With frustration edging into her voice, Jeanette said, "It feels like you're saying there's something wrong with my parents' church. That's the church I grew up in; that's the church we got married in, and apparently I'm good enough for you. What's wrong with the rest of them?"

"I'm not saying there's anything wrong with them," I replied, perhaps a bit defensively. "My guess is that they're like most every other church in the country. *That's* what I think is the problem, and I don't want to be a part of it. Where are the new believers? I'm not talking about seven-year-olds accepting Christ in Sunday school, though that's good. Where are the adults who are being discipled and are on fire to get to know Jesus? Doesn't it ever feel to you like the people there are walking through life asleep?"

Sighing, Jeanette said, "I know what you're saying. I see it. And I guess I *am* it too." The fight was gone from her. "It's just that things have been so crazy and so unsettled. I think I just want some stability for us as a family, and the church has been good to us."

"I know," I conceded. "I want that too. I'm just not sure how to find it or, better yet, how to help create it. This is the first time in my life when the next step isn't obvious. Then there's this amazing life with Christ I experienced while I was in France—sharing Christ and discipling real people. I think I needed to see the church in St. Louis this morning, to know that what I experienced in Europe can happen here, too. I realize you weren't in France with me to experience what I did, so I'm being drawn to something you may not understand. That's not fair, but I need you to trust me."

"Bob, you know I love you, and I will follow you anywhere," Jeanette said, gripping my hand. "I realized this morning that I can't even remember the last time I thought about sharing the gospel—probably not since before Alyce was born. I want to be used by God too. I want to experience some of the things you wrote about in all those letters. You're right; I haven't seen anything like that here. But if we really do this—if we move to be part of what's happening in St. Louis—*you* are going to have to tell my parents." She gave me a gentle elbow to the side, and I was grateful to see a twinkle in her eye.

After a moment, she asked, "Do you think we'll ever get to go to France together? I would love to see that little town where the hospital is. It sounds beautiful. I want to share that part of your life with you."

Is that it, God? I wondered. *Am I searching for something that can only be found there? Or am I different when I'm there?*

"I don't know," I said. "I would like to go there with you, and everyone in town is dying to meet you and Alyce. Maybe when the war is over. In the meantime, we have a week before we need to answer the church in St. Louis, so let's each commit to praying about it separately, and then let's talk about it on Wednesday. That's three days from now. Let's find out what God wants."

+ + +

As it turned out, God wanted something else entirely. Tuesday came, and with it a shock we didn't expect.

When the postman pushed the bundle of letters through the slot in the front door, an official-looking letter from the US Navy landed on top of the pile. Opening it, I found orders to report for duty the following Monday as chaplain to the Chicago naval station.

I left for Chicago the next day to find a place to live. Jeanette and Alyce would join me later in the month as I completed my commitment to Uncle Sam.

SOLDIER FIELD

ON MY WAY TO CHICAGO, I traveled through St. Louis to break the news to Jerry Richards in person. When he heard, he was both gracious and persistent.

"Bob, I understand completely," he said, a tinge of disappointment in his voice. "You have to fulfill your commitment to your country." Then he continued in his normal, upbeat tone. "But the Chicago naval station isn't that far by train or car, so maybe you and Jeanette can come and lend a hand on weekends when we do rallies. You know we desperately need people like you."

I took his words to heart, and when we helped out at one of the church's weekend youth rallies, I met Torrey Johnson, who had recently founded Youth for Christ.

"Bob Evans!" Torrey bellowed as he shook my hand. "That's a name I keep hearing. I'm really happy to meet you."

"I'm honored to meet you as well." I returned his hearty

handshake. "I've been following all that's going on with the youth these days. It's amazing what God is doing."

We talked for a long time about youth rallies, evangelism, and our spiritual journeys. There's something about telling another person how you experience God that bonds you together, and when we parted that day, I felt like I'd found a new best friend. Torrey had that effect on people, and I could see why he made such an impact with the younger generation.

+ + +

A week later, I was shocked to receive a letter from Torrey Johnson asking if I would share my story later that spring at an event at Soldier Field in Chicago. I read the letter and, without a word, handed it across the kitchen table to Jeanette. After she read it, she looked at me with eyes as big as saucers. Then she read the letter again.

"Bob, this is unbelievable!" she squealed. "Do you know that I went to Soldier Field once when I was at Wheaton to see the Green Bay Packers play the Bears? It's immense! How could Youth for Christ possibly fill that place? Do you have any idea how significant this could be?"

"Who won the game?" I asked.

"Uh, the Packers won. But that's not the point!" She shot me a confused look. "This is one of the largest stadiums in the Midwest, and they are asking *you* to share your testimony there. Do you understand? Your life story could impact thousands!"

Truth be told, I wasn't thrilled about standing in front of thousands, but I didn't want to dampen Jeanette's moment. I was much more comfortable with one or two—maybe ten—folks. However, as I prayed about it, I realized that what really concerned me was the unpredictability of my symptoms from my injury in France. I periodically experienced headaches, memory loss, and confusion. What if the symptoms crept up as I was standing in front of thousands of people? Still, I kept my fears to myself.

Jesus, I know you wouldn't set me up to make a fool of myself and of you. I'm trusting that you are in this, and I will follow you.

I accepted the invitation and began to prepare. I soon learned that Torrey Johnson had taken out a second mortgage on his home to raise the down payment for renting the stadium. I admired that type of commitment.

Three weeks after V-E Day, I was standing in the visitors' entrance to the field where last year's national champion Green Bay Packers had lined up to storm the field behind Coach Curly Lambeau. *Great things have come from here before,* I prayed. *Please, Lord, do something great through me today!*

As I prayed in the visitors' tunnel, one of the main attractions of the event took the field to thunderous applause. The "Flying Parson," Gil Dodds, was trying to break his own world-record time for running the mile. First, though, he gave a short testimony of what it means to live out Hebrews 12:1: "Let us lay aside every weight, and the sin which so easily ensnares us, and let us run with endurance the race that is set before us."

Dodd was famous for warming up in one pair of running shoes and then changing them before the race. When asked why he did that, he explained that the extra weight of sweat in the shoes from the warm-up could mean the difference between winning and losing the race. Dodd missed setting a new record that night, but it didn't matter to the jubilant crowd.

Well, thankfully I don't have to go on after someone really popular, I thought wryly as I began what felt like a ten-mile walk to the stage.

It was a surreal feeling to step behind the Sontronics Halo microphone that I'd heard referenced so many times on the radio and then hear my own voice echo into the massive stadium. For a second I envisioned Moses standing before Pharaoh's court when he told Pharaoh to let his people go. I tried not to be distracted, but I'm sure I fumbled my words a few times as I told seventy thousand people the story of how God used my time in Europe. I concluded with these words: "The enemy of our souls plotted death and destruction for Europe through the maniacal greed of war, but Jesus secretly plotted hope. And as with my story, he planted those seeds of hope throughout the continent to blossom into a new generation of Christ followers who will rise up and change the face of Europe forever."

Photographers from the *Chicago Tribune* snapped pictures of each moment, and I even had a bit of fun posing with Gil

Dodds as though we were about to start a race. But nothing compared to the awe I felt as I stood in the press box, watching as hundreds of people responded to Percy Crawford's simple message of salvation.

Later that evening, I stood in the massive parking lot as bus after bus pulled out, thinking of all those who had come forward. *Who will disciple all these people?* I thought. *Where will they go to learn how to live like Jesus?*

After that day, I put in my time with the Navy, but my heart and soul were with Youth for Christ. I helped plan rallies and events with a singular goal: to help young people encounter Jesus Christ.

CHAPTER 41

YOUTH FOR CHRIST

TORREY JOHNSON AND I saw each other occasionally throughout the remainder of the year and soon realized we were kindred spirits. After I was discharged from the Navy in January 1946, one of the first phone calls I received was from Dr. Johnson. He wanted to offer me a job.

The YFC headquarters had been established only recently, in September of the previous year. They were located in Winona Lake, Indiana, just west of Fort Wayne, but the plan was to relocate to Chicago. I eagerly accepted the position, and Jeanette, Alyce, and I made the temporary move to yet another part of the Midwest.

I was eager to jump into ministry again. With the war now officially over, the country was trying to get back on its feet. Many of the soldiers returning from the war were filled with questions and longings that the world, still reeling from the war's devastation, could not answer.

Yet as fruitful and fulfilling as my ministry with YFC was,

I felt that a part of me was still in Europe. Whenever a story about Europe appeared in the newspaper, I read it eagerly, like a letter from home. Jeanette saw the struggle within me and began to pray that God would open a door for us to minister together in Europe.

In March, I received a phone call from Jerry Richards. "Have you seen a copy of today's *New York Times?*" he asked. "The front-page photo features Billy Graham and four others praying before boarding the first commercial flight from Chicago to London. That should be you, Evans! *You* are the Europe expert!"

"Um, I'm hardly an expert," I corrected. "Remember, it took me just a few days to get wounded and a few months to get kicked out. Visiting a couple of countries in Europe hardly makes me an expert."

"I know, I know," he conceded. "But you know a lot more than you give yourself credit for. That's why I sent a letter to Torrey Johnson. He needs you in Europe!"

Still uncomfortable, I replied, "While I really appreciate your confidence, I'm not sure I can be of much help. I was just a chaplain in the military who happened to spend some time in France."

"Nonsense, Bob," Jerry said. "Since I've known you, Europe has been on your heart. This morning I read the story of the lame man by the pool in John 5. Do you remember what Jesus asked him? 'Do you want to be made well?' When I read it, God brought you to mind, and that's why I called. Do you want to go to Europe?"

Taken aback by his question, I stammered. "I . . . I am not really sure. I think about France all the time, but I haven't seriously considered going back for more than a vacation to introduce Jeanette to the people I met. More longing than intent, if you get my meaning."

"Where do you think those longings come from?" Jerry asked. "I believe God speaks to us through the desires of our hearts and draws us toward his will through our longings. There's a reason you have such a deep love and passion for Europe."

"I suppose you're right," I admitted. "And truth be told, as amazing as it was to speak at Soldier Field, my best times of ministry were in that little café in Draguignan. Tell you what, will you agree to pray with me about this over the next couple of weeks? I need to hear God clearly on this."

"You got it, pal," Jerry said. "I'll give you a call."

As Jeanette, Jerry, and I prayed, all the unique moments in France came back to me: God's voice in the mornings as I studied his Word from the bench overlooking the sea, those moments walking home along deserted streets after meetings with folks in the town, and the passage in Scripture that talked about the priest from a foreign land. All of it seemed real and relevant. *Have you been planning this all along?*

+ + +

The first answer to our prayers came after Torrey Johnson and Billy Graham returned from their well-publicized trip to Europe. Torrey pulled me into his office and promoted me to international director of Youth for Christ with this admonition: "There's a lot of work to do in Europe, and I think we mentioned your name every day while we were there. We need you to help us get traction for the Kingdom there while this door of opportunity is still open."

For the first time since I returned home, I began to think practically about how we could engage Europe with the gospel. My dreams were tentatively beginning to form into reality.

CHAPTER 42

ACROSS THE OCEAN AGAIN

A DEFINITIVE ANSWER to our prayers came in the spring of 1947, when the owner of the Andes candy company in Chicago called and asked me to meet with him. The owner was a well-known Greek-American Christian who had a passion to see his countrymen come to Christ.

Tensions had bubbled in postwar Greece after the German and Italian occupation, and in March 1946, the struggle escalated to a full-scale civil war. Now, a year later, skirmishes between the Western-backed Greek government and the Yugoslavian-backed Communist party had increased. International news stories highlighted the need for humanitarian aid for the rural families caught in the cross fire.

The owner of the candy company, whose extended family still lived in Greece, was desperate to help the land of his heritage and offered to finance a survey trip for two other men and me. We hoped to see what doors God was opening and lay the groundwork for evangelistic teams from YFC to go to Europe when college let out that summer. Finally, I had my chance to establish a beachhead for YFC in Europe. There was only one disappointment in this plan: once again, I would have to leave Jeanette and Alyce at home.

This trip would be my first real transatlantic flight, as "Mr. Andes" had bought us three round-trip tickets to London aboard American Airlines. Instead of spending seven days aboard a ship, we would leave from Chicago and arrive in London the same day. From London, we'd take a ferry across the channel to France and board a train for Athens.

The plans were finalized quickly, and I departed on a rainy day in late April. My job was to go a week ahead of the other two men, find a place to stay, and try to make contact with churches that might be willing to house a team of evangelists.

Jeanette and Alyce dropped me off at the stop in downtown Wheaton. As I kissed Jeanette good-bye and boarded the sleek, silver bus, I had no way of knowing that in just a few days, I would find myself back in an escalating war zone.

+ + +

When I arrived in Greece, I was disappointed to find that the state of affairs there had deteriorated significantly and that ministry was nearly impossible. People stayed in their homes and hunkered down, trying to avoid being killed. Travel outside of Athens was out of the question, and even within the city, anything that could be construed as "encouraging people to assemble" was illegal.

I was able to speak at a couple of Protestant churches within Athens, and a number of people accepted Christ, but due to the extreme conditions, it was dangerous to follow up with people. This became even more evident when my host woke me up in the middle of the night and took me by backstreets to the harbor and helped me board a boat out of Athens.

I was devastated to have to telegraph back to the United States that it wasn't advisable to send any evangelistic teams at the moment. I encouraged my colleagues to change their tickets and meet me in Poland instead.

Poland was recovering after the war, too, but gratefully, we found open doors there. We connected with the Evangelical Christian Union, and day after day I preached with my colleagues—Peter Deyneka, Helen Zirnov, and Martha Moennich—in youth meetings that lasted six or seven hours. At the end of every meeting, young men and women crowded the stage to receive Christ.

We used interpreters during our messages, but when young people came forward, we simply knelt down and prayed with them, our spirits connected by something deeper than language. It was the purest thing in the world to pray to God without any thought of how those around me responded to my words.

I was struck by the intensity of emotion these young people showed as they repented of their sin and committed themselves to living for God. Most of them had little memory of life without war, and they wanted to be part of rebuilding a new, hopeful Europe. Their brokenness and grief over the millions who had died in the war without knowing Christ, and their countrymen who still didn't know him, bolstered their fervor to be part of a movement for God in Europe. *What I would give for all the good people back in American churches to experience this kind of fresh, raw passion!* I thought.

+ + +

On one memorable day, twenty-five young men came forward together and committed themselves to spending the next year traveling and preaching the gospel to youth throughout Poland. They had no plan other than to believe God's promise that he would provide. The audience was so moved that everyone gathered around them, prayed for them, and took a spontaneous offering. I stood there with tears streaming down my face as people who had next to nothing emptied their wallets into hats and bags to send out these new missionaries.

But along with the incredible spiritual response in Poland, I also witnessed devastating poverty and physical need. It was difficult at times to stay focused on sharing the Good News and preaching when I wanted to buy everyone in the audience a good meal. I made a mental note: *We must respond to this need not just with words but with deeds. As soon as I get back, the first thing I'm going to do is convince Youth for Christ to send crisis-response teams, with funding in hand, to ease the suffering of the people. No one is concerned about what happens in eternity when they don't know where their next meal is coming from.*

After Poland, we went to the refugee camps in Germany, which still held thousands of stranded Eastern Europeans. I was grateful God sent me to Poland first so that when I entered the refugee camps, I was better accustomed to being around people in great need. The response to the gospel was unprecedented in the camps, and people came to Christ by the tens and hundreds every day.

Next up were the United Kingdom, Holland, and Germany. We made contacts there among churches that were eager to organize youth rallies like the ones Billy Graham and Torrey Johnson were making famous.

After weeks of exploring, I was more convinced than ever that Europe was ripe for evangelistic teams, youth rallies, and long-term missionaries. My experience in Draguignan hadn't been unique: almost everywhere I went in Europe, I saw similar situations and similar opportunities. My mind spun with possibilities.

+ + +

Upon returning to the States, I made my report to Torrey Johnson and my colleagues at YFC. Excitement pulsed through the organization. By this time, Billy Graham had officially joined the YFC staff, and the organization was almost overwhelmed with the opportunities set before it. I had gotten to know Billy before the war, when he was a student at Wheaton and I was a pastor in nearby Dixon, Illinois. Europe had left a mark on Billy like it had on me. He insisted that YFC make reaching Europe one of its highest priorities.

Europe was in great spiritual need, and it was time to get serious about devising a strategic response. We made some phone calls to gather Christian leaders and evangelists from around the world to meet in Europe to discuss a big-picture plan.

We believed the continent was ready for the hope of the Good News.

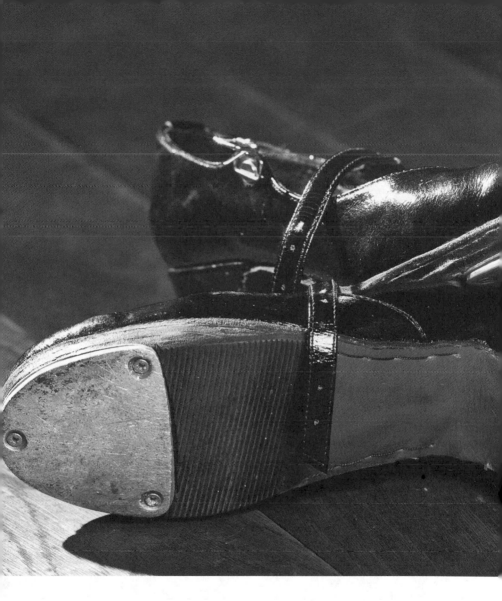

Paris, France
March 7, 2016

JAZZ JONES

CHAPTER 43

LEARNING A NEW DANCE

AFTER FINISHING LANGUAGE SCHOOL, my goal was to find a place to meet local women and interact with them on a weekly basis. The problem was that in a city the size of Paris, the possibilities were almost endless. I wanted to try something I'd never done before—something fun that would allow me to learn with other beginners.

I considered my options. Maybe theater, archery, art, or knitting? Then one day, as I watched a musical with Ginger Rogers and Fred Astaire, it hit me. Tap dancing! That was it! This was something I'd always wanted to learn, and I was excited about the prospect of taking a class with other local beginners. I searched online for *un cours de claquettes*, a tap-dance class.

In France, all clubs and associations start at *la rentrée*, the time at the beginning of September when everyone returns to school and work after their summer holidays. I found a website for tap classes with a retro-classic musical theme. I e-mailed the teacher to see if it was possible for me to join the class even though it was March and the class would soon be over for the year. She said I could come for a free trial to check it out, and if I was interested, I could sign up for the fall. I must not have performed too badly that first day, because at the end of class, she said I could continue with the group until the class ended in June. My plan was off to a good start!

I ordered my first pair of tap shoes and had them ready for class the following week. In the beginning, there wasn't much conversation between the other ladies and the two young couples in my class. When we arrived each week, we all went to the dressing room, where we exchanged our street shoes for tap shoes and took our places until class started. My classmates arrived at different times, and everyone left as soon as the class was over, so my hopes of connecting with people seemed limited.

Then one day, I took my place in the back row next to a girl who was having difficulty catching on to the choreography. In the dressing room after class, I complimented her on her sparkly gold shoes. (Mine were basic black.) Hearing my non-French accent, she asked where I was from.

"Je suis américaine. Je viens d'Hawaï," I said.

I decided that the next week I'd suggest meeting up with her during the class's spring break. I thought we could practice the dance together, and maybe it would even lead to a friendship outside of class. Unfortunately, she wasn't in the last two classes before the holiday or the ones after. I was disappointed, but I was learning that God opens and closes doors in ways we can't always predict. The key is to always look for opportunities and take them when they come up.

+ + +

With my background in dance, I was able to catch on to the choreography pretty quickly. Sometimes, while waiting for class to start, the other women asked me for help with some of the steps. Our class was preparing for the *spectacle*, or recital, in June. At this recital, each of our teacher's tap classes performed a dance they'd been working on throughout the year. Regrettably, I wasn't going to be able to participate since I'd already booked a train ticket for Germany to spend a week there working with Sven on wedding preparations.

When I told the teacher and the rest of the class that I wasn't going to be at the *spectacle*, they expressed their sadness. But when they heard the reason, they were elated, and I received many kind *félicitations*. Everyone the world over likes the joy and excitement of a wedding, and they all agreed it was more important than the recital.

Something clicked in that moment, and suddenly the ladies wanted to know why I was living in Paris. What kind of work did I do? What did Sven do in Germany? The questions and answers flowed, and I began to feel a deeper connection with the women there. And now we always had a topic to discuss: how the wedding preparations were coming. With that, I began to feel more at ease talking with everyone at the class, and I came to this happy realization: I was becoming one of them.

My initial plan as I got to know my classmates was to invite them all out for coffee or drinks after class. That's what I would have done in the States, but it clearly wasn't the right tactic here. It would be too much for me to go from casual chitchat before class to such a big offer. I was finding that living in a new culture and trying to read the signs and understand what's acceptable and what's not can be a little intimidating. Thankfully, Bill, my team leader, always had helpful suggestions. In this situation, he recommended that I ask people intentional questions every week to get to know them. So far, this plan seemed to be working well.

As it turned out, all of us did go out for drinks after the last class—and I wasn't the one who suggested it. At the café, I mostly listened to the conversations and asked a few questions. At one point, the conversation turned to me, with more questions about what Sven and I did for work. I was able to paint a picture of some of the ways we were helping people in the communities where we lived. The atmosphere felt relaxed, and, in the moment, I realized how much I enjoyed my classmates and the relationships we were forming. At the end of the evening, one of the women collected our e-mail addresses and sent them out so we could keep in touch, as many of my classmates intended to continue on with the class in the fall.

As I walked home that night, I praised God for how he

was working in this situation and blessing my simple plans. Without my having to force it, I now had more friends to add to my list of people to pray for. I was excited to continue these relationships in the fall, and I began to pray that I would find one "person of peace" in the group who would be open to meeting regularly to study the Bible.

Then a big dream began to form in my mind: *Wouldn't it be amazing if that led to a larger group of women I could gather for a Bible study?*

CHAPTER 44

ADDING CHAPTERS TO THE STORY

MY DAYS WERE QUICKLY FILLING UP as I made connections with people and built on those relationships. The seeds of friendship I'd been planting were turning into a garden of Kingdom possibilities.

One day Margot invited me to attend her and her significant other's chorale concert. I continued to be amazed by her love for life and the variety of activities she was involved in as a seventy-three-year-old. I was honored to receive the invitation, especially since it was the first thing we'd done together outside of our periodic language meetings.

In talking with Bill about this relationship, he offered practical suggestions on how I could incorporate ministry into my meetings with her just by asking for her help as a French speaker. My first attempt was to bring along a print-out of Jesus' first miracle in John 2, in which Jesus turns water into wine. I had her read it aloud to me once so I could listen to her pronunciation, and then I read it back to her. I prayed that God would penetrate her heart as she read it, knowing the power of God's Word. After we had read it a few times, Margot remarked that this was a well-known story.

Interesting, I thought. *How is it that an atheist is familiar with Scripture? Maybe she sees benefits in knowing some of the sacred texts, or maybe she remembers the story from somewhere in her childhood.*

These were small beginnings, but each time I was with Margot, I hoped she would learn a little bit more about Jesus. As long as she was open, I would continue to bring her snippets of the Good News.

And one day, if she was willing, I hoped to ask her to help me prepare for a *Découverte la Bible* (DLB) study. This is the French version of an evangelistic technique called Discovery Bible Study, a program developed to introduce nonbelievers to the core of the gospel. The concept is simple: participants read a passage of the Bible and then discuss a series of questions. I hoped that Margot would help me practice leading the study in French, and perhaps I'd even get to hear some of her answers, along with her thoughts on how other French people might respond.

And then there were my neighbors, Jean-Claude and Brigitte. I stopped by to see them a couple of times but never received an answer. I eventually left a note on their door with my cell number, inviting them out for a drink. The next day, I noticed the note was gone, but it was two weeks before I received a response.

Finally, they left a note on my door explaining that they had left on holiday the day after they received my note. They were pleased with the invitation and suggested a time and date to meet. Brigitte included her cell number on the note, so I texted her to confirm the date and time. In the end, we had drinks and snacks at their place, and that was when I found out she was due to have a baby in September. I was excited to hear the news, especially since the beauty and magic of a newborn often changes people's views on God. *Lord,* I prayed silently, *let that be the case for them.*

Brigitte told me she'd likely stay home with the new baby, as the laws in France allow for an extended maternity leave. *That could also provide opportunities for the two of us to get together,* I thought. *Perhaps I can even offer to babysit for them from time to time!*

We had a lovely time chatting. They were patient with my French, particularly when I didn't understand something and asked them to repeat it or explain it. Our conversation felt natural and laid-back. They told me how they met and a bit about their background.

I asked them for fun ideas for Sven and me to do in Paris, and they animatedly discussed the options while Brigitte wrote them down for me. Jean-Claude suggested that the four of us do something together when Sven came to visit in July. Again, God was one step ahead of me! I was pleasantly surprised that they brought up something I had intended to suggest myself.

At one point, the conversation turned to my work and my

desire to create community and do Bible studies with people. Jean-Claude mentioned with a shrug that they didn't believe in anything, but they didn't seem opposed to my ministry at all. That seemed to be a difference between Europe and the United States: people in Europe who claim to be atheists are rarely antagonistic about the beliefs of others. There seems to be an openness to letting people believe whatever they like.

I was starting to feel like I had community here. And now, with another neighbor on the way, I had another entry for my prayer list.

Arriving in Interlaken, Switzerland

Wheaton, Illinois
May 3, 1948

BOB EVANS

CHAPTER 45

GOD IS ON THE MOVE

JACK WYRTZEN HAD BEEN A GUEST SPEAKER at the Beatenberg Bible Institute, a small Christian college in the Swiss Alps, and he suggested it as a possible location for our planning conference. After some thought and prayer, the YFC team agreed that Switzerland would be ideal for a gathering of evangelists from around the world. Switzerland's staunch position of neutrality throughout World War II had left it largely untouched, along with being accessible for believers from all areas of Europe—former Allied and Axis countries alike.

After getting the green light from Torrey and Billy, I mailed letters to all the contacts I'd met on my recent trip to Europe and asked them to spread the word, if they could. We would meet high above Interlaken in the tiny mountain town of Beatenberg to discuss how the world evangelical movement could have a united response to the vacuum of hope in Europe.

Those were heady days. The sense of God being on the move in an unprecedented way permeated our meetings. We felt strongly that the need of the hour was a unified strategy on how we, the church, could effectively engage with what God was doing. We prayed like I'd never prayed before, holding overnight vigils to pray for people to come to Christ and for various youth rallies and events.

Perhaps because of the miracles we saw daily, none of us batted an eye when Billy Graham announced the audacious theme for the Beatenberg conference. "The Evangelization of the World in Our Generation" seemed not only possible but probable. Yet as the conference began to take shape, something else was brewing as well: a debate between members of the group on which of their two deeply held beliefs should hold priority in reaching Europe—evangelism or discipleship.

Another question that arose was who the keynote speaker should be. Though the conference was organized and sponsored by Youth for Christ, we made a concerted effort to promote it as a multi-organization event, not a YFC event. With Billy Graham, Bob Cook, Torrey Johnson, and Jack Wyrtzen planning to attend, we already had some of the world's leading evangelists. Therefore, I suggested we invite Dawson Trotman, the founder of The Navigators, to challenge the delegates. We were thrilled when Daws agreed to take the lead spiritual role in what would become a watershed moment in the global evangelistic movement.

+   +   +

The months of preparation sped by, and before I knew it, it was time to board a plane for Switzerland. By this time,

Jeanette, Alyce, and I lived in Wheaton, Illinois, where the new headquarters of YFC was located.

Alyce was four years old and a bundle of energy who challenged both of us. Curious about everything, she asked more questions every day than I could put a number to. This was just one of the reasons Jeanette wasn't excited to see me leave home for the month-long trip.

"Look, Bob," Jeanette began. "I understand why I can't go. I really do. But it doesn't mean I have to like it. For years you've been telling me how much you want me to see what you experienced in Europe, and yet every time there's an opportunity for me to do that, there's some reason why I have to stay home."

"I know, I know." I put another shirt into my suitcase. "I just can't justify taking the whole family, given that I'll be so busy the whole time. And you know money is tight."

"As I said, I know all of it." Jeanette passed me a pile of extra socks and underwear. "I just wonder if there will ever be a time when it's 'justified' to take me along to this place that occupies so much of your heart. But let's forget it for now. I don't want to spend our last hour together arguing. I know you would take us if you could. I think I'm just worried about you being gone, and I'm going to miss you. You're hearing a whole mix of emotions from me right now." She let out a sigh. "Sometimes I can't believe I'm married to someone who is organizing worldwide conferences. Remember when you were going to be a simple pastor and I was going to be a simple nurse?" She slipped between me and the suitcase.

"I just want to make sure you don't forget about us when you're gone doing amazing things. Remember that we are amazing too."

"All right, all right," I said, pulling her close. "I promise I won't go to Europe again without taking you along, and I promise I'll be careful and come home quickly."

After I finished packing my bag, the cab driver arrived to take me to the airport, where I'd join the rest of the Youth for Christ delegation.

Hugging Alyce tightly, I said, "Okay, Princess, I need you to be good and not make too much trouble for Mom. Do what she tells you, and I'll bring something special for you from Switzerland or Holland."

"Okay, Daddy. I'll miss you. Mommy said to ask for chocolate, but I would like a doll instead. How long are you going to be gone?" She looked into my eyes as I knelt before her.

"Thirty-five days," I said, suddenly feeling that was too long. "I'll be back in the middle of September, and I'll send you some postcards along the way. I'll be back before you know it."

"I love you, Daddy," she said, squeezing my neck.

"I love you too, sweetheart."

I turned toward the door. Jeanette was leaning against the door frame with a soft smile on her face. "Remember, Mr. Evans, you promised. Next time we're going along."

I embraced her. *She's going to hold me to that,* I thought.

"I promise." I picked up my bag and hurried out to the cab.

CHAPTER 46

A FIRE THAT STILL BURNS

AFTER ARRIVING BY TRAIN in downtown Interlaken, my fellow conference attendees and I gathered our luggage, exited the station, and greeted the bus driver holding a YFC sign. He led us to an aging Mercedes bus owned by the Bible school, and we were soon winding our way up the mountain road toward the school.

The glimpses of Swiss scenery I caught between thickets of trees as we drove along nearly took my breath away. *I will bring Jeanette and Alyce here someday,* I thought, the promise I'd made still fresh in my heart. *Everyone should have the opportunity to see the beauty God created in Switzerland.*

The bus had to stop and wait a number of times on the way up the mountain for goats and shepherds to cross. When we finally arrived at the Bible school, we concluded we were probably the main attraction in a town of three hundred people.

The view of the valley and lakes below us was mesmerizing.

Sunlight shimmered on the dark-green water, and red-roofed houses peppered the emerald landscape. The bright-blue sky was punctuated by billowy white clouds, and snowcapped mountains stood sentinel all around. I could hear the faint tinkling of bells that hung on the necks of cows and sheep in nearby pastures. This scene was its own worship service to our Creator.

Tearing my eyes away from this magical scene to refocus on my purpose for being there, I exited the bus and followed the driver to the meeting hall of the school. There we registered, received our room assignments, and dispersed to settle in and freshen up before the evening meal. I claimed one of the lower bunks in the rustic dorm room before heading outside to take a walk in the majesty of God's creation.

+ + +

Two days later, the delegates began to arrive—250 people from 46 countries. The guest list was graced by Egyptian pastors, US Army soldiers, Chinese and Philippine evangelists, and professors of theology from Oxford and Cambridge, to name a few. The group here truly represented the Kingdom of God on earth, and those of us who had organized the event couldn't help but smile when we saw each other. Maybe this was how Paul and Peter felt when they held the first Jerusalem Council and multitudes of previously unidentified believers showed up.

The first day of the conference was pure gold—one world-class speaker after another. Dawson Trotman opened with a challenging rallying cry of not settling for the "milk of babes." "We are men!" he declared. "Men of God from all over the globe, and in this desperate hour, the world needs men! Men who will do the hard, daily work of growing spiritual reproducers. The need of the hour, after the decimation of the war, is to repopulate God's global church with disciples who will make more disciples and who will fan the flames of the great spiritual engine of the Kingdom." He finished his message with these words: "The hour of the harvest is here. It will not wait, so let's roll up our sleeves and get down to the real business of the Kingdom." The audience erupted in applause, and I almost expected the people to leave the hall and get back on the buses that brought them so they could return to their disciples at home.

We spent hours praying and discussing how best to reach the nations. Meetings were punctuated by *kaffee und kuchen* breaks. The delectable refreshments completed the trifecta of perfection for mind, spirit, and body. The first night we collapsed into bed, simultaneously exhausted, elated, and admonished.

On the second day, Dawson discovered a fire pit high on the mountain overlooking Interlaken. He suggested that after the evening meal, anyone who wanted to could carry along a few pieces of firewood and make the one-mile trek from the Bible school up to the mountain meadow, where we would hold a worship service.

The fire crackled before us in the fading light of the sunset. It was breathtaking to see pink and orange hues reflected off the snowcapped Alps. Forming an impromptu choir, our voices belted out the opening verse of "Eternal God, Whose Power Upholds" as loudly as we could. The words reverberated off the mountain walls around us.

"Eternal God, whose power upholds
Both flower and flaming star,
To whom there is no here nor there,
No time, no near nor far,
No alien race, no foreign shore,
No child unsought, unknown,
O send us forth, Thy prophets true,
To make all lands Thine own!"

We sang until our voices threatened to crack from exhaustion, caught up in the momentous event we were part of. *It must have been like this when David's mighty men gathered at night to toast the day's victories and battles,* I thought. *God's men reveling in the great adventure God called them into.*

And then I wondered whether David's mighty men were as prone to boyish behavior as the group of renowned Christian leaders around me, who may or may not have taken turns flinging burning coals high into the air out over the cliffs below like homemade fireworks.

As the evening wound to a close, men began straggling back to the school, and the crowd dwindled. I found myself lingering around the fire pit with Torrey Johnson, Billy

Graham, Jack Wyrtzen, Bob Cook, and Dawson Trotman, who stirred the remaining embers with a stick.

Billy spoke into the fading glow of the fire. "Men, I really think this is it. God is setting up the end of all things, and we get to be a part of it. I'm not a history scholar, but I can't think of a time in the last two thousand years when so many people from so many places came to Christ at the same time. It has to mean something, right?"

"I know what you mean," Daws chimed in. "Who would have thought it would take a world war to bring about a world revival?"

"Tell you what, Dawson," Billy said. "You take the military guys in the States. Torrey and Jack, you've got the students. Bob, I've never seen someone more made for Europe than you. I need to decide on what piece of the pie I want, but I'm still young, so I have time to choose."

"Maybe you should take Ding Dong, Texas. I've heard folks down there like to dream big too," Torrey said with a laugh, kicking a piece of coal toward Billy.

Dawson grinned. "Maybe you should take it *all*. We could all use the help, seeing as how you gave the rest of us such simple tasks."

"Hey, I didn't give them to you. God did!" Billy said in mock offense.

The playful repartee continued, but the words buzzed in the back of my mind as I stared into the flames. I could barely breathe, and it wasn't because of the altitude. *Made for Europe.* It wasn't the first time those words had come to me, but that night, in that moment, they hit home. As I poked at a log with a stick, the reality of God's call on my life sunk in. I really was meant to be the priest from another land sent to Europe. But what in the world did that look like?

After a few minutes, the other guys noticed I hadn't said anything, and despite my attempts to hide it, they saw the tears streaming down my cheeks.

"You okay, Bob?" Dawson asked. "What's going on?"

"What if Billy's right?" I asked quietly. "What if God is asking us to do something that radical? Isn't that what you've been trying to challenge us with, Dawson? Evangelize the world, and disciple them all before we die. Guys, I'm already past thirty. We need to take this seriously."

Great, Evans, I thought. *Way to go overboard and kill the moment.*

Into the silence, Dawson Trotman spoke, "Thank you, Bob. You're right. We came to this mountain to dream God-sized dreams. Let's not assume that God isn't here as well to make them come true. It would be just like him to do that. I think the sunset tonight was just his little reminder that he holds all the power in the universe."

"Yeah, I was just giving you a hard time, Billy," Torrey said. "You're right. I would give anything to see the youth of the world reached."

"I don't really know what God has for each of us," I began, "but you need to know that I think God has been calling me to Europe my whole life. Just a few minutes ago, he spoke it so clearly to me that I know I can't do anything else. I have to reach Europe!" I finished in a gasp that was half declaration, half question.

"Come on, guys," Billy said, suddenly serious. "Let's gather around Bob, lay our hands on him, and pray. He's not joking. I think God just spoke here, and we need to listen."

So we huddled to pray beneath a canopy of stars that were beginning to twinkle in the fading twilight. We were simply men desperate to be used and desperate to see others come to know the God we loved. Tears of passion flowed as we asked God to move, to act, to save.

When we finished, the fire had burned away to glowing embers. Billy came over to me and put an arm around my shoulder. "God asked something of you tonight," he said, "but you aren't alone. God has put Europe on my heart too. We will reach it together."

Jazz and Sven

Paris, France
June 15, 2016

JAZZ JONES

CHAPTER 47

A PLACE TO BE PRESENT

ANOTHER CONNECTION I MADE in the community was a new café that opened just a few doors down from my building. The three workers there were pleasant and greeted me with a smile and a friendly *bonjour* whenever I entered.

When excitement for the Euro 2016 tournament started to heat up, I went in a few times to watch the games with others who had gathered to eat, drink, and cheer on their beloved team: les Bleus. In the middle of a game one night, I had the sense that I was at home—that I belonged. At first, I couldn't explain it; I just felt at ease and comfortable, like I was supposed to be there. It wasn't just that the decor was done in my favorite color, purple. Paris *was* becoming home.

That night, I decided this was going to be "my café" and that I was going to be a regular. My goal was to go there at least twice a week around the same time. I hoped that would provide opportunities for me to speak with the workers and some of the other regular customers. The idea wasn't entirely mine; it was a missional principle: the power of presence.

It's rare to meet someone at random, share the gospel in one sitting, and lead them to the Lord. It does happen, and every so often we celebrated something like that on our team, but mostly the Good News is shared slowly over time, in the context of relationship. For that to happen, one must be present and available for the Lord to use. One of the wonderful things I was finding about Europe was that it was built for presence and community. There was a cultural value to spending time with neighbors in coffee shops, pubs, and cafés, and my desire was to be the tangible presence of Jesus in this café.

+ + +

One day something happened that showed the benefit of my frequent visits. I was in the café during happy hour to write a newsletter to my supporters. For a while, I was the only customer there. One of the two workers that day, the *monsieur*, left on an errand. Then the *madame*, the cook, got a phone call and walked to the café door. Turning to me, she said she was going to leave for a bit. Although I was surprised by her announcement, I replied with a *"D'accord"* and a smile. As she left, I prayed no other customers would arrive in their absence.

About fifteen minutes later, the *monsieur* returned. He looked around for the *madame*, calling out her name. I told him she had left but promised to be back shortly. His eyebrows shot up with surprise. *"Donc vous avez gardé le café pour nous,"* he said, noting that I'd kept an eye on the place for them.

"Eh, *oui*," I confirmed.

"Merci beaucoup, madame."

The fact that the workers left me alone in their open café—and that I hadn't even paid my bill yet—illustrated a certain level of trust. I did belong here.

CHAPTER 48

PRAYING THE STREETS

AS PART OF OUR TWO-DAY TRAINING with a short-term ministry team from the States, we took to the streets to find "people of peace." During training, we had learned an evangelism tool called "the three circles" that we were eager to try. This simple diagram illustrates man's brokenness, God's intended design, and the Good News that can bridge the two. The nice thing about the tool is that you don't need apps, tracts, or even a Bible to talk about it, just something to write on and people willing to listen for a few minutes.

Short-term teams are a vital part of our ministry in France. They boost the "manpower" as we create connections in a neighborhood. Some teams, like this one, simply come to saturate a neighborhood in prayer.

We split into groups, and I was partnered with Sally and Joseph. We walked the drizzly streets one afternoon, praying as we walked and asking God to point us to the people we should talk to. For Joseph and me, this was to be a "watch and learn" experience so we could lead teams like this in the future. Sally led the interactions with the people we met, and I translated. It was exciting to think that a year ago I had needed the translator, and now I was helping others share the Good News in French.

After walking down a nearly empty street, we came across a young African man who was waiting at a covered bus stop. The skepticism in his eyes was obvious as we approached.

"Bonjour!" I said.

Sally started off by saying that we were walking around the neighborhood to pray for people. She asked him if there was anything he needed prayer for.

"Non," he answered quickly.

Despite his deflection, I had a feeling that there must be something we could pray for, so I asked him if he and his family were in good health.

"Oui."

I thought for a couple seconds more. Then, prompted by the Holy Spirit, I asked if his family had found employment. *"Oui . . . sauf moi."* Everyone had a job but him.

I told him that we'd love to pray that God would provide employment for him.

Confused, he replied that he didn't know how to pray for a job.

I told him we'd gladly pray for him right then and there.

When he nodded, Sally prayed, and I translated. He even gave us his contact information to pass on to Bill for follow-up. There's something powerful and precious that happens when a person realizes that someone—perhaps even God himself—knows and cares about his struggles.

+ + +

On one day following the training, part of the US team and a few from our Paris team had another outreach opportunity. We went to a food distribution center at a church in Château Rouge, a neighborhood in northern Paris. We talked and prayed with the women who were waiting there for food to arrive. Many of the women appreciated our prayers; others were skeptical. Some of the women were believers, some were Muslim, and some didn't profess any faith at all.

After only a few months of full-time ministry, doors of opportunity were opening everywhere I looked. I realized at one point that the challenge wouldn't be finding new ways to engage but discerning which opportunities were the ones God had designed specifically for me.

I remembered that Bob Evans had felt conflicted by all the needs in Europe too. How did he decide to start GEM? I hadn't gotten that far yet. I determined that even though I was becoming very busy, I would make the time to finish reading his story.

Beatenberg Congress on World Evangelization

Beatenberg, Switzerland
August 11, 1948

BOB EVANS

CHAPTER 49

DISCIPLESHIP

OF COURSE, the conference wasn't all mountaintop vistas and hymn-sings. The 250 delegates from around the world came with different ideas about what should be done to advance the Kingdom. On the last full day, I was surprised to find myself passionately on the minority side of a heated argument about conversion and discipleship. Certainly I believed that conversion is an essential part of discipleship, but the prevailing argument was just to get as many souls into the Kingdom as possible. Given the increasing popularity of large-venue evangelistic events like youth rallies, it was hard to argue that this wasn't the best way to do things.

And yet something inside me, maybe from my childhood in Cameroon or my time in France, led me to believe that Jesus' call to make disciples involved more than a conversion experience. We needed to help people learn to live like Jesus, not just believe that he died for their sins and that heaven awaited them. If they didn't have a heart to reproduce spiritually, then no matter how many people came into the Kingdom, the movement would stall with that generation.

This conversation came to a head one night at supper when some of the guys were talking again about seeing hundreds come to Christ at one event. As I listened, I was transported back to the night I stood in the parking lot of Soldier Field and watched buses pull out of the lot, headed to destinations unknown. Something in me snapped.

"Guys, what happens after that?" I asked, cutting off the speaker. "Seriously! What happens next for these folks who walk out of the stadium or the church or the tent or wherever they're gathered and go their separate ways? How do they learn how to practice what they've just become?"

Silent stares met my questions, so I continued, "I saw hundreds of people receive Christ one night in Chicago, and we handed them a sheet with ten Scripture verses, a New Testament, and a "Footprints in the Sand" bookmark as they filed out of the stadium. It was the most important decision of their lives, and we sent them back out into the world like lambs to the slaughter."

"Don't you believe that God is sovereign, Bob?" one man asked. "Surely he has it under control."

"It's not about God's sovereignty; it's about the practical issue of a person learning to do something new—to live a different way. As a kid in Africa, I learned to fly-fish in the rivers around our village. If someone had given me a list of the top ten fly-fishing tips and a book on fly-fishing and said, "There you go! Now you're a fly fisherman," I probably never would have caught a fish. I might have tried, but ultimately I would have given up. But that's not what happened. My father took me fishing, and he showed me how to tie the fly on the line, how to hold the rod, and how to cast. I learned more in one afternoon with him than I could have in a month with a book, no matter how good that book was. Discipleship is the same. We need to show people how to live like Jesus, and we need to do that in the context of their lives and their questions and struggles. That takes time—one-on-one, life-on-life time! Maybe someone can do this with a couple of people, but surely not with thousands! Jesus did this with the twelve he was with almost every waking moment for three years, and they still struggled. I'm pretty sure I'm not as good at it as he was."

"Come on, Bob. How can you argue with results?" another man asked. "Thousands of people coming forward—certainly God is in these events."

"Look, I'm not saying God isn't at work." My voice took on a more conciliatory tone, my fervor now spent. "What I'm saying is that we can't let it stop there. If we do, we're being irresponsible—these are real people's lives. And more importantly, these people need to become the next generation of disciplers. If we don't train them, we'll lose them, and this movement will stop."

"But isn't training the church's job?" another man asked.

"Sure, church is part of it. But just like fishing, a person can only learn so much from a seminar or a sermon. Who's going to answer their individual questions? That is especially true in Europe right now. When I was recovering in France,

I discipled the town priest right alongside the town's favorite restaurant owner. Both needed help. I think massive evangelistic campaigns in Europe without some plan to prepare people to walk alongside all these new believers is dangerous. How can we help laypeople grow in their ability to disciple other men and women? Look around this room—there's only a handful of women. We men can't meet this need by ourselves. I'm not sure we're ready to launch this movement yet."

"But what if God is ready?" Billy said.

"Then I think maybe we should talk about dividing and conquering," I said, cognizant that few people had seen more evangelistic responses than Billy had. "Maybe we should put in place some folks who are focused on preparing the soil— getting existing churches ready to receive new people—and others who are focused on the harvest—getting people connected with those who can walk through life with them."

"Guys, I think Bob is right," Billy said. "Personally, I feel torn this week. As many of you know, I've been asked to step in as president of Northwestern College in Minneapolis. One reason I'm inclined to take the job is that I'd be doing exactly what Bob is talking about: helping laypeople become better at discipling others. And yet God has gifted me to be an evangelist. All week long, I've been wrestling with the very tension Bob is bringing up. There is a small percentage of gifted evangelists, but we need millions of competent disciplers—that's what we're all commanded to do. I think that's what Paul was getting at when he wrote about the different parts of the body and the unique roles we play."

"Exactly," I agreed. "For every great evangelist, we need countless skilled disciplers. If a thousand people respond to an altar call, we need a thousand men and women ready to engage with them and show them how to live like Jesus and become grounded in the Word. It would be even better if we could identify churches or groups they could join to find other people on the same journey. Then they could learn together and ultimately pass on what they've learned. My concern is that both in America and here in Europe, most churches don't provide this kind of landing place. Churches today seem to be full of people who attend because they need something or because it's just what people do, not because their lives are being transformed. If we don't change that, we'll be dead in the water."

"Well said, Bob!" Billy chimed in. "I guess we know what we need to pray for."

That put a halt to the conversation, as no one wanted to argue with the young firebrand. Ironically, it was a conversation Billy and I would continue to have many times over the following decades as I helped to organize his European events.

That night in my journal, I wrote, "I want to be a part of the discipleship solution. I want to see thousands come to Christ, too, but if I have to choose, I want to help people live as believers, not just become believers."

CHAPTER 50

A CHANGE OF PLANS

THE DAY HAD COME to leave the beauty of Beatenberg and the exhilaration of the conference to begin the journey home. I had planned to spend a few days after the conference exploring some of the countries on our list of potential Youth for Christ launching points, but when I awoke on departure day, I realized I needed to take some time alone with God to process what had happened during the conference.

One of the delegates had mentioned a hotel he liked in Paris, which was one of the cities I wanted to explore, so I called and made a reservation for three nights at Hôtel de la Madeleine near Place de la Concorde at the eastern end of the famous Champs-Élysées. With the hotel secured, I asked the receptionist at the Beatenberg Bible Institute to send three telegrams on my behalf: two to cancel meetings in Amsterdam and Brussels, and one to Jeanette.

Jeanette. Conference amazing. God spoke. Staying now in Paris. Hôtel de la Madeleine. 3 days until flight home. Canceled rest of trip. Pray for me. Love you. Miss you. B.E.

Checking my watch, I realized I needed to hurry to get on the next bus down to Interlaken if I was going to be able to catch the train to Basel, where I would switch to a French train bound for Paris.

"Danke sehr," I said, thanking the receptionist in what little German I had learned throughout the week.

She smiled. "You are welcome, Mr. Evans," she replied in perfect English. "God bless."

In minutes, I was staring out the window as the bus crawled down the mountain amid the grinding and squealing of brakes. God's breathtaking beauty again scrolled by in front of my eyes, but it didn't register this time; I was reliving the various conversations I'd had over the past week, both with the other delegates and with God. I noted the conversations that had caused my emotions to kick in and my passions to flare. *Why do I care about this so much, God?* I prayed.

Looking at my ticket to Basel, I chuckled at the Swiss. My train was to leave at 9:37. Not 9:38 or 9:39 but precisely 9:37. *Well, I guess this is the country that's known for watches. I guess I'll see how punctual they really are.*

+ + +

When the bus deposited me at the train station, I realized I had twenty minutes to buy some gifts for Jeanette and Alyce. Inside the store, I found a shelf that offered Swiss merchandise: cowbells; a variety of chocolates from Cailler, Sprüngli, and Lindt; cheese samplers; and a variety of hand-made Heidi dolls with thick braids jutting out from their traditional Swiss bonnets. I chose a large Cailler dark choco-late bar for Jeanette and a cheerful Heidi doll for Alyce and, after a second's hesitation, a small cheese sampler for me—I would need something on the train, after all. I paid with the few Swiss francs I had left, packed my treasures in my satchel, and headed for track 4 with a few minutes to spare.

I positioned myself near the large clock suspended above the platform and watched as the minute hand clicked to thirty-four. Peering down the track, I could see a headlight and a plume of smoke as the train to Basel rounded a distant corner and slowly came into the station. *There's no way the train can get to the station in time,* I thought.

But sure enough, the train came to a stop with a final wheeze exactly as the minute hand clicked to thirty-seven. *I guess Swiss engineering must extend to train conductors too!*

Boarding the third car, I made my way to seat 26A and stowed my luggage before dropping into the seat. Relief flooded through me as I realized the conference I'd helped to arrange had concluded without a hitch, and all the delegates were happily on their way home.

What an amazing few days, God. You may have launched an international movement in that tiny mountain town. The whistle blew, and with a guttural chug, the train lurched into motion. Checking my itinerary one last time, I real-ized my connection in Basel allowed only nine minutes to switch trains, which didn't leave a lot of margin. There wasn't much I could do about that now, however, so I searched my satchel and pulled out the packet of cheese. The package contained five thick cuts of cheese: Emmentaler, Gruyère, Tilsit, Appenzeller, and Raclette. I savored the Swiss snack as the train hurtled toward Basel.

I made my connection in Basel, and after a nap, I awoke as the train approached the outskirts of Paris. Staring out the window, I thought back to all my childhood dreams of seeing this great city. In a million years, I never could have imagined entering the city with the eyes of a missionary, seeking God amid the beauty and ruins of postwar Paris. Though much had been done to repair the devastated city, everywhere I looked I saw some shell of a building that had yet to be rebuilt.

CHAPTER 51

AN EVENING IN PARIS

I SURVEYED MY ROOM AT THE MADELEINE, which was surprisingly spacious by French standards. It included a tiny balcony with a chair, a round folding table complete with a vase of fresh flowers, and the ubiquitous ashtray. It seemed like every room of every building in the country was set to cater to the nation's fascination with smoking. Three more ashtrays adorned the room, and the lingering aroma of cigarettes indicated that they had been well used.

I tossed my Bible and journal into my well-worn satchel and headed out with the expectation of a big-game hunter on safari. My heart was set to hear from the Lord, and I was committed to discovering answers to the questions swirling inside me.

"I know you're there, Lord," I whispered as I descended the stairs. "But where will I find you? What will you have to say?"

As I pushed open the hotel's front doors and proceeded

out into this city I had longed to visit for most of my life, I felt alive with possibility. I was in awe of God's extravagant generosity to draw me here, of all places in the world, to clarify my purpose and set my path for the next chapter of my life.

As I walked from the hotel toward Place de la Concorde, I was struck by the beauty of late August in Paris. The effects of the war had all but been erased in these past four years, and everywhere I looked I saw flower boxes exploding with geraniums in varying shades of red, pink, white, and coral. Around the square in front of la Madeleine, colorful umbrellas shaded restaurant patrons who sat outside, enjoying an afternoon coffee or a visit with friends over a glass of wine. Here and there I heard snatches of music from street entertainers at the various cafés.

Where should I go, God? Where will I find you?

Skirting the massive Place de la Concorde, I wandered west, realizing I was walking without intention or knowledge about where I was going. Where were my feet taking me? The plaza itself was a work of art—or perhaps a collection of works of art. I was surrounded by massive fountains, their streams backlit in the late-afternoon sun. Bikes and cars entered and exited in random directions as if in a spontaneous ballet. Over the trees, I saw the tip of the Eiffel Tower pointing skyward in the golden afternoon light.

As I approached the street, I saw small huts of vendors nestled among the trees, offering crêpes, wine, and other delicacies. Others were surrounded by stands of flower bouquets or newspapers. Artists with their masterpieces leaned up against the trunks of the towering trees, trying to entice passersby to take a closer look.

From the street I spotted the roofs of the famed Louvre to the east, but when I turned to the west, my breath caught in my throat. There, in the center of the wide avenue, perhaps a mile away, stood the Arc de Triomphe. In that moment, the reality of the war and my part in it flooded back to me. The image I'd seen in newspapers of Hitler leading his troops around that global monument flashed through my mind and my heart, and I stood there staring at one of the world's most iconic symbols of freedom. *Costly freedom,* I thought, considering all the lives lost.

The crowd of Parisians enjoying their afternoon stroll along the Champs-Élysées flowed around me while my mind struggled to reconcile this scene with the grainy propaganda photos I'd seen of the German army parading along this same street almost a decade earlier. Joining the milling throng, I began to follow the path of ancient trees lining the street that would lead me to the great arch.

The crowd around me was an intriguing mix from many walks of life. I saw American soldiers, families with their children, young lovers walking hand in hand, musicians, and vendors hawking their wares. There was another class of people moving in and out of the crowd, almost unseen. Their clothing was mismatched and clearly worn, and they slipped in and out with downcast eyes. Some held small signs begging for assistance. Some stood to the side, surveying the crowd, while others walked against the flow, jostling unsuspecting folks and moving on with newly acquired treasures. Automatically checking my wallet, I decided to move it to my satchel, clutching it a little tighter. Like the buildings that had yet to be rebuilt, the Gypsies were remnants of the war—people who had come to the city in hopes of eking out a life.

The contrast touched my heart. Affluent people desperate to forget the past and move on with life flowed together with those who had yet to be blessed in any observable way, all seeking a better life. Suddenly the spare change in my pocket became a gift to bestow and not a treasure to be buried.

This is Europe, the Spirit within me whispered. *This is why you are needed here.*

+ + +

I soon found myself standing outside the giant traffic circle around the Arc. A worn French flag fluttered gently in the evening breeze, a symbol of yet another costly triumph and the hope it represented to the nation—perhaps to all of Western Europe. And yet, as we learned in the brief respite between the first and second world wars, peace among people is fleeting.

There will be more wars, I thought. *Sinful people will see to that. Europe needs something more—something lasting that only God can provide.*

I then heard the Spirit's gentle challenge to my heart: *You were one small part of securing peace in Europe for now. Will you be part of bringing a Kingdom of peace here that will stand the test of time?*

As the last golden rays of sunlight slipped behind the buildings to the west, I realized that I had been standing there for quite some time. Returning to the present, I felt hungry for more than answers. I recalled the many colorful restaurants near my hotel and decided I'd seen enough of Paris for one day. Heading back down the hill, I saw one of the ever-present crêpe vendors packing up his cart, and I hurried over to order something for the walk back to the hotel.

Savory or sweet? I pondered.

"Bonsoir, monsieur, êtes-vous ouvrez?" I asked.

"Ah, an American who speaks French. *Bonsoir. Oui,* the griddle is still hot. What would you like?"

"Do you have any chicken?" I suddenly realized I hadn't eaten anything substantial all day. "I put on a few miles today, and I could use something hearty."

"I have some beautiful chicken here," the chef said. "I also have some vegetables left over—tomatoes, onions, and cheese, of course."

"That sounds amazing." My mouth watered in anticipation. "A little extra cheese, if I may, please."

"Bien sûr," the chef said, ladling out a generous portion of batter. In a few seconds, he expertly turned over the slightly brown, paper-thin pancake.

"Sir, you look fit," the chef commented, never taking his eyes off the spinning wheel. "Are you military?"

"Former military." I chuckled. "I was with the southern invasion force down by St. Tropez, but I was wounded and didn't get much farther than that. Now I'm a missionary of sorts."

"Well, that sounds like quite a tale." He folded the crêpe as melted cheese oozed out of the edges and then placed it in a piece of wax paper. "You will want to wait for a few minutes; the cheese and meat are very hot."

"It looks delicious. How much do I owe you?" I took the packet from his hand.

"You owe me nothing. Your service to my country has purchased a lifetime of crêpes. If it weren't for men like you, I would not be standing here today making a living." A troubled look clouded his face. "You said you are a missionary. I can't say I know what that means, but for many of us, God seems to have left our country. I come from a religious family. When I was a child, we all went to Mass, but now none of us do. Not even my parents. Though if I am honest, when they stopped going to church, it was like something died in them. For me . . . I don't know. How could God allow all that has happened? Yet it also seems like our rescue from tyranny was miraculous. I don't know what to believe. My life seems to be both blessed and empty, if that makes any sense at all."

"It does," I said with a nod. "All day as I walked around your beautiful city, I've been struck by the contrasts God has allowed to exist. I'm sorry. I don't even know your name, and here we are talking about life and God."

"Ah yes, forgive me," he said. "Most people just come by and tell me what they want. Not many stay to talk. My name is Marcel Bertrand."

"Bob Evans," I said, shaking his hand. "I can't say I fully

understand all you've suffered throughout the war, but I can say I had more than a firsthand glimpse in the south of France. It is confusing, and yet in the midst of the horrors, my greatest joy was seeing God show up and offer hope to hopeless people. Please forgive me if I'm being too forward, but don't give up on God. Look for hope and the ways he's working, and I think you will find him. There is beauty here among the ashes. This may feel unusual to you, but may I pray for you and for your family and business?"

"Well, that's a first," he said, surprised. "I guess you can. That is very kind of you."

I laid a hand on Marcel's shoulder. "Jesus, I want to pray for Marcel and his family today," I said quietly. "He has blessed me this evening with an incredible gift—a pleasant conversation and this delicious crêpe. Like Marcel, I have questions too. I don't always understand why you allow certain things to happen, and yet I know without a shadow of a doubt that you are good. I pray that in the coming days, Marcel and his family would experience something good that can only come from you so they know you haven't abandoned them or left France. I also pray a blessing over his business. Will you show favor to Marcel and bring him a steady stream of customers so he can support his family? I know that you know Marcel. You made him, and you love him. Show him in the coming days that this is true. Amen."

"Thank you, Bob," Marcel said. "No one has ever prayed for me like that before. I am glad I was still here to meet you. Now take a bite of that before it gets cold," he said with a smile. "I don't want you to think I don't make the best crêpes in Paris! If you are here for a few days, come back, and I will make you another variety."

"Merci!" I said before biting into the cheese-encrusted corner. With my mouth full, I managed to exclaim, "This is wonderful! Thank you!"

+   +   +

On my leisurely stroll back to the hotel, I realized I'd been so caught up in the magnificence of the city that I hadn't done what I'd come here for.

Okay, God, thank you for the gift of this wonderful evening in Paris, but now I need to hear from you. Remembering all the restaurants around my hotel, I decided that some good French dessert and a strong cup of coffee were just what I needed to bring clarity to my quest.

As I made my way around the Place de la Madeleine, one restaurant in particular caught my eye. It sat on the corner of the square with a number of outside tables covered by bright-red umbrellas. Each umbrella was emblazoned with the name *Fauchon.* In the front window I saw tiered trays of delectable-looking desserts and chocolates, including one of my favorites: éclairs. I took it as a sign.

CHAPTER 52

MADE FOR THIS

TAKING A SEAT at one of the tables facing the square, I ordered a coffee and an éclair and pulled my Bible and journal from my satchel.

Well, Jesus, I prayed silently, *I feel like you have been drawing me here since the night I stepped off the LCI-45 along the shore of St. Tropez. But it's more than this place, isn't it? You've been speaking to me every step of the way. But what have you been saying?*

First, there was Ed and the guys. That was when I initially realized ministry was really just living life with people and helping them in their search for God. Before that, I'd spent much of my life studying to minister to a congregation by teaching them the Word of God. While some of that training was helpful, nothing prepared me for those raw, spiritual relationships with guys who were far from God but desperately wanted more. Those men couldn't get enough of the Bible, and I realized how much I needed to learn the

Word myself so I could share it without always having a Bible handy. And yet God was right there with me.

All I knew for sure was that what I experienced on the beaches of St. Tropez and in the village of Draguignan was what I wanted more of—having Jesus touch another person through me and seeing that person turn around and impact someone else. "That was 2 Timothy 2:2 in real life," I declared into the warm Parisian night.

Then there were Kristophe, Bernadette, and Father Matthias. I met them where they were, and half the time, I didn't know what was coming next. I certainly hadn't known what to expect the night that Kristophe had me come to his home secretly!

I don't think I'd considered before how uniquely each of those people connected with God. There was nothing set or programmatic about it. For my part, I injected Jesus into their agenda rather than coming with my own, and it seemed like God had already prepared them to hear. Or perhaps they were so broken and desperate that any drop of hope was like water to a parched soul.

It was unsettling, because I realized I couldn't do this without God. But it was also exhilarating—very different from delivering a prepared sermon. Suddenly theology had to become practical and responsive. The teaching made sense because of the relationship we had. It felt like I was joining God in what he was already doing in their lives, and I learned to trust that the Spirit would lead me in the moment. It wasn't all up to me.

But none of that prepared me for Ed's death. That hurt, and I just about gave up. It felt like God gave me an amazing gift and then took it away. Those were hard days, and it was only when God reminded me that Ed was with him that I was able to move forward. I wasn't sure I fully understood the urgency of the gospel until I saw him lying there in that bed. Even in the midst of war, we had somehow felt immortal and impervious. Some lessons you only need to learn once, though.

And then, suddenly, I had to leave. When I got on that ship, I had to entrust all those folks to God's care. I wasn't able to help them with everything they needed, but I think they saw how I kept going back to Scripture, to God, and to other people to find the answers. No doubt they missed me when I left, but when the next question came up, they didn't skip a beat. They leaned into their growing community.

If I returned to Europe, I needed to work in such a way that I could always leave, and that meant strengthening nationals so they could carry on if something happened to me. They had to become the solution.

It might have all seemed like a dream if I hadn't returned home to find God at work there, too. Hearing the reports of youth rallies springing up all over, seeing the church in St. Louis and realizing that discipleship can happen anywhere, and seeing all those people streaming forward to receive Christ at Soldier Field assured me that God was doing something significant. I felt like God was tearing me apart, rearranging my motives and desires, and putting me back together again.

I reflected on all the conversations at the conference about evangelism and discipleship. *What if it's not one or the other but both at once?* I wondered. *When did the disciples start to believe? They followed Jesus from the beginning, but some denied him even at the end.* I stared into the empty coffee cup. *Maybe helping a person come to believe is discipleship. For that matter, almost everything about discipleship is helping a person to believe in God more.*

I sighed, putting my journal and Bible back into my satchel. *I think that's enough for today. I'll be mulling this over all night as it is.*

Noticing that I was getting ready to leave, the waiter approached. *"L'addition?"*

"Oui." I nodded. *"Puis-je avoir un autre de ces éclairs, s'il vous plaît?"* I asked, indicating one of the delectable éclairs still sitting on the plate in the window. I'd hate to see it go to waste, after all.

"Mais bien sûr." The waiter nodded, returning momentarily with the bill and a wrapped éclair. I wandered back to my hotel, lost in thought. Perhaps I hadn't gotten any lightning bolts of guidance, but maybe clarity would come with the morning.

CHAPTER 53

TAKING THE RISK

AS THE FIRST CLATTER OF CARTS along the cobblestone streets and the grumble of engines from early deliveries broke the stillness of the predawn night, I became aware of words running over and over through my head. *Teach Matthias so he can reach the town. Teach Kristophe so he can help Bernadette. Teach Bernadette so she can tell the story of God's redemption. Teach . . .* As wakefulness overtook the mantra, my eyes focused on the pink-orange sky visible through the window.

"God, I think I know what you're asking of me," I said as I looked out the window. "But I'm not sure I'm up for the risk. I have a wife and a daughter. I have a good job. I'm one of the leaders of the evangelism movement that's sweeping the world, working alongside some of your greatest evangelists today. What we're doing in Youth for Christ is important, and I get to play a part in that. Why would you want me to risk all that? Why did you lead me there in the first place?"

Silence seemed to be the only answer to my heartfelt questions.

"I know," I continued. "I have done the stadiums, but is that really what I've been called to do?"

And that was the crux of it, wasn't it? That was what God brought me to Beatenberg to learn. I wasn't the person for the stadium; I was the person for the day after or the day before. That was what Ed needed, and Kristophe and Bernadette and Father Matthias. In fact, more than anything, Europe needed men and women to help the Matthiases and Bernadettes become the kind of believers who could share what God was doing in their lives with others.

I'd always known that, but perhaps in my vanity I'd hoped to be one of those guys who stood on a stage or a street corner and watched God bring in the harvest. But I should have known better. During my years growing up in Cameroon, my parents modeled true discipleship for me as they humbly lived with villagers and opened their home and their lives so new believers could see what it looked and felt like to live as a Christian. Their Kingdom message was poured out in cups of tea and served over time on wooden plates of food.

Rolling out of bed, I sat at the small desk in the corner of the room with my Bible and journal. Almost everyone else at Beatenberg was desperate to see more rallies and events in Europe, where we hoped hundreds and thousands would come to Christ. If that came to pass, we would have to do something to get the European Church ready to receive them, and it seemed like God was asking me to be a part of that.

"Father, I have no idea how to do this, but I'm your man. I believe you want me to do this."

On impulse, I opened my Bible to the passage God kept bringing to mind:

> The things that you have heard from me among many witnesses, commit these to faithful men who will be able to teach others also.
>
> 2 TIMOTHY 2:2

That's it, isn't it, God? I thought. *This is what you made me for.*

"What would that look like?" I said aloud, closing my Bible. Turning to a blank page in my journal, I scrawled these words:

What I know:

- Because of the war, and perhaps other wars in the past, the Church in Europe has been weakened. Fewer people are turning to God and the local priest for answers because it seems like they have none.
- People are coming back to God, though, through evangelistic work and through care and love for the refugees and those displaced by the war. The problem is that there aren't enough churches or mature believers to disciple them all.

- The French I learned as a kid opens doors and relationships. I don't think the task before me can be done without knowing the language—perhaps not perfectly, but at least conversationally.
- People in Europe are relationally open, and many of them are hurting. It wasn't hard to create relationships and bring up spiritual topics.
- It wouldn't be enough to come back to Europe and connect relationally in just one town. To make the kind of impact needed to transform Europe spiritually, the strategy has to be one that will impact many communities.

I reflected on the things I'd been reminded of in the past day: my upbringing, my training, my love for learning, my experiences, and the desires of my heart that had been awakened in Beatenberg.

What if we started a school? I thought. *But it couldn't just be any school. Europe didn't need another Wheaton or Oxford where people could learn about God; they needed a place where they could live as disciples and practice the things they learned with real people. It would be a practical school—a school of discipleship where Kristophes and Matthiases alike could come and learn things they could implement the following day.*

My hand almost couldn't keep up with my mind as I scribbled down ideas and thoughts, trying to capture everything that was being unlocked inside me.

+ + +

Hours later, as the bright light of late morning streamed through the window, I glanced at my watch and realized I'd have to hurry if I wanted to eat breakfast at the hotel, as the dining room would close in just fifteen minutes. Leaving my work, I bounded down the stairs, my mind alive with possibilities and questions.

To my relief, the breakfast bar was still open, and as I entered the door to the tiny eating area, the smell of fresh croissants and coffee met me. *This is what heaven will smell like,* I thought, savoring the moment. The few other hotel guests in the room nodded and welcomed me with polite *"bonjours."*

As I sat down and began to butter a croissant, a voice in my head sprinkled seeds of doubt. *Start a school in Europe? Who in the world would help you do this when it's the antithesis of what all the other famous evangelists are doing? You're going to risk everything—your job, your reputation. You know what Jeanette's parents will say. You don't have a clue what it would take to open a school or if anyone even wants one. Just play it safe. Besides, Alyce is almost ready to go to kindergarten, and raising children requires money. Jeanette will never go for this.*

The thoughts came at me so powerfully that as I sat there, butter dripping off the croissant, I felt life and joy fading.

I suddenly felt foolish. Big dreams were easy when I was walking on the streets of a historic city like Paris. I must have just gotten swept up in the moment.

You can still help in Europe a bit. That will be enough, the internal voice continued.

Looking at my plate, I closed my eyes in resignation. What had I been thinking? *I'm not up for something of this scale. I'm not the kind of guy to risk everything on a whim.*

Suddenly an image blossomed in my mind. I was standing in a crowded boat, which bobbed up and down in the gentle swell of the Mediterranean Sea. Fear and doubt rocked in my heart as surely as the boat did in the sea. Then I sensed a presence at my side as a big man moved through the crowded boat and stood at my side. "What do you think, Evans? Is God watching us?"

My eyes snapped open, and with a spark of determination, I dismissed the enemy's lies. An enemy held Europe under his sway, and just as during the war, the time had come for another invasion. It would take every bit as much courage and resolve now as it had then, when I'd stepped into that boat as the first chaplain to accompany an invasion force.

"Father," I prayed aloud in the quiet breakfast room, "I'll do it. I will start a school to help strengthen European believers and laypeople so that everyone you're bringing to faith here can be rooted and established in Christ. I have no idea how. I have no idea what anyone will say about this. But if it's your will, I'll do it."

Suddenly aware that other patrons were staring at the lone American talking to himself, I looked around and said sheepishly, *"Bonjour. Il fait beau, n'est-ce pas?,"* commenting on the nice day.

A few people nodded their heads, and then everyone returned to their breakfast.

After I finished my croissant and coffee, I went to my room and recorded my vow before God in my journal. I would be coming back to Europe. I would finally make good on my promise to Jeanette to show her the places and people in France I'd come to love.

"I'll do my part if you do yours, God."

Remembering the tragedy in Nice, France

Paris, France
July 14, 2016

JAZZ JONES

CHAPTER 54

BASTILLE DAY

A YEAR EARLIER, while I was at GEM's first-termers retreat, Sven had enjoyed the Bastille Day fireworks with a group of language-school friends at the foot of the Eiffel Tower. He told me that, even though the place was packed and his group had barely made the last train back to school, it was the best fireworks show he'd ever seen. Since Sven moved back to Germany at the end of December, he and I took turns visiting each other every month. It was his turn to visit me, and Sven was eager for me to experience it with him this year.

Sven asked if I wanted to watch the fireworks from the Champ de Mars or just stay at my place and try to stream the show online. I'd heard there would be live music at Champs de Mars, and I didn't want to stay home, but I wasn't sure I was prepared for the huge sea of people that would gather in front of the tower. We opted for a compromise: we'd view the show outdoors but from a distance. We looked at a map and agreed on the Jardin des Tuileries, the gardens that run west from the Louvre toward Place de la Concorde. The area is big and open, and it offers a great view of the Eiffel Tower.

It had been eight months since the last attack, but I couldn't help but think that such a gathering would be a perfect time for another act of terror. I was sure security would be beefed up, but I still couldn't bring myself to join the throng of people.

I made dinner in my flat for us, grabbed some raw veggies, and packed everything in Tupperware. To save time, we rode the bus to the gardens instead of walking. Scoping out the area, we saw that other people had come up with the same idea and had claimed various parts of the lawn. We managed to find a spot at the west end of the gardens facing Place de la Concorde that offered a good view.

Sven and I enjoyed our dinner alfresco while we waited for the fireworks to start. Despite the fact that it was the middle of July, the evening air was rather cool. We bundled up the best we could with the jackets we'd brought. The Hawaiian sarong we'd hoped to use to sit on instead became a makeshift cloak. We chuckled at the thought of warming ourselves like this in the middle of summer and then settled in to wait for the show.

We talked, people-watched, and tried to ignore the chilly wind that sought to penetrate our thin layers. With my Hawaiian blood, I'm often the first person to declare it is cold, but this time, it wasn't just me. Everywhere we looked, people were pulling their scarves tighter and huddling together to keep the cold at bay.

By ten o'clock, the sun hadn't quite set yet. The lingering daylight was one of the things I loved most about summer in France. More people joined our area, and as the size of the crowd grew, my worry about being in the midst of it grew as well. Thoughts of a potential attack flitted, unbidden, through my mind. I tried to push those thoughts away and prayed that God would keep us safe.

When eleven o'clock arrived, the lights on the Eiffel Tower began their frenetic sparkling, as they do every hour on the hour after sunset. I marveled as blue, white, and red lights cascaded up the tower. Everyone around us cheered with anticipation, knowing we were just seconds away from a spectacular show.

We were not disappointed. The theme for the 2016 show was *Paris est une fête*: "Paris is a party." It did feel like a party, just with a lot of strangers. But for that half an hour, all of us strangers bonded with *oohs* and *ahhs* and *whoas* over the extraordinary displays of colored lights and fireworks.

+ + +

Wanting to soak in the moment, I took only a few photos with my phone. When I tried to pull up the camera, I swiped the screen the wrong way, and a French news feed appeared. I was alarmed to see a current headline with the words *Nice*, *attentat*, and *morts*. My mind whirled. *There were deaths due to an attack in Nice?*

I lowered the phone onto my lap, stunned. I clicked on

the link to read the details about what had happened. Sven noticed that I'd turned my attention away from the fireworks.

He reached over and laid a hand on my arm. "What's wrong?"

Not wanting to alarm others, I leaned over and told him the tragic news.

"Oh no!" he exclaimed, trying to keep his voice down. "Are you okay? Should we head home now?"

"I'll be all right," I said. "Thanks. We can stay." But I had trouble concentrating on the rest of the show.

After a huge round of applause from the spectators, Sven and I joined many others at the bus stop to make our way home. During the ride, my mind was on overload. *I can't believe there's been another attack in France! Those poor people in Nice! They were just like Sven and me, celebrating France's national holiday. It feels like such a blatant disregard for human life. The attacker didn't distinguish between age, gender, or nationality as he plowed into the street with a truck. It seems like all he cared about was the destruction of human lives.*

When we returned to my flat, Sven and I sat on the couch, and I spilled my thoughts. When I was done, he took my hands and we prayed for Nice, for those injured, for the friends and families of those who had been killed, and for the country of France as a whole. We also thanked God for keeping us safe.

How much more could one country bear?

CHAPTER 55

A DATE WITH HISTORY

A FEW DAYS AFTER SVEN WENT BACK TO GERMANY, I decided that my act of moral defiance against yet another attack would be to finish reading Bob Evans's story instead of watching endless news clips and worrying about what might happen next.

One scene from his story caught my attention. It was about a local chocolatier called Fauchon, which still existed all these years later. I'd seen it before and knew it was across the river at Place de la Madeleine. I felt strangely drawn to the place. I wasn't sure if it was just the description of the delicious éclairs, but it felt significant somehow.

So that day, I decided to make a pilgrimage across town to the place where the idea of my mission agency had begun. It also seemed like a fitting place to put to rest the event that inspired me to start reading Bob's story, as well as this most recent attack. Plus, I really did love a good éclair.

When I looked online, I was disappointed to find that the

café was closed for renovations. The bakery was still open, however, so I decided to pick up some éclairs and find a chair in the Jardin des Tuileries, where I could savor them in the sunshine and reflect on the whirlwind of the past nine months.

So much had happened in my life: surviving a terrorist attack, getting engaged, finishing language school, planning a wedding, and starting full-time ministry. It was almost too much to comprehend.

As I stepped out the front door to my apartment building, a grin spread across my face. I was free to discover a new (to me) pâtisserie and enjoy a delicious pastry. Walking with joy and purpose, I headed toward the metro.

After emerging from the packed metro at Madeleine, I made my way around the massive building. All around me, throngs of tourists and Parisians walked about in streams of humanity heading for the various exits to the square, enjoying a perfect summer day in Paris. I made my way upstream to the northeast corner of the square, where I could already see the red umbrellas and awnings of Fauchon.

I stood there for perhaps five minutes, trying to picture the scene from the late 1940s, with Bob seated at one of the quaint tables. *What would you say today, Bob?* I wondered. *The world has found new reasons to kill and destroy each other, and the France you loved is probably gone. In your day, people struggled to find God again and were desperately looking for something. Today most of them aren't really looking, but they still desperately need God.*

+ + +

I was glad to find that the outside seating was open and a few tables remained unoccupied. *Score!* Glancing at my watch, I realized it was almost four o'clock, just in time for the famous French *goûter*, the afternoon snack to bridge between lunch and a late dinner. I decided to order a coffee and an éclair. *Who knows?* I thought. *I might end up sitting exactly where Bob sat almost seventy years ago.*

When I entered the shop, I got in line behind a few other patrons and started perusing the vast variety of desserts and treats. I stuck to my original plan and chose an éclair, just as Bob had ordered. I could come back to sample the other delights another time. As I placed my order, I was struck by the expression of the young lady behind the counter. Her head was covered with a beautiful floral scarf in the Muslim tradition, though not the traditional hijab.

What struck me most was the sadness behind her eyes. *I wonder what her life is like here in Paris,* I thought as she selected an éclair from the plate in the front window. She went about her job with efficiency and professionalism, but she kept her conversations with the customers short and to the point. I did see a hint of a smile on her face after I paid for my purchase, genuinely smiled at her, and said, *"Merci beaucoup."* I made my way to one of the tables outside, taking a seat facing the crowd.

Father, she seems so sad, I prayed silently. *Do you want me to talk with her? If you do, I'll need your boldness, and I'll need the Holy Spirit to guide my words.*

The server arrived a few minutes later with my coffee and placed it in front of me without making eye contact. I settled into my seat and took in the sight before me: a fluffy, chocolate-covered éclair sitting next to a steaming cappuccino. Taking the first bite was like tasting a piece of heaven.

I paused for a moment and looked out at the square before me. *What did it look like in Bob's day?* I wondered. I saw the Nike store across the square and chuckled. *Well, I guess some things are different.*

The musicians in the square began to play the French national anthem, and even from where I sat, I could hear the clink as euros were tossed into their open instrument cases. I took the last bite of éclair and sipped my coffee, basking in the moment. *God, thank you for the little gifts you give.*

The young woman came back and asked if I'd like another cappuccino. I shook my head and smiled, and then a sudden thought crossed my mind: right after the attacks, I don't think I would have seen a young woman; I would have seen a Muslim. Even in a setting like this, my guard would have been up, and I'm not sure I would have considered reaching out to her. *God, you have been changing me,* I thought.

I felt my phone buzz but chose to ignore it. However, within moments, I became aware that all around me, other patrons' phones were chiming, whistling, and chirping too. Just as my phone buzzed again, I heard the woman at the table next to me exclaim in disgust, "*Non!* When will this end?"

What has happened now? I wondered as I fished for my phone.

All the headlines blared this news: the Islamic State had claimed responsibility for the attacks in Nice, announcing their intent to target citizens of nations fighting them. It was no surprise that this was an act of terrorism, but something about seeing it spelled out like that gave it an air of finality.

It was as though all the events of the past nine months had converged in this one place and time. When Bob Evans had sat at this same restaurant almost seventy years ago, France was just pulling itself back together after a world war that had been fought within its borders. Now the country was the scene of another kind of bloodshed and fear.

According to one article I read, France had suffered more terrorism-related deaths in the previous eighteen months than it had in the past one hundred years. The reasons for the instability and violence might have changed, but at the heart of it all, people are still people. They're trying to find their way amid the shifting currents of a world that is far from God. When Bob sat in this square, he dedicated his life and ministry to lost people. I was here because I wanted to do the same.

As I looked back over my time in France, I realized it wasn't primarily marked by the events at the stadium but by the people God had brought into my life. I thought about Margot, Jean-Claude, Brigitte, and Ilias, who were experiencing glimpses of the Kingdom of God that they might not have otherwise experienced. Every one of those individuals, even though they hadn't accepted Christ yet, was worth the risk and all the challenges I faced here, so far from the safety of home.

Father, please be close to all the people who are being affected by this tragedy, I prayed. *I ask for your protection over the nation of France, the police, and the government as they respond. And please help the Church around the world. May we respond with your grace and love, not fear and hatred. Please give me opportunities to be a light for you in the darkness.*

I checked my phone again for the time and realized it was just after 5:30 p.m. I needed to think about heading home. I noticed the server approaching once more, and looking at her face, I saw signs around her eyes that she had been crying.

"Are you okay?" I asked.

Looking away and trying to compose herself, she responded that she was fine.

"You look like something is really bothering you," I prompted. "Is there anything I can do for you?"

"I'm sorry," she began, wiping her cheeks with her free hand. "I shouldn't be bothering customers with my problems. I was just coming to see if you needed anything."

"It's really no problem," I assured her. "I'd be happy to help if I can."

"Did you hear what happened in Nice?" Without waiting for me to respond, she went on, "Why is this happening in France? My family moved here sixty years ago. I was born here, but now, when I walk down the street, I feel people looking at me as if I'm the foreigner or as if I'm a terrorist.

I don't like what's happening any more than anyone else does, and now I'm afraid to go out sometimes because people will think I am one of them." She took in a breath and plunged ahead. "My family is Muslim—kind of. We rarely go to the mosque, but I still wear my scarf to honor my father's wishes. I'm tired of being afraid! Ever since last November, I'm afraid. My brother, Hasim, was at the concert at the Bataclan. He wasn't killed, but he saw everything, and they held him for more than a day for questioning, just because our family comes from Lebanon. I was going to go to the concert with him—that could have been me. And now, after all this in Nice, it will start all over again." She stopped abruptly. Heaving a big sigh, she continued, "I'm sorry for going on— I'm just tired of the fear and hatred. But you didn't come here to hear all that." She suddenly looked a bit embarrassed.

Jesus, what do I say to her to comfort her? I prayed. "What's your name?" I asked.

"Aisha."

"Aisha, I know what you mean about being afraid," I began. "I was in the football stadium when the attacks happened last November, and I was very afraid. For the next several months, all that affected me a lot. In fact, it still does sometimes. When I was out on the streets, I was always looking around to see if something would happen. But I believe in God, and I know that he's in control and will protect me. You said that you were Muslim. Do you believe in God?"

"I'm not sure," she responded. "I'm not even sure my father really believes. I think maybe the traditions just keep him connected to his childhood and to our Lebanese culture. Frankly, it seems like religion is at the heart of so many of our problems, and I'm not sure I want anything to do with that."

"Yes, religion causes many problems," I said. "But there's a difference between religion and believing in God. In fact, it's God who has given me the hope I need to overcome some of my fears. I think all this violence and killing must break God's heart. According to the Bible, it's not what he wants for people."

"You have actually read parts of the Bible?" She looked shocked. "I'm not sure I've ever met anyone who has done that. Certainly not a young person, anyway. I didn't think there was anything in there that's relevant for today."

"You might be surprised," I said with a chuckle. "Do you work here often? This café is kind of special to me, and I suspect I'll be coming back from time to time."

"Yes," she said. "I work here five nights a week to help pay for university."

"Well, maybe when I come in, if I've found something in the Bible that is relevant to today, I can show it to you. Would you be open to that?"

She nodded. "I have to admit I'm a little curious."

"Great," I said with a smile. "I'd like someone to talk to about those things. Right now, do you think I could pray for you and your family and the people in Nice? It feels like something we should do."

"Sure, I guess."

We prayed and then went our separate ways.

Aisha, I thought as I mentally added another name to my prayer list. I walked across the square toward the metro, smiling to myself and wondering what Bob would say if he saw a missionary like me talking to a young Muslim woman about Jesus in the very restaurant where he'd decided to start GEM. I looked across the square toward the restaurant one last time before descending the stairs into the metro. *I think he'd be proud.*

Evans family headed to Europe

Chicago, Illinois
August 21, 1948

BOB EVANS

CHAPTER 56

HOME AGAIN

MY EYES FLUTTERED OPEN as the plane made its descent toward the world's busiest airport. My three days in Paris and the plane ride home had given me time to think about the conference in Beatenberg. I knew what God was calling me to do—he'd made that clear. But there was still some wrestling taking place in my heart. His prompting for me to go to Europe felt inconvenient and intrusive. And it affected more people than just me.

I've been in my new job as vice president of Youth for Christ for less than a year, God, I prayed silently. *I don't feel right about abandoning them. And what am I supposed to say to Jeanette and Alyce? They're just now getting settled into our new home and life in Wheaton!*

The only response was the droning of the four Double Wasp engines.

Also, do you want me dead? I prayed. *Jeanette's parents are already upset that I moved their only grandchild a few hours away. What are they going to say if we take her to another continent?*

You were made for Europe. The thought bounced through my brain again.

But I have an okay salary, I told God, covering ground I'd already covered many times before. *I like my job. I like my office. I like our church in Wheaton. I like that I can see a football game if I want to. What if I'm only imagining this or wishing it's true because I miss my friends in France?*

But then the other side kicked in. *I did feel alive there,* I admitted. *God, you were very present in my life then. Besides, I don't know of any missions organizations that send missionaries to Europe. Even so, I'm not sure that Billy's passion for Europe will be enough to sway the staff and board of YFC that we should pursue Europe. After all, thousands of people are coming to Christ in the United States as well, and Europe is considered a Christian continent.*

I was still rehearsing the arguments in my head when the plane bumped down and then settled onto the runway. As the plane pulled up to its designated spot near the terminal, I saw Jeanette and Alyce standing near the edge of the runway.

Oh, Jeanette, I'm sorry, but I think our lives are about to get messy, one way or the other, I said to myself as I saw her holding Alyce's small hand and shielding her eyes against the sun's glare. I began the slow shuffle toward the door, at once troubled and eager to see my two girls.

As my foot hit the ground, I saw Alyce's face light up in

a gleeful smile. She strained to run to me as Jeanette tried to hold her back. When I had covered half the distance, Jeanette finally gave up and let Alyce come bounding to my waiting arms.

"Hey, Princess," I said as her slight form crashed against me and she threw her arms around my neck. "I've missed you." I returned her hug with a big squeeze of my own.

Squirming out of my grasp, she beamed up at me, her expectant blue eyes meeting mine. "Did you bring me a doll, Daddy? Did you?"

"Doll?" I said. "I thought you said you wanted a *ball*! Or was it chocolate? I forget."

"Don't be silly, Daddy!" There was only a hint of worry in her voice. "Mommy wanted chocolate. I wanted a dolly."

I reached into my satchel. "Well, let's see if I can find that ball in here. I've got a real nice black one for you in here somewhere."

Concern flickered in her eyes until my hand closed around the little Swiss doll I'd picked up in Interlaken. Alyce's eyes lit up as I handed it to her. "Hmm, I guess I did get a doll!"

"She's perfect, Daddy!" Alyce squealed. "Thank you!"

By this time Jeanette had made her way to me. "Well, it looks like you're a hit," Jeanette said with a grin. "She has been beside herself waiting for you to get here and wondering if you'd remember her doll."

"Hello, dear." I pulled my wife into a deep embrace. "What about you? Have you been beside yourself wondering if I'd remember what you wanted?" I reached into my satchel again. "I picked up something for you in Interlaken, but I was afraid it might get damaged." I pulled out the small box of Cailler chocolates wrapped in a colorful silk scarf. "So I bought this packaging to wrap it up in."

"Well, Mr. Evans, it seems you have thought of everything," she said, leaning in for a kiss.

With luggage in hand, we made our way to the parking lot, and Jeanette started to drive us home. We chatted for a while as I described Switzerland, but it didn't take long before the warmth of the fall day, combined with the motion of the car, lulled me to sleep. The next thing I knew, Jeanette was patting my knee to let me know we were home. I stumbled from the car into the house and collapsed into bed.

Home, I thought. *But for how long, Lord?*

CHAPTER 57

ARMCHAIR OBEDIENCE

MY EYES SNAPPED OPEN, and I was greeted by the deep dark-ness of early morning. My body, still used to European time, decided it was time to get up. Slipping out of bed, I padded toward the kitchen, not wanting to wake Jeanette and Alyce.

When I got to the kitchen, I looked at the clock and dis-covered it was only 4:07 a.m. I couldn't even make a cup of coffee for fear that the percolating pot would bring Alyce pre-maturely from her room. Settling for a glass of water instead, I grabbed my Bible and headed into the living room, where I switched on the table lamp and settled in for an early version of my time with the Lord.

Lord, where are you in all of this? Reveal your plan to me, I prayed as I settled into the chair. *What exactly was it that you told your disciples about following you?* I flipped through the pages of Matthew. *Ah, here it is:*

> Jesus said to His disciples, "If anyone desires to come after Me, let him deny himself, and take up his cross, and follow Me. For whoever desires to save his life will lose it, but whoever loses his life for My sake will find it. For what profit is it to a man if he gains the whole world, and loses his own soul? Or what will a man give in exchange for his soul? For the Son of Man will come in the glory of His Father with His angels, and then He will reward each according to his works."
>
> MATTHEW 16:24-27

I had hoped that perhaps there was some wiggle room in this passage. But as I stared at the page and saw Jesus' words there in black and white, I felt the gentle voice of the Spirit prompting me: *What are you going to do with that, Bob?*

Placing my finger in the Bible, I closed it and leaned back in the chair, staring at the ceiling. In the shadows cast by the lamp, the familiar furniture and curtains of the room seemed to surround me like a jury, silently bearing witness to my struggle.

"Jesus!" I spoke out loud. "What you're asking me to do feels like jumping off a cliff blindfolded. And I'm not only concerned for myself; I'm worried about Jeanette and Alyce, too. Besides, I have no idea where to even start!"

Tears of frustration began trickling out of the corners of my eyes.

Suddenly I pictured the scene in John 21, where Jesus meets his disciples along the Sea of Tiberias for breakfast. This was the first time Jesus had been with Peter since the triple betrayal, and Jesus wanted to restore his relationship with Peter. The question Jesus asked Peter three times in that scene was the same question I felt God was asking me now.

Bob, do you love me?

Of course I love you, Jesus.

Then it's time for you to go and do what I created you to do.

I sighed in resignation. *Why Europe, Lord? And why now?*

A crystal-clear answer entered my thoughts. *Many people can serve me here. Who will go to Kristophe and Matthias and Bernadette?*

I recalled the simple, radical prayer I'd prayed overlooking the Bay of St. Tropez, and I whispered the words again: "Jesus, show me what to do, and I will do it."

On impulse, I riffled through pages of my Bible until I found one of the first verses I'd memorized as the son of missionaries:

Jesus came and spoke to them, saying, "All authority has been given to Me in heaven and on earth. Go therefore and make disciples of all the nations, baptizing them in the name of the Father and of the Son and of the Holy Spirit, teaching them to observe

all things that I have commanded you; and lo, I am
with you always, even to the end of the age."
MATTHEW 28:18-20

I finally heard God's voice saying what he'd been saying
to me all along: *I am with you always.*

With unshakable resolve, I closed the Bible and declared,
"Jesus, if you are in this, I'm in it too."

Now I just have to convince Jeanette, I thought.

For the first time, I truly began to pray for God to make
a way for us to serve him in Europe. I was still deep in prayer
when I became aware of another presence in the room. I
looked up to see Jeanette leaning against the doorway and
holding a cup of coffee in each hand. The golden light of
dawn had begun to filter into the room through the blinds.

"You sure got up early," she said, offering me one of the
cups.

"Yeah," I sighed. "I think my body is convinced I'm still
in Europe. It's interesting that I never used to notice the time
change when I traveled by ship."

I sipped the steaming coffee in an attempt to forestall the
speech I'd been preparing. Swallowing the life-giving liquid,
I looked up into her eyes. "Jeanette, there are some important
things for the two of us to talk about. You may want to sit
down."

"Oh," she said with a conspiratorial smile. She settled into
the armchair next to mine and crossed her legs. "So you've
finally decided to stop resisting God's call to Europe?"

Silence hung in the air between us. I could only stare at her in disbelief.

"What?" she said with an air of satisfaction. "Mr. Evans, did you think you're the only one God speaks to? Your telegram said to pray, so I took that little notebook of names and addresses from your dresser and called them all and asked them to pray for you. A bunch of us got together the first night and prayed that God would speak. You did mean for us to *actually* pray, didn't you?"

Well, God, you sure knew the woman for me!

CHAPTER 58

LAST TO KNOW

AS IT TURNED OUT, I was the last one to get the message about God's plan for me. Later that week, when I hesitantly made my way into Torrey's office to break the news to him that I had to leave YFC to pursue my call in Europe, he looked at me in surprise.

"I thought all that was settled around the fire in Beatenberg. I was just waiting for you to come up with a plan and a time frame."

Grimacing, I thought, *It's not nice to tell everyone else first, God.*

"I realize YFC doesn't have money to send me to Europe, so I'm going to need to take some time to go out and raise funds. But I think the state of the Church in Europe is a compelling situation that people will want to get behind."

"Yeah," Torrey agreed. "We have to keep momentum here in the States, and we'll need to bring in someone to replace you here, but Billy thinks we can raise enough money to hire your replacement and offer you some financial backing to help you get settled over there."

"Billy!" I exclaimed. "How in the world does *he* know about this? I didn't know until yesterday morning!"

Torrey chuckled. "I knew you were going to Europe since the day we were walking around Soldier Field. You never stop talking about the place! Everyone who knows you figures you're going back there, one way or another. I, for one, can't think of a place that's more in need of discipleship and training than Europe. This is the right thing, Bob!"

I just stared at him, stunned. *Am I really that slow, God?* "Your offer is incredibly generous," I finally managed to get out.

"Here." Torrey passed a piece of paper across the desk. "I made a list of some of the churches from the YFC network that might be interested in what you want to do in Europe. If you need any introductions, let me know. Otherwise, I'd suggest letting them know you're going to work for us part-time as our international director and asking if you can share at one of their services."

Glancing at the list, I saw the names of twenty churches throughout the Midwest. I was surprised to see Calvary Baptist Church of St. Louis there. After another moment of reflection, however, my incredulity was erased. Given my conversations over the past twenty-four hours, I suspected Jerry Richards had prophesied I would go to Europe in that first letter to Torrey Johnson several years ago.

"I think I'll spend the rest of the month in the office to get things squared away, and then, if it's okay, I'd like to begin visiting these churches in November."

"Sounds great, Bob," Torrey said. "Just let us know if you need anything, and we'll see what we can do. The staff prayed for you this morning, and I promise we'll keep praying until you're fully funded and ready to go."

I reached across the desk to shake Torrey's hand. "You have no idea what a privilege it is to work with men like you, Torrey."

Instead of taking my hand, Torrey walked around the desk and placed his hand on my shoulder. "The privilege is mine, Bob. You're our first European missionary!"

With that, he closed his eyes, and with a short but meaningful prayer, he anointed me for missionary service. There was one line I knew I'd never forget: "Just like Bob was one of the first men into Europe as a serviceman, Father, we send him now as the first of an army of your disciples to invade Europe with hope and your Good News."

CHAPTER 59

SEEDS OF HOPE

THE FIRST MONDAY IN NOVEMBER, I kissed Jeanette and Alyce good-bye and began a two-week circuit of church visits through the Midwest. With a couple years' savings and my active-duty pay from the Navy, we'd been able to scrape together the money for a used Pontiac Streamliner. My first stop would be in southern Wisconsin; then I'd drive through Iowa and Missouri. After that I'd make my way through Indiana, and I'd finally head back to Illinois.

When I pulled into the parking lot of Calvary Baptist in St. Louis about a week into the trip, I was surprised to be met not only by the pastor but also by Jerry Richards.

"Jerry, it's great to see you!" I said. "But why aren't you at work? Is everything okay?" I wondered what could lure Jerry out of the office on a workday.

"Well, Pastor here said you were coming, and I wanted to talk to you about something," Jerry said. "Come on. We were just going out for lunch—my treat. Are you up for some home-cooked Italian?"

"Sure thing!" I realized it had been a number of hours since I'd eaten.

Before long we were seated for lunch at Mancinni's, a restaurant in a quaint neighborhood of St. Louis known as The Hill.

"I'm not sure what you like, Bob, but if I were you, I'd try a large order of their toasted ravioli. It's a local delicacy," Jerry said, thumbing through the menu.

When the waitress arrived, I was surprised to see her put a fourth place setting on the table.

Jerry leaned back in his chair. "So, Bob, how was Switzerland? I've been dying to hear."

Jerry and the pastor listened as I shared about what had transpired: the 250 international delegates, the breathtaking views, the late-night campfire, the hikes alone with God, and even the disagreement about conversion and discipleship. I explained my belief that this wasn't an issue of either/or, but that we need people who are just as dedicated to discipling believers as they are to bringing them to a saving knowledge of Jesus. "That brings me to what I keep finding is the most shocking part of this story," I said.

"Hold on, Bob," Jerry interrupted. "Here comes our food."

Wow, have I been talking all this time? I felt embarrassed as I turned to see the waitress and someone who looked like the chef coming our way with four steaming, fragrant plates of food. I was even more surprised when the chef pulled up the fourth chair and set the remaining plate in front of himself.

He wiped his hand on his apron before extending it to me. "Lou Mancinni."

I took his meaty hand. "Bob Evans. Pleased to meet you."

The pastor offered to pray over our meal, and when he said "Amen," I picked up my knife and fork and prepared to experience toasted ravioli. But before my fork made contact with the pillow of pasta, Jerry said, "Okay, Bob, can you continue with what you were telling us?"

Slightly disappointed that the mouthwatering pile of pasta on my plate would have to wait, I set down my fork. "Do I need to start over for Lou?"

Jerry waved his hand. "Nah, that's fine. He knows enough of the story. Just finish what you were telling us."

"Well, as I was saying, the most shocking part of the story is that God has clearly called Jeanette and me to go to Europe as missionaries, so we've been sharing all God is doing there with everyone we can. We've also been pulling together a team of people and churches who will pray for us and support us. I've been serving God for a long time, but this missionary part is a little new to us."

"Are you wondering yet why I asked Lou to join us?" Jerry said with a grin, clearly enjoying his little mystery.

"Well, yeah," I confessed. "Having lunch with the restaurant owner isn't exactly normal." I corrected myself: "Well, not normal here. I guess I ate lunch with a restaurant owner in France almost every day while I was there."

"You don't know me, and I don't know you," Lou began. "But my nephew Joey went with Jerry and some of the other guys from Calvary Baptist on a bus up to that big rally you spoke at in Chicago. I'm not sure what all happened there, but when Joey came back, he said that after he heard your story about France, Jesus saved him. It's been years since he went to that thing, and he hasn't been the same since. He was kind of on the wrong path before the rally, but now he's one of the youth leaders at the church. I've never seen anything like it. So when he insisted that it was God, we decided to check it out for ourselves. Well, wouldn't you know it, over the course of about six months, our whole family became Christians. So I guess, in part, we have you to thank for that."

Wow, I thought. I was thrilled by the ripple effect of all those people accepting Christ.

"Anyway," he continued, "when I heard you were coming through, I asked if there was any way I could meet you and shake your hand."

"Well, I . . . I didn't realize," I stammered. "I was just sharing the story of what God has done in my life. What has happened in your family is pretty amazing! God is incredible like that."

"Yeah, he is," Lou agreed. "But that's not really what I wanted to talk to you about. I was talking to Jerry Wednesday night at church, and he told me you're going back to Europe so God can add to that story you told. This new toasted ravioli thing has really taken off here, and the restauraunt is doing well financially, so we decided we'd like to help you go back to Europe. How does $1,000 a month sound to you?"

At the mention of the ravioli, my hand had unconsciously reached for my fork again, but now it fell away, all thought of food gone.

One thousand dollars a month! The shock must have been written all over my face, because all three men broke out into delighted grins.

"Of course, Unified Metal Works isn't going to be out-done by pasta, so we thought we'd match that." Jerry was obviously pleased with their little game.

"The church can't give quite that much, although we wish we could," Pastor Jones added. "But we're going to commit to $500 a month. The church has also agreed to hold a rummage sale, with all the proceeds going to your launch fund. If half of what Jerry has told us is true, we're proud to be on your team. Do you know that George, Jerry's nephew, has been meeting with some Navigators on his ship? Everywhere you go, God seems to plant little seeds of change."

A million thoughts flashed through my mind in that moment. I recalled that in the last few days, I'd spent a lot of time complaining to God and telling him why this wouldn't work. But one by one, God had met all my concerns. I hadn't exactly been demonstrating complete faithfulness and obedience, and yet he had gone above and beyond in blessing me.

That moment in Mancinni's restaurant was another turning point, a reminder to expect great things from God, not be surprised by them.

When I could finally speak again, I began to thank them. But like most men of that era, they tried to deflect the words, explaining that it was the least they could do and that it was all God's money anyway. While that was true, of course, it was God's money in the hands of godly stewards, and I was exceedingly grateful.

Lou brought any further attempts at gratefulness to a close when he stood up and announced, "This calls for some of Mama's cannoli!"

I called Jeanette as soon as I could to tell her that our time frame for leaving for Europe had moved up significantly. She agreed and let me know that a letter had just arrived from Billy Graham with a check for $3,400 and a note that read: "I said we would do this together, Evans. This should help get that school going." As I hung up the receiver, I thought, *If people knew what a wild adventure it is to be a Christian, they'd be lined up at the door.*

CHAPTER 60

NEW YORK

THE MONTHS OF PREPARATION flew by, as did the good-byes and gatherings with friends. It had been only nine months since I'd told Jeanette, or rather since she'd told me, that God was taking us to Europe. The process of raising support had been a roller coaster of surprises—both good and bad—and yet God had been front and center through all of it.

As generous as some of our friends had been, we were shocked that some family members and lifelong friends who had grown up in the church were not as enthusiastic. Some friends who were in leadership in a local church told us we were "foolish" for wanting to be missionaries to Europe. "Don't you remember World War II?" they asked. *How could I forget?* I thought wryly.

"That's God's judgment on the continent for leaving God," they continued. "He has abandoned them. The center of God's work today is here in America. I don't know why you two are wasting your lives."

Jeanette and I had nothing to say to that, and we wondered if that would be the last time we would talk to them. Moments like those were painful.

Having grown up on the mission field, I was familiar with the idea of utter dependence on God, but it took on new significance to be in this position not as a child but as a father.

I'm making a life-changing decision for her, too, I thought as I watched Alyce twirl through the living room. *Do I have the right to do that?*

The Spirit's reply came into my heart: *To whom are you trusting her, Bob? Me or you?*

I trust you with her life, Lord. It was a prayer I would offer many times in the days ahead. *Sometimes I wonder how you put up with me, Jesus. Here I am about to be a missionary, and yet I struggle with simple things like trusting you. I am like a child sometimes. Grow my faith, and let me be a good example for Alyce of what it means to follow you. And protect her heart, no matter what we do or where we go. She is yours, Lord.*

Up and down, around and around the roller coaster went until, one day, we opened a letter from a relative on the East Coast. We realized, once we registered the gift it contained, that we were fully funded. God had done it, and now it was time for us to do our part.

+ + +

In the final weeks leading up to our departure, we pared down years of possessions to the bare minimum. We separated out things for friends and donations for the Salvation Army until our home was a maze of boxes and crates.

First we would make the trek to New York City, where we'd booked passage on a steamship bound for the Italian city of Naples. In discussions with the leadership of YFC, we had determined that Paris made the most sense for our base of operations for the coming years, given that I already knew French and had made a number of connections there the previous fall.

The day before our departure, Jeanette and I arose early so we could pack up the car. As we ate breakfast, I noticed that my normally sweet wife had an intense look on her face—the look of a gladiator about to enter the arena for a fight to the death. I thought about asking her what she was thinking, but something about her demeanor gave me pause. As it turned out, I found out soon enough.

"Do you really think we need to take all these teacups?" I asked as I lifted another box marked "Fragile" and headed toward the door.

"You can't seriously be asking me that, Bob," she said. "What are we going to drink out of?" She wiped the sweat from her face. "And this from the guy who is clearly taking every book he's ever owned. I bet they have some books over there already. You could probably leave one or two here."

"You know I'm only taking the bare minimum," I said defensively.

"Bare minimum?" she exclaimed. "The Pinckneyville

public library had fewer books than you're trying to pack into that car. Six boxes?"

"Well, I suppose there are quite a few," I conceded, knowing that they'd take up almost half the space we had. "But they're all essential. Besides, you have two boxes marked 'shoes,' and I'm only taking the pair I'm wearing. The few times I've been to Paris, the women have been wearing shoes—they must have some of those there, too."

"They also have winter, spring, summer, and fall. Have you thought about that? Besides, I have Alyce's shoes in my boxes too."

In the end, we both were forced to compromise when we realized our boxes exceeded the space in our car. We labeled more boxes for the Salvation Army and said good-bye to more pieces of life as we knew it.

+ + +

The next morning at 5:00 a.m., the three of us loaded into the front seat of the Pontiac, Alyce sitting between Jeanette and me on the bench seat, holding a small suitcase on her lap. I went to our neighbor's house and placed the key under his flowerpot so he could give it to the real estate agent later in the week.

As we sat in the car while the engine warmed up, I reached over and grabbed Jeanette's hand. I could see the tears in her eyes as we stared at the only home we'd ever owned—the place that held many precious memories of our married life together. We shared a silent moment of thanks and grief before I released her hand, grabbed the gearshift, and pulled away for the last time.

It was a strange feeling to drive through the silent streets of Wheaton in the predawn light. I took a couple of short detours so we could see our home church and the YFC offices before we turned the car eastward toward New York.

We stopped overnight with friends and family along the way, and when we finally saw the sign welcoming us to New York, we were both relieved and exhausted. Carefully negotiating the narrow East Coast streets and traffic, we made our way toward the massive New York Harbor.

Our ship would be boarding the next day, and we'd made arrangements to leave the car in the parking lot of Sudan Interior Mission (SIM). Once we arrived at the dock, a crane would lift the car and place it in the hold while we boarded via the gangplank. After a number of wrong turns, we finally found the SIM lot and piled out.

"Okay, let's leave as much in the car as possible," I instructed. "The person I talked to from SIM said this lot is patrolled. Just grab the suitcase with the clothes you need for tomorrow. Once we're on the ship, we can go down and get anything else we need. I'm going to pay the attendant and have him call us a cab to get to the hotel. I'll be right back."

I made sure all the doors and trunk were locked, and then I picked up my bag and walked with Jeanette and Alyce to wait for the cab. After loading our suitcases into the trunk, Malcolm, our talkative Irish cabbie, slid behind the wheel. As we accelerated away from the docks, Jeanette braced herself in the passenger seat while Alyce clung to my arm and squealed with joy as the cabbie weaved and bobbed through traffic, negotiating the narrow streets like a spooked horse heading back to the barn.

Once we arrived at the Harborside Inn, I paid Malcolm, grabbed our bags, and headed for the hotel door. I could hear the whooshing of the surf down the street, and the crisp tang of the cold sea air tickled my nose.

After we checked in, we got cleaned up and settled in for our last night of sleep in our homeland. Malcolm would return for us in less than seven hours, and we knew it would be an eventful day. We had no way of knowing at the time just how eventful.

CHAPTER 61

CHOICES

I **WOKE UP** thirty minutes before the alarm, afraid to oversleep and miss our cab. I gently woke Jeanette, and she went to rouse Alyce, who was sleeping on a cot near the foot of the bed. I quickly repacked our suitcases while Jeanette helped Alyce dress for the short ride back to the parking lot.

When it was almost time to go, Jeanette reached into her purse, pulled out a small package, and handed it to me. "I've been saving this for a day like today," she said. "It's one of the most precious things I've ever purchased."

I unwrapped the package in the dim light. It was the book I'd sold to her all those years ago when we'd met at Wheaton.

"I know you had to get rid of a lot of your books before the trip," she whispered. "But I thought I'd save this one. It's a reminder that we're taking all the important things with us."

+ + +

As unlikely as it seemed, the day had come. Today we would follow Jesus in obedience and leave the United States as missionaries to Europe. Thinking back to all the twists and turns that had led us here, I marveled at our creative God. I wondered if Kristophe and Matthias had received my letters and if they knew I was on my way back to their country.

I tried to take it all in as we walked into the lobby. This was it—the dream was becoming a reality. In seven short days, we'd be in France, with no set plans of coming back to the States. I looked at Jeanette, and I could tell there were similar thoughts swirling behind her blue eyes. Today was the first day of a new chapter of our lives.

As the cabbie pulled away from the hotel into the empty streets of New York, I smiled at Jeanette. "Promise kept, dear. I said I'd take you to Europe the next time."

She chuckled and shook her head. "This isn't exactly what I had in mind, but I wouldn't miss this adventure for anything, Mr. Evans."

"Well, you didn't specify how long you wanted the trip to be," I proclaimed in mock defensiveness.

"I'll be more specific in the future, you can be sure," she replied. "In a million years, I never would have guessed I'd live in France. You are full of surprises, Bob."

We spent the rest of the ride in silence, both lost in our own thoughts.

Before we knew it, the cab was pulling up in front of the dark entrance to the parking lot. I paid the cabbie, giving him an extra tip for such an early trip. When he left, we were suddenly aware of how lonely the parking lot was at this hour. Nothing stirred. In the distance we could hear the faint crash of waves and the call of the gulls.

"Okay, Jeanette, here are the tickets for you and Alyce. When we get the car, I'll drive you to the passenger terminal, where you two can get in line. Then I'll take the car to the loading dock and see if there's a way I can board from there. If things go as planned, I'll meet you at our cabin, and then we can explore the ship together. Do you have your identification and passports?"

After a moment of rustling, she replied, "Yep, here they are."

"All right, let's go."

We strode into the dimly lit parking lot and made our way down the long aisles of cars to space 217C, near the back corner of the lot. As we entered the last row, I noticed a car with the driver's-side window broken out and thought, *So much for the lot being patrolled.*

A hundred feet or so down the row, there was a car with all its windows broken.

Then, in the distance, I saw the nose of our Pontiac covered in glass.

"No!" I ran toward the car, already knowing what I'd find when I arrived.

Our car had been destroyed. All the windows were

broken, and it was empty except for broken glass and five heavy boxes of books, which had been ripped open and then abandoned. I glanced over my shoulder and saw Jeanette and Alyce huddled close together in the dim light.

This can't be happening. Why would you let this happen, Father? I screamed inside.

Motioning for Jeanette to stay where she was, I slowly walked around the car. They had taken everything.

A fierce, guttural scream ripped from my lungs. I brought my fists down onto the hood of my car, or what was left of it. The thieves had even managed to take one of the wheels before being scared off.

"Where is that security patrol?" I said through gritted teeth.

Turning from the devastated car, I walked back to Jeanette. She asked the obvious question: "How bad is it?"

"They took everything!" I screamed through my tears. "They destroyed the car and took everything. What are we going to do? I have to find the security guy or call the police or something. Maybe they caught the guys," I said, though I knew that was ridiculous.

"Stay here," I commanded. "I'll go find someone to help." Then I ran off toward the attendant's booth.

When I arrived, I banged on the door, waking the sleeping guard. Rubbing his eyes and stifling a yawn, he opened the window to his booth.

"Can I help you?"

"Help me? Help me!" I shouted. "We've been robbed. Our car is destroyed. Call the police—right now!"

With each sentence, the attendant's eyes got a little wider. "What? Where were you? Why are you down here at this time of night?"

"Wake up!" I shouted. "Our car was in your parking lot. We are leaving for France today, and our car has been broken into and everything inside was stolen."

"You kidding me?" he asked, now fully awake.

"No, I'm not kidding! And I'm not the only one—we saw a handful of other cars too. Call the police. Now!" I tried to calm down, realizing that my shouting was only confusing him.

He called the police, and in about ten minutes a patrol car arrived with two officers.

"What seems to be the problem here, sir?" the taller man asked.

"We've been robbed, and we need to be on a ship in a couple of hours. Have you caught any thieves tonight?"

"No, not really," the shorter man said. "It's been a quiet night so far."

"Well, not here, it hasn't!" I exclaimed. "Come with me."

I led them toward our car, and when I got to our row, I saw that Jeanette and Alyce were in front of the car. Jeanette was on her knees, crying uncontrollably.

How could you let this happen, God? We got rid of almost everything! We kept only the stuff that really mattered, and now it's gone!

413

I made a mental list. Her grandmother's teacups. Our wedding pictures. All of Alyce's toys and clothes. Everything we owned—gone!

"Ma'am, please move away from the vehicle," one of the officers said. "There's broken glass everywhere, and we don't want you to get hurt."

Jeanette let out a desperate sob and stood with my help. She wept against my shoulder, and I wept with her. Alyce was crying, too, not used to seeing her parents upset. We stood huddled there with our three remaining bags.

I tried to assure them of what I myself couldn't come to grips with. "It's going to be all right," I said. "The police are here now—they'll figure this out. We'll just cancel the trip and get this sorted out. I bet the police will be able to recover our stuff. What thief is looking for teacups and little girls' dresses?" I didn't believe a word of it, but it had a calming effect.

After explaining to the officers why we were in New York and that we were supposed to be on the ship in less than two hours, I settled in to answer the myriad questions from the police. Why were we here? Where had we stayed? Why were we out at 5 a.m.?

Finally one of the men, who introduced himself as Officer Phillips, said, "Bob, I'm so sorry this has happened, but I don't know what to do. Your vehicle is a crime scene, so we can't move it. I guess I'd suggest you find someplace to stay and regroup. Maybe we will catch the folks, though frankly, with no witnesses in the dead of night, I doubt it. There has been a rash of break-ins up and down the docks this past month, and we don't have a clue who's responsible."

I nodded. "I'm sorry I yelled earlier," I confessed. "It was just so shocking. One minute we were driving from the hotel, about to set sail for our new life in France, and the next minute everything we owned, including our car, was either gone or destroyed. I just lost control, and I'm sorry."

Officer Phillips chuckled. "That doesn't even scratch the surface of what I would've done—you can bet on that. You're right to be furious. Look, I will personally do everything I can to get this taken care of. Here's my card—call me in a couple of days. We have to get back to the station to get started on this, but let me know if there's anything I can do for you. Again, I'm sorry this happened."

"Thank you, sir." I sighed. "I know you'll do everything you can. I think we're okay for now."

I walked over to where Jeanette and Alyce stood. "Well, I guess we're not going anywhere today."

Jeanette looked at me defiantly for a moment. Then, reaching into her purse, she pulled out the tickets. "Bob, this is it!" she whispered. "God has met our every need to get to this point. My heart is breaking, but I can't help but think that this is our moment. We have each other, and we have Jesus. I think we need to get on that ship. If you're ready, I'm with you, no matter what happens."

I gazed at her resolute face and thought, *She has never looked more beautiful to me than she does in this moment.* I drank in her confidence and faith, both in God and in me.

Grabbing her shoulders, I leaned down and kissed her like the day we got married.

I turned and shouted to the two policemen who were walking toward the entrance of the parking lot.

"Officer Phillips! Could you give us a ride to Pier 9? We have a ship to catch."

EPILOGUE

WITH THE HELP OF OFFICER PHILLIPS AND HIS SIREN, Bob, Jeanette, and Alyce made it to the ship before it sailed. As expected, the police never recovered any of the stolen property, although the car was sold for about one-third of the price Bob had paid for it.

When the Evanses' supporters heard about the tragedy, they rallied around them and raised an additional $13,000 to help them replace all they'd lost. One donor even gave a substantial gift that she insisted Jeanette use to replace her tea set. For years after that, Jeanette would make a cup of tea when she needed to be reminded that God truly cared about her and knew her heart. That small but specific gift would be an anchor for her as she withstood a number of trials and tragedies in her years on the mission field, including the loss of their teenage son, Bruce, in a motorcycle accident.

Bob continued to work for Youth for Christ in Europe

from 1949 to 1952, handling the logistics for Billy Graham's early crusades in the United Kingdom and mainland Europe. In those early years of working with the crusades and other outreach tours like the Palermo Brothers, Bob's conviction about the importance of discipleship continued to grow.

This eventually led the Evanses to leave YFC so they could pour all their energy into the ongoing training of believers. The first thing they did was to open a Bible school in Chatou, France, called the European Bible Institute, which was dedicated to training lay leaders in the fundamentals of the Bible. The inspiration for this move came to Bob one day when he was reminiscing about his time in Draguignan with Father Matthias and Kristophe.

What could be done to help guys like Matthias and Kristophe? he pondered. He wanted to help people who were curious about the faith, along with young spiritual leaders, grow in their faith and leadership ability. He and Jeanette landed on the idea of starting a school for practical theology—not just another place to study the Bible but somewhere to learn and grow in community with other students who were applying what they learned in local ministries.

In 1952 Bob founded a new organization called Greater Europe Mission. He flew to Illinois, and the organization was founded in Wheaton.

Over the years, many people have asked about the meaning behind the name. Why "greater"? Anyone familiar with Bob and Jeanette's Midwest roots will be reminded of a phrase often used about Chicago and its surrounding suburbs: "the greater Chicagoland area." From the beginning, Bob had his eyes set on a few places that were within the reach of Europe but not quite Europe, such as North Africa and the western countries of Asia.

As GEM has grown, it has opened twenty-two Bible schools, spanning the far reaches of Europe, from the Nordic Bible Institute to Mediterranean locations such as Greece. Schools have been formed in Portugal, Spain, Germany, and the Netherlands, and the most recent one was founded in the 1990s in Zaparozhye, Ukraine, after the fall of the Berlin Wall.

From its humble beginnings, Greater Europe Mission now has more than three hundred full-time missionaries serving in twenty-seven countries. Though its roots are in education, the mission has never lost Bob's personal drive to see people come to Christ and be discipled. Sixty-five years later, it is still pursuing that same mission. In fact, its mission statement is "Reaching Europe by multiplying disciples and growing Christ's Church."

For the first forty years, Bob led the Mission from Europe with the help of trusted leaders such as Noel Lyons, Walter Frank, Bob Johnson, and Don Bruggman. He passed the leadership baton to the organization's first official president, Ted Noble, in 1992.

Today, GEM is strong and growing and finds itself in one of the most strategic mission fields in the world. Political upheaval and financial instability in Europe are shaking the faith of comfortable and complacent Europeans who are beginning to wonder if the great European Union experiment will ultimately succeed.

In addition, the continent is facing the largest migration of people since the end of World War II. As of 2016, sixty-five million people have been displaced due to political and religious unrest. Add to the mix a growing sense of nationalism and increasing terrorism threats throughout the continent, and Europe sometimes feels like a very risky place to share the gospel. Even so, there is unprecedented openness to the things of God—a kind of openness that hasn't been seen since Bob Evans's early days of ministry.

+ + +

PARIS, FRANCE

AUGUST 10, 2016

JAZZ JONES

We are nearing the end of this book, yet the story is not complete. Or I should say *stories*, because every relationship is an amazing God story that is unfolding. That's the way it has been for missionaries all across the planet for more than two thousand years. It's true whether they traveled to new continents like I did or walked across the street or down the hall of their apartment building.

It's risky to take the gospel to others—not because of terrorists or shaky world politics, but because it means accepting God's call to trust him in new and deeper ways, to leave behind what's comfortable, and to go on an adventure with him. I don't know all the chapters ahead of me. I hope that some of them include Aisha, Margot, Ilias, Jean-Claude, and Brigitte experiencing God's love firsthand and having their lives changed for all eternity. I'll be looking daily for those doors to open, and when they do, I pray I'll be ready to share the hope of God with my friends here.

I didn't ask for the trauma of being in the middle of some horrific events here in Paris, but I did ask God to bring me here and to use me. Sometimes people ask me why I stay here instead of going home to Hawaii, where it's "safe." Given all I've learned in the past year, my answer is always the same: God has called me to share his love and hope in Paris right now. I believe he will continue to use me here until he calls me to serve him somewhere else.

So I challenge you to find the ways God is calling you to step up and join the adventure of serving him wherever you are. Joining God in his work is not always easy, whether you go next door, down the street, to the other side of the state, or to another country. You may find yourself way outside your comfort zone—and that's okay! As long as you're being obedient and humbly following the Lord, he will give you the courage, boldness, and wisdom to overcome any obstacle and go through any difficult situation. I can tell you without a doubt that God is ready to equip and lead you to do whatever he has planned for you.

When it comes to taking risks, I suggest that we all take a cue from Bob Evans: "It's always good to remember we're immortal." Your life is never at risk when you are serving God where he has called you to be. The greater risk is to live your life on the sidelines, letting your days and opportunities slip by.

God's got your back, so go for it!

REFLECTIONS FROM GEM'S PRESIDENT

WHAT A PAIR OF INSPIRING STORIES! Two missionaries separated by nearly seven decades but united by the same passion, commitment, and sacrifice—and the same heart to see hurting people experience the hope of Jesus.

I've heard the old saying "When God calls, he always equips." I've assumed this meant God gives us the gifts and abilities we need to do the job. But what about the faith we need to meet and overcome obstacles? What about the cost?

Bob, Jazz, and thousands like them in the last two thousand years have had to discover both the call and the resolve that God placed within them to pursue obedience—despite all odds. When God calls, it can feel overwhelming. Others might not understand it. Some may try to persuade against it, whispering that it is "too risky" or "doesn't make sense." However, here is the truth: real life, the life God wants for us all, is the one he calls us to. We are invited to jump off the cliff and into the adventure with him. The only real risk is missing the opportunity to make our lives matter for something larger than ourselves.

I grew up in England and became a follower of Jesus when I was seventeen, after trying hard to ignore God for a number of years. I was a construction worker and then a police officer. At twenty-three, I was pursuing my own life plan, when God interrupted and called me into a life of ministry. He called me to leave behind the safety of my proverbial nets and work with him to reach people. I served as a youth pastor, an evangelist, a church planter, and a mission strategist, mainly in the United Kingdom.

In 2012, I encountered Greater Europe Mission when the organization sent hundreds of short-term missionaries from the United States and Canada to help with outreach during the London Olympics. In the years afterward, we kept bumping into each other.

In September 2015, God interrupted my life again. As I watched the stream of desperate refugees crashing onto the shores of Greece, God broke my heart for them. I instantly knew I had to get involved in reaching this new wave of Europeans, as well as those who had lived in Europe their whole lives. I left my job with another ministry and joined GEM full time in January 2016. I felt an urgency like I'd never felt before to reach Europeans. I knew God was doing so much in Europe right now, and I had to dive in or miss my chance to make a difference. As president of Greater Europe Mission and an ambassador of the gospel to Europe, I have the immense privilege of stepping into the shoes of the great Bob Evans.

You could ask the hundreds of GEM missionaries why they serve God in Europe. Each would have a unique story with this common theme: God called them to the most unreached continent on the planet to reach and disciple those who desperately need him. Both native and new Europeans need Jesus.

I realize that *unreached* is a loaded word these days, but anyone who has walked the streets of Europe in recent years knows that, while church buildings still stand, the Church— God's people—is sparse.

At the same time, signs of new life are everywhere. The Church in the UK is growing. New church plants in many European cities are effectively reaching local people. And God is doing something remarkable right now with the conversion of Muslim people.

Every day we at GEM hear stories of new Jesus followers who have met Jesus in a dream or in an open church or through the witness of faithful neighbors. I recently met a man who was an Egyptian Christian living in London. He was serving for a week in Athens at a day center for refugees, and he told me he had led thirty-two Muslims to Jesus the previous week.

It's time to dive in, friends. God is on the move, and he's calling us to join him.

GEM is looking for people like you to serve in Europe with us. We need lots more Jazzes—people who are willing to commit to come and see how God can use them. We take people on short-term teams or on three- to twelve-month internship programs, and, of course, we take people like Jazz, who become long-term missionaries to Europe.

GEM desires to partner with churches around the world that want to make a Kingdom impact in Europe during this strategic moment in history. Some churches send people, some send teams, and some commit to stand with a person, project, or place. All are welcome.

We also need people who will support our missionaries and our organization. Every GEM intern and missionary must raise his or her own financial and prayer support to minister in Europe. Others, like me, have perceived that this is a critical Kingdom moment in Europe and want to invest their resources to see spiritual transformation happen in Europe and from there to the whole world. Will you prayerfully consider giving regularly to the work of GEM?

I'm asking you to pray, give, or go. Here's how you can respond now.

Pray: Join our global Euro Prayer Team.

Give: Become a regular donor and support GEM's strategic and vital work.

Go: Register your interest by joining a team, taking a vision trip, participating in an internship program, or becoming a missionary with GEM.

You can find out more about our programs and opportunities at www.GEMission.org.

+   +   +

I believe with all my heart that the spiritual needs of Europe are every bit as desperate today as they were almost seventy years ago, when Bob Evans started Greater Europe Mission. The social and cultural issues have changed, but spiritually, Europe is very much the front lines of a world at war. The two great religious powers of our day—Islam and secularism—strive to pull the continent apart. This is not a safe and peaceful time in Europe. We're not inviting you into a comfortable ministry situation without challenges. But take heart: you are not alone.

Jesus took a risk when he left the comfort of heaven to live among us. Herod tried to kill him when he was a child. He faced plots and political opposition. Ultimately, he was betrayed, crucified, and put to death. We know, of course, that Jesus conquered it all, but he willingly faced this because you and I were the prize that was worth the risk.

People's eternal and desperate need is to experience the saving, redeeming power of Jesus. I pray that *you* will see that it's worth the risk—and join us.

Jon Burns
President and CEO, Greater Europe Mission

AUTHOR'S NOTE

THIS BOOK IS A PAIRING OF TWO STORIES: one past and one present. While some of the characters and conversations in Bob Evans's story are fictional, his experiences and the historical events that serve as a backdrop are all true. Jazz's story is fresh and raw, the way only something pulled from the headlines of our crazy world can be. We hope that you have been both entertained and challenged by the echo of sacrifice and risk for eternal rewards that exists between the founder of Greater Europe Mission's amazing call into ministry and the sacrifices and challenges faced by modern-day heroes of the gospel.

The modern church in North America owes a great debt to Youth for Christ, the Billy Graham Evangelistic Association, The Navigators, and a host of other ministries born out of the '40s and '50s youth movement.

This book portrays Bob's wrestling with the debate from that era related to conversion and discipleship. His story is in no way intended to indicate that one is more important than the other. Bob's journey of discovering who God made him to be simply led him to invest in deeply discipling people.

This story is also not intended to stereotype the ministries mentioned above. Evangelism and discipleship are two sides of the same coin, and we are all called to be engaged in both practices within our network of relationships.

I would like to thank the history department of The Navigators and the Billy Graham Center for Evangelism at Wheaton College for their assistance in assembling a realistic timeline for Bob's story. To the best of my ability, I have upheld the accurate timeline of events throughout the book.

I hope and pray that the retelling of this segment of modern missional history is an inspiration to others to engage in God's mission wherever they are.

John Gilberts

ABOUT THE AUTHORS

 **JOHN GILBERTS** serves as chief of staff and director of global partnerships for Greater Europe Mission (GEM).

John grew up in the Northwoods of Wisconsin, where school wasn't called off unless it was −40 degrees or twelve inches of new snow had fallen since midnight. Many days he walked to the bus stop when it was −38 degrees.

John became a follower of Jesus at age sixteen. Nine of his classmates had been challenged at summer camp to name one person they believed was "too hard" for God to reach. They unanimously chose John.

For a year, the nine kids prayed for and pursued John with the gospel. Beneath the stars one night at a campsite near Chicago, John gave his life to Christ. From his first moments as a new believer, John has been used by God to bring others into the Kingdom.

John earned a BA in theology and music from Moody Bible Institute and an MBA from the University of Phoenix.

John enjoys photography, playing the guitar, lingering in French cafés like Bob Evans did, and working on his fly-fishing skills.

He and his wife, Molly, live in Colorado Springs, Colorado.

+ + +

JAZZ JONES BECKER is the daughter of an Army officer and a wise mother. Jazz enjoys a close relationship with her two younger sisters, who live in Hawaii. Jazz's family has US East Coast roots, but she has moved twelve times. Europe has always felt like a second home to her.

Jazz was homeschooled the last two years of high school, and then she studied contemporary Christian music (with a studio recording emphasis) at Greenville College in Illinois for two years. She transferred to the University of Hawaii at Mānoa and earned a BA in second language studies. Jazz also studied French at Les Cèdres language school and the Sorbonne in Paris.

Thanks to God's grace and her parents, Jazz has followed Christ all her life.

In 2012 God led Jazz to serve him in Paris. She was appointed by Greater Europe Mission to join the France team and arrived in Paris in 2014.

Jazz enjoys music, going to the beach, reading, traveling,

writing, sports, foreign languages, and quoting movies with her sisters.

Jazz and Sven were married in 2016 and live in Paris.